Leading Schools Successfully

D0488036

Leading Schools Successfully: Stories from the field considers international research focussing on leadership in schools. Based on the ISSPP (International Successful School Principalship Project) which has conducted over one hundred multiple perspective case studies of successful school principals from more than a dozen countries, the book captures the exhilaration of being a principal who grows and sustains success from those practitioners who are acknowledged as exhibiting outstanding leadership.

Whilst much is known about successful school leaders, the book reinforces the argument that it is neither possible, nor appropriate, to generalise specific strategies that should be adopted to ensure success for all schools, at all times, in all settings. Instead, success calls for a high level of judgement, wisdom, artistry and sheer hard work on the part of principals, adapting for their particular context the knowledge about leading schools successfully. Reflection sections in each chapter ask the reader to consider the further issues that each chapter raises.

Topics considered include:

- the importance of school principals to school success
- turning around under performing schools
- values-led leadership
- sustaining successful leadership
- leading in multi-cultural settings
- issues and implications for the future.

With international contributions from experts in the field, the book offers a new perspective on leadership in schools and will be of interest to school principals and researchers.

Christopher Day is Professor of Education at the University of Nottingham, UK, and leads the Teachers' Work and Lives and School Leadership Research groups in the Centre for Research in Schools and Communities.

David Gurr is Senior Lecturer in Educational Leadership at the University of Melbourne, Australia.

Leading Schools Successfully

Stories from the field

Edited by Christopher Day
and David Gurr

Routledge
Taylor & Francis Group

LONDON AND NEW YORK

First published 2014
by Routledge
2 Park Square, Milton Park, Abingdon, Oxfordshire OX14 4RN

Simultaneously published in the USA and Canada
by Routledge
711 Third Avenue, New York, NY 10017

First issued in paperback 2016

Routledge is an imprint of the Taylor & Francis Group, an informa business

© 2014 Christopher Day and David Gurr

The right of the editors to be identified as the authors of the editorial
material, and of the authors for their individual chapters, has been
asserted in accordance with sections 77 and 78 of the Copyright,
Designs and Patents Act 1988.

All rights reserved. No part of this book may be reprinted or
reproduced or utilised in any form or by any electronic, mechanical,
or other means, now known or hereafter invented, including
photocopying and recording, or in any information storage or retrieval
system, without permission in writing from the publishers.

Trademark notice: Product or corporate names may be trademarks
or registered trademarks, and are used only for identification and
explanation without intent to infringe.

British Library Cataloguing in Publication Data
A catalogue record for this book is available from the British Library

Library of Congress Cataloging-in-Publication Data
Leading schools successfully : stories from the field / edited by
Christopher Day and David Gurr.
    pages cm
    1. Educational leadership – Cross-cultural studies.
    2. School management and organization – Cross-cultural studies.
    3. Educational change – Cross-cultural studies. I. Day, Christopher,
ACP. II. Gurr, David, Dr.
    LB2806.L3835 2013
    371.2–dc23   2013004270

ISBN 13: 978-1-138-65215-6 (pbk)
ISBN 13: 978-0-415-85498-6 (hbk)

Typeset in Baskerville
by HWA Text and Data Management, London

David Gurr would like to dedicate this book to his children, Jim, Ari and Zoe.

Christopher Day would like to dedicate this book to his ISSPP colleagues for their continuing commitment to understanding the work of successful school leaders and in respectful memory of Eduardo Flores-Kastanis

Contents

Contributors

Helene Ärlestig has a PhD in education and works as an Assistant Professor at the Centre for Principal Development, Umeå University, Sweden. Her research focus is on educational leadership, organizational communication and principals' professional roles. She is also interested in assessment and evaluation from a leadership and governing perspective. Helene is involved in the ISSPP, UCEA/ Belmas network ISLDN, International School Leadership Development Network on social justice and the EPNoSL, European Policy Network on School Leadership. She is the convener for Network 26, Educational Administration at the ECER, European Conference of Educational Research. She has written several articles and chapters in both Swedish and international publications. Helene teaches and is Director of Studies at the Swedish National Principal Program at Umeå University and a former principal.

Ora Bar Yaakov was principal of the Rabin School, a 7–12 grade high school with 1,300 students, located in a low SES neighbourhood in Beersheba, Israel. Appointed to start the school from scratch in 1995, Ora led a successful pedagogy of teachers' personal relations with each student, which resulted in a sense of belonging, high academic achievement, and low violence and dropout rate. After retiring in 2011, she became head of a principals' preparation program at Ben-Gurion University of the Negev.

Jeff Bennett is an Assistant Professor in the Educational Policy Studies and Practice Department in the University of Arizona College of Education. He has held professional roles as an urban high school social studies teacher, department head, and school-community specialist. Well acquainted with living and working in both diverse and international contexts, Jeff's passion for collaboration, community building, and civic engagement at the University of Arizona located near the border with Mexico in the U.S. Southwest, targets preparation of the next generation of educational leaders. Specifically, his research focuses on collaborative and capacity-building leadership for change in diverse communities and employs both qualitative and quantitative methods. He is active both in the International Successful School Principalship Project (ISSPP) and the University Council for Educational Administration (UCEA). Jeff has presented his work at AERA, UCEA, ECER, and

ISSPP. He has also published work in peer-reviewed journals such as *Educational Administration Quarterly*, *Leadership & Policy in Schools*, *International Journal of Educational Management*, *Journal of Cases in Educational Leadership* and various book chapters.

Christopher Day is Professor of Education at the School of Education, University of Nottingham. He has worked, also, as a schoolteacher, teacher educator and school's adviser. He has extensive research and consultancy experience in England, Europe, Australia, South East Asia, and North America and with the OECD in the fields of teachers' continuing professional development, school leadership and change. He is the Editor of 'Teachers and Teaching: Theory and Practice' and Founding Director of the 20-country longitudinal research project, *Successful School Principalship* (http://www.ils.uio.no/english/research/project/isspp/). Recent books include *The International Handbook on Continuing Professional Development* (co-editor and contributor, Open University Press, 2004); *A Passion for Teaching* (RoutledgeFalmer, 2004); *Teachers Matter: Connecting Work, Lives and Effectiveness* (lead author, Open University Press, 2007); *Successful Principal Leadership in Times of Change: International Perspectives* (lead-editor and contributor, Springer, 2007); *The New Lives of Teachers* (Routledge, 2010); *Ten Strong Claims about Successful School Leadership* (lead author, National College, 2010); *Successful School Leadership: Linking with Learning and Achievement* (lead author, Open University Press, 2011); *Sustaining Successful School Leadership* (co-editor and contributor, Springer, 2011); and the editor of the International Handbook on Teacher and School Development (Routledge, 2011).

Joy Doherty is a consultant in educational research. She completed her doctoral thesis on Successful Principal Leadership of an Independent School in Victoria, Australia at the University of Melbourne in 2008 as part of the International Successful School Principalship Project. She has a background in secondary education in Government, Catholic and Independent schools in South Australia and Victoria and has worked on various projects with the Victorian Curriculum and Assessment Authority. She has lectured at Deakin University and tutored at the University of Melbourne in Language and Literacy subjects in the Bachelor of Education and Diploma of Education programs and has co-authored two text books on English Language for senior secondary students. Recent publications and presentations have focused on her doctoral research. Her research areas are successful school leadership, the development and sustainability of professional learning communities, sociolinguistics and volunteerism. Joy is a member of the Australian Council for Educational Leaders.

Lawrie Drysdale has a background in teaching, human resource development, lecturing and research. His career spans over 30 years in education. He is a Senior Lecturer in Educational Leadership at the Graduate School of Education, the University of Melbourne where he coordinates postgraduate courses in educational management, and teaches subjects in leadership, human resource management, marketing, school effectiveness and improvement. His research interests are in marketing in education, and successful school leadership, and he is a member of the

International Successful School Principalship Project (ISSPP). Lawrie has written extensively in both academic and professional journals and he is member of the Australian Council for Educational Leaders and was made a Fellow of the Victorian Branch in 1996, and a National Fellow in 2012.

Thad Dugan is currently a doctoral student in Educational Leadership Program at the University of Arizona and a practising school administrator in the Tucson Unified School District. As a school administrator, he has been an assistant principal, and principal, school counsellor, instructional coach, and special education teacher. Prior to his work in public education, he worked with students with autism. His research areas include leadership for social justice, successful school leadership in the Southwest context, and turn-around school leadership. He has presented work at AERA, UCEA, ISSPP, and a variety of local and state conferences. He has also published work in a peer reviewed journal , *Journal of Cases in Educational Leadership* (2012), as well as book chapters in *Global Leadership for Social Justice: Taking it from the Field to Practice* (2012) and *Educational Leadership: Building Bridges Among Ideas, Schools, and Nation* (2012).

Eduardo Flores-Kastanis was a Professor in the graduate program in education at the Universidad Autonoma de Chihuahua in Mexico. Since 1991 he was involved in participatory research projects with Mexican elementary and secondary public schools trying to improve the organizational structure and administrative practices in these schools to facilitate the work of teachers and improve student learning. His major research interests focus on how organizational structure and administrative practices impact on the work of teachers. Eduardo was appointed National Researcher by Mexico's National Council of Science and Techonology (CONACyT) in 2007. Since 2008 he participated in a Mexican network of 10 higher education institutions which belong to the ISSPP.

Encarnacion Garza is an Associate Professor at the University of Texas at San Antonio in the Department of Educational Leadership and Policy Studies. His major emphasis in teaching is the preparation of future school principals and superintendents that will serve primarily minority children. His research is focused on the preparation of school leaders who serve in schools with predominately minority student populations. As a scholar-practitioner whose scholarship employs a critical theory perspective, his research focuses on three themes: 1) the study of minority student success, 2) the preparation of principals as leaders for social justice, and 3) the exploration of school district/university partnerships with respect to preparing principals as social justice advocates. As lead faculty for the partnership with a local school district, he is active in the international study of leadership as a researcher and participant in the International Successful School Principalship Project (ISSPP).

David Gurr is a Senior Lecturer in Educational Leadership within the Melbourne Graduate School of Education at the University of Melbourne, and has a 33-year background in secondary teaching, educational psychology, school supervision, and research in educational leadership. He is a founding member of the International

Successful School Principalship Project, and co-led an Australian team that was awarded a national grant for this project in 2005. He has more than 100 publications and has presented at more than 80 international conferences. David has been the Vice-president of the Australian Council for Educational Leaders and past Editor of *Hot Topics*, Monograph and the academic journal, *Leading and Managing*. He has received several honours from ACEL including being awarded the National Presidential Citation in 2004, a national fellowship in 2006, and the Hedley Beare Educator of the Year award in 2012.

Loke Heng Wang is a Head of Department in a primary school in Singapore. He has led teams of teachers in the areas of Character and Citizenship Education, the School Excellence Model and Mathematics. As a passionate advocate in developing people, he has nurtured teachers to take on leadership positions. He was awarded his PhD from the University of Melbourne, in 2010 for research in exploring the characteristics and practices of the principals in schools in Singapore that forms part of the International Successful School Principalship Project. He received the National Day Commendation Award honoured by the President of Republic of Singapore in 2007 for his outstanding contributions to the public service.

Stephen Jacobson is currently Professor of Educational Administration, and was formerly chair of the Department of Educational Leadership and Policy as well as the Associate Dean of Academic Affairs for the Graduate School of Education at the University at Buffalo (UB)/State University of New York. His extensive publications have examined teacher compensation, school finance, the reform of leadership preparation and effective leadership in high needs schools. He was the 2007/08 President of the University Council for Educational Administration (UCEA) and, in 1994, received UCEA's prestigious Jack Culbertson Award for outstanding contributions by a junior professor. He is the lead editor of *Leadership and Policy in Schools*. In 1999 he was President of the American Education Finance Association.

Betty Merchant received her PhD in Administration and Policy Analysis in 1991 from Stanford University. She is Dean of the College of Education and Human Development at the University of Texas at San Antonio and Professor in the Department of Educational Leadership and Policy Studies. She has taught at all grade levels, K-12 in a broad range of cultural contexts, including tribally controlled Native American schools. Her research focuses on the differential effects of educational policies and practices, particularly for students traditionally marginalized by mainstream educational settings; school leadership and educational decision-making within increasingly diverse contexts.

Yvonne Minor-Ragan has dedicated her life and her life's work to building communities and helping others. Led by her philosophy that 'if you want to improve the quality of life of a community it must be done through education', she has been a leader in revitalizing US public schools. She has been very active in the community. Yvonne was brought to Buffalo by M&T Bank as part of their educational initiative. She has worked with teachers, parents, students, and M&T to turn around what had been one of the lowest achieving schools in the Buffalo System, PS 68. Because of her innovative and strong leadership PS 68, reconstituted as the Westminster Community Charter School, was named as one of the most improved schools in New York State. Now the President of Buffalo Promise Neighbourhood, Yvonne has received many awards in recognition of her service to that region, including several Educator of the Year awards, the Governor's Award for Excellence in Education, the prestigious National Milken Educator Award, and an Honorary Doctorate from Canisius College.

Jorunn Møller is Professor at University of Oslo, the Department of Teacher Education and School Research. Her professional interests are in the areas of educational leadership and governance, reform policies and school accountability. The interplay between structure and agency is a key aspect in her studies. She has been involved in a range of research projects on school leadership and educational reform and is participating in international research networks in the field of school leadership (ISSPP), and in the field of policy and governance across Europe (LE@ DS). She is currently leading a PhD program focusing on 'Educational Leadership, School Reform and Governance, and has supervised a number of candidates who have successfully been awarded their PhD. In addition, her work includes responsibility for a Master's program for school leaders and in-service education for principals and superintendents. Her most recent funded project, which started in November 2011, is 'Legal Standards and Professional Judgement in Educational Leadership', a project which is designed to disentangle the complexity of legal standards and school leaders' professional judgment with a focus on students' right to a good psychosocial learning environment and special needs education. The project is cross-disciplinary and funded by the Research Council of Norway. Jorunn Møller has been a visiting Professor at the University of Cambridge, the University of Wisconsin-Madison and the University of Sydney. During 2009–2012 she was elected Vice Dean for research at the Faculty of Educational Sciences.

Lejf Moos is a Professor of the Department of Education (DPU) at Aarhus University, Copenhagen. He taught and studied education, school development and school leadership in Danish and international research projects, such the International Successful School Principal Project. On the basis of the research he has produced a number of books and journal articles in Danish and in English. The latter is: Moos (Ed)(2013) *Transnational Influences on Values and Practices in Nordic Educational Leadership – Is there a Nordic Model?* (Springer). He is active in European policy networks and is the president of the European Educational Research Association and a member of the World Educational Research Association Council and many editorial boards.

Elizabeth Murakami Ramalho is an Associate Professor in the Department of Educational Leadership and Policy Studies at University of Texas at San Antonio. She is a native South American who received her MA in Curriculum and Teaching, and her PhD in Educational Administration with specialization in International

Development from Michigan State University. She is an actively involved researcher in the International Successful School Principalship Project, and is focused on successful leadership and social justice issues for Latino populations, and urban and international issues in educational leadership. Her single and collaborative research in P-20 urban and international schools has been published in journals including the *Journal of School Leadership*, *Educational Management Administration and Leadership* (EMAL), and the *Journal of School Administration*. Her latest co-edited book focuses on a social justice agenda for P-20 professionals and is entitled 'Educational Leaders Encouraging the Intellectual and Professional Capacity of Others: A Social Justice Agenda'.

Ross Notman is an Associate Professor in Education at the University of Otago and Director of the Centre for Educational Leadership and Administration. He was the foundation Head of Department of Education Studies and Professional Practice at the new University of Otago College of Education for 2007–8. In 2009, he was a Visiting Fellow at the Teacher and Leadership Research Centre at the University of Nottingham. He was awarded a Fulbright Travel Scholarship in 2010 to Indiana and Alaska to study and compare innovative leadership programs for rural principals. Ross's major research interests focus on teacher and school principal development, particularly in the field of the personal dimensions of principalship. He is the New Zealand project director of an international research study, across 14 countries, into the leadership practices of successful school principals, and an eight-country study of how to prepare educators to be leaders of high-needs schools. He has also been the director of a New Zealand government-funded research project that examined values teaching and learning in the New Zealand school curriculum. Ross is a member of the editorial board for the *Journal of Educational Leadership, Policy and Practice* and was a recipient of the Minolta Dame Jean Herbison Scholarship in 2005. He has been a national council member of the New Zealand Educational Administration and Leadership Society since 2003.

Petros Pashiardis is a Professor of Educational Leadership and the Academic Coordinator of the 'Studies in Education' Program with the Open University of Cyprus. He has also worked at the University of Cyprus from 1992–2006 as an Associate Professor of Educational Administration. Before joining the University of Cyprus he worked as a schoolteacher, an Education Consultant with the Texas Association of School Boards and an Assistant Professor with the University of Texas-Permian Basin where he was heavily involved in research and teaching on the School Principalship, on Strategic Planning in Education program. He has worked or lectured in many countries including Malta, Great Britain, India, New Zealand, Greece, Germany, South Africa, Switzerland, Australia, and the United States. He has also been a Visiting Professor at the University of Pretoria, in 2004 and a Visiting Scholar at the University of Stellenbosch, South Africa. On his own or with others, he has authored well over 100 articles in scholarly and professional journals many of them on aspects of leaders and leadership. In 2008, he co-edited the *International Handbook on the Preparation and Development of School Leaders*, together with Jacky Lumby and Gary Crow. For the period 2004–2008, Professor Pashiardis has been President of the Commonwealth Council for Educational Administration and Management. He is now on the Board of Governors of the Commonwealth Foundation.

Raihani is a Senior Lecturer at Universitas Islam Negeri (UIN) of Riau, after having recently completed a postdoctoral fellowship at the University of Western Australia (2009–12). He has published two monographs and is now working on a book entitled *Creating Multicultural Citizens: A Portrayal of Contemporary Indonesian Education*.

Vassos Savvides is a doctoral student in Educational Leadership and Policy at the Open University of Cyprus. He holds a BA in Educational Sciences and an MA in Educational Management and Evaluation. He worked as a Lecturer in Primary Education and a research assistant at the Open University of Cyprus. Currently, he is a Training Officer at the Cyprus Academy of Public Administration. His research interests include school leadership, educational effectiveness, organizational culture, and civic and citizenship education. He has participated in a number of international comparative research projects such as the International Successful School Principalship Project and Leadership Improvement for Student Achievement.

Monika Törnsén has a PhD in education and is Assistant Professor at the Centre for Principal Development at Umeå University, Sweden. Her focus is on pedagogical leadership and supervision, leadership in relation to the core processes of schooling, learning and teaching and the mission of schools i.e. the school's national objectives as a whole, staff-related issues and school results. Besides the International Successful School Principalship Project (ISSPP), she is involved in the European Policy Network on School leadership (EPNoSL) which aims to improve school leadership in Europe through a collaborative network in which members co-construct, manage and share knowledge intended to inform policy in the area of school leadership, and in a EU-Comenius project named Professional Learning through Reflection promoted by Feedback and Coaching (PROFLEC). Monika, a former teacher and principal, teaches at the National School Leadership Training Program and on courses in pedagogical leadership with an emphasis on the core of schooling – the teaching and learning program – and quality enhancement.

Celina Torres-Arcadia is full-time faculty member at Tecnológico de Monterrey, Campus Monterrey, Mexico. Since 2006, she has been an active member of the research group Schools as Knowledge Organizations in the graduate program in education of the Tecnológico de Monterrey. The group's aim is to promote initiatives oriented to identify and promote schools' administrative practices that enable better conditions for teaching and learning. Since 2008, Celina has also led the Mexico research group in the International Successful School Principalship Project (ISSPP). In this project she collaborates with the leaders of other research groups of other 14 countries, and has led the development of the first digital knowledge base to support sharing best practices between principals along Latin-American schools. Her major research interests focus on organizational identity, and particularly how the identity concept is related to the school learning profile.

Dorit Tubin is an educational sociologist, and a Senior Lecturer in the Department of Education, Division of Educational Administration, and head of the Center of Promotion of Professionalism in Education, Ben-Gurion University of the Negev, Israel. Her main field of interest is educational organizations (schools, universities), the mechanisms that explain their behaviour, and the factors that enhance or hinder their improvement. Her current research consists of successful school leadership, school organizational structure and marketing, innovative learning environments, and the interactions between schools and national identity.

Gunn Vedøy holds a PhD in Educational Leadership from the University of Oslo, Norway. Her main research interest is in compulsory education in both a national and international context, concerning such issues as multiculturalism, leadership, ICT, religion and adapted education. The theme of her doctoral work was leadership, democracy and compulsory education for students from linguistic and cultural minorities in Norway. She has been a part of the Norwegian research team in both the International Successful School Principalship Project (ISSPP) and the project ISSPP – revisited. She has also been involved in an EU project concerning the development of educational leadership and ICT. Gunn has worked as a teacher in primary and adult education and in teacher training programs. She is currently employed as a researcher at the International Research Institute of Stavanger (IRIS) where she is involved in projects concerning Education, migration and minorities, and innovation in the public sector.

Teresa A. Wasonga is a Fulbright scholar and Associate Professor of Educational Leadership at the Department of Leadership, Educational Psychology, and Foundations at Northern Illinois University, USA. A graduate of University of Missouri–Columbia, she has put her learning into action by co-founding an innovative High School for disadvantaged highly intelligent girls in Kenya – a school good enough for the richest and open to the poorest. In addition to teaching and research on leadership in the United States, she has done research in Kenya leading, partly to this publication. Teresa has worked as a Visiting Professor at the Institute for Educational Development–East Africa, Aga Khan University in Dar es Salaam, Tanzania; and the University of Eastern Africa–Baraton, Eldoret, Kenya. She has published in several educational journals including *Journal of School Leadership; International Journal of Educational Management; Leadership and Policy in Schools; International Studies in Educational Administration; Education and Urban Society; UCEA Review; Multicultural Perspectives;* and *Educational Considerations.* Recent book chapters include: 'The silent minority: invisible bridges among African immigrants in America'; 'Perspectives on K-12 learning and teacher preparation in East Africa'; and 'Mitigating the impacts of educational policies in rural Kenya'.

Foreword

Brian J. Caldwell

The International Successful School Principalship Project (ISSPP) is the most comprehensive and coherent international comparative study of the principalship ever undertaken. It has been in progress for more than 10 years in over 15 countries, engaging the world's leading scholars and practitioners in the field of educational leadership. If ever there was a sound basis for outstanding policymaking it surely has been constructed in this project.

The publications that have drawn on the findings constitute a field of study in their own right, as documented in the first chapter of the book, which is the fourth to be published, complementing scores of refereed publications of shorter length and more than one 100 research-based case studies. It is fitting that the fourth in the series presents these studies in the voice of the principal.

The body of knowledge that has been constructed over more than a decade satisfies every criterion for quality longitudinal research. The studies have been guided by a robust conceptual framework that was sensitive to context. Account was taken of extant research, always assured given the eminence of the scholars who participated. Quantitative and qualitative methods were utilized. The large number of case studies was complemented by other approaches to the collection and analysis of data. These were not one-shot case studies in most instances because some principals were visited on many occasions, often over several years. The project as a whole is iterative in the way that findings at each stage are taken into account in the next. It is for these reasons that no one publication should be read as an account of the project as a whole, but each should be complete in terms of purpose and methodology, and this criterion is satisfied at a high level in the pages that follow.

Some policymakers and scholars are sceptical of international comparative studies or, indeed, any effort to draw lessons for the local setting from what has been achieved in another country where the conditions may differ in often dramatic fashion. Such scepticism is not warranted in this instance. The editors have been involved from the outset, are leaders in the field of leadership and are at the top of their game. They have synthesized the findings in the final chapter in remarkable fashion. It is this kind of project that can lead to new theory and what is presented comes as close as any effort I have seen. I am satisfied that all concerned with the preparation and ongoing development of principals can design and deliver programmes of support on the basis of these findings, no matter what the setting. A newly appointed principal in a small school in a remote setting can learn as much, and be as inspired as much, as the experienced principal in the largest schools.

There are three noteworthy strengths of this book that resonate strongly with my interests. The first relates to a common theme in other international comparative studies that show that it is neither possible nor appropriate to generalize particular strategies that should be adopted to ensure success for all schools in all settings. I was particularly interested to see what was reported for principals in different contexts, given that some lead 'turnaround' schools while others lead schools that have sustained high performance for many years. It is striking that the broad themes can be generalized but the particular ways that particular strategies are employed differ from setting to setting. Success therefore calls for a high level of judgement, wisdom and artistry.

A second strength lies in the strong and unequivocal affirmation that successful principals must not only be at the forefront of knowledge and skill in learning and teaching but must also be actively engaged in one way or another. In one instance the principal of a very large school is teaching a class and learning beside his colleagues to ensure all are at the leading edge of knowledge.

Finally, and this observation will come as no surprise to those who know my endeavours over the years, these principals do not need to be told what to do, and are not, and need not, be unnecessarily constrained by centrally-determined command-and-control or carrot-and-stick policies and procedures. They are self-leading and self-managing and they set a high priority on helping their colleagues develop the same capacities. The research reported in these pages reinforces my view that a high priority in each jurisdiction in public education and governing bodies of schools in the private sector should be to build the capacity of all leaders to do the things that these principals are doing so well.

Brian J. Caldwell
Managing Director and Principal Consultant
Educational Transformations

Professorial Fellow
University of Melbourne

Chapter 1

Leading schools successfully

David Gurr and Christopher Day

The International Successful School Principalship Project (ISSPP) has, since 2002, sought to understand the characteristics, dispositions and qualities of successful principals in successful schools. It has done this across more than 15 countries and has produced more than 100 multiple perspective research informed case studies, more than 80 journal papers, 20 individual book chapters, four project books, three international books, and five special issues of journals.

The first project book of the ISSPP (Leithwood & Day, 2007a) comprised of country reports from the initial group of seven countries. The view of Leithwood and colleagues (e.g. Leithwood *et al.*, 2006; Leithwood & Riehl, 2005) that successful school leadership is transformational and comprises at least four core dimensions of setting direction, developing people, developing the school and managing the instructional program was found to apply across many countries, despite their differing social, economic and educational histories. However, these core dimensions were extended, for there was also evidence for additional practices such as strategic problem solving, articulating a set of core ethical values, building trust and being visible in the school, building a safe and secure environment, introducing productive forms of instruction to staff, and coalition building. More importantly, perhaps, it was clear that successful principals promote equity, care and achievement. In effect, they exercise both transformational, and instructional values led leadership.

The second and third project books saw a move to cross-national analysis, with book two exploring instructional leadership, organizational learning and culturally responsive practices across countries (Ylimaki & Jacobson, 2011), and book three the sustainability of successful leadership (Moos *et al.*, 2011). Ylimaki and Jacobson (2011) found that successful leadership is: *context sensitive* in that global, national and local contexts need to be considered to fully understand the behaviour of principals; best thought of as a *layered and multidimensional*, with, for example, instructional leadership influence distributed within a school, and *having multiple foci* such as academic improvement, satisfying accountability policies, and promoting democratic education; *socially* constructed from the interaction of the life experiences and knowledge of principals with their work; promotes *sustainability* of success through the interaction of values, influence skills, and emotional and intellectual qualities of leaders. Moos *et al.* (2011) found several factors which seem to be important for sustained success: diagnosis, discernment, emotional understanding, self-renewing communication (negotiation and deliberation) and distribution of leadership; personal qualities and beliefs such as resilience, commitment to making a difference, and engaging the school and wider community; balancing discourses (e.g. social justice and high achievement); utilizing both transformational and instructional leadership practices; professional learning (whether it be through compulsory or voluntary programs); and, managing accountability expectations.

This book marks a special contribution to the work of the ISSPP. For the first time, a collection of the stories behind the research is presented, told by the principals themselves through a series of conversations with ISSPP researchers. It tries to capture the exhilaration, privilege, opportunity, and some of the issues and concerns that go with the principal role. It is a celebration (without being a valorization) of the work of principals throughout the world; and what we find is not only illustrations of their values, qualities, skills and practices but also their sheer, sustained hard work over time, the hope they bring for better education for children and young people, the constancy of their commitment, and their continuing palpable passion.

The book draws upon two sources of inspiration. First, within the ISSPP we have been concerned from the outset to provide a sense of as well as the facts of the work of successful principals. In the first three books, the mixed method research of the ISSPP helped to theorize and provide rich, more nuanced understandings of successful school leadership, the voices of the principals themselves were often in the background. This fourth book, in contrast, provides a window into the lived experience of being a successful principal. The second inspiration is a collection of 16 stories of successful Australian principals focused on the exhilaration of being a principal (Duignan & Gurr, 2008a). Principals were selected based on professional nomination, as were the writers of the chapters. In synthesizing the stories from these books, several themes emerged. The principals clearly articulated their educational philosophy and had a strong sense of moral purpose. They had a passionate belief in the significance of their work, an unwavering hope for a better future, and commitment to making a difference for all students. Their leadership was seen as a service to others, and they focused much of their work on developing people, including themselves. They developed professional cultures across their schools and communities that were collaborative, collegial and inclusive. They also demonstrated a range of personal qualities that helped them in their work, such as: having a love of learning, having a 'can do' attitude, and accepting of the demanding and difficult work. Above all they enjoyed and gained much satisfaction from their work as shown by one of the principals, John Fleming (who is also part of the ISSPP research):

> I love my job, I love it. It is not all hard work and drudgery, and, how am I going to get through it?' It is actually exhilarating.
>
> (Gurr & Duignan, 2008, p. 2)

Recently, Notman (2011) has produced an edited collection of 11 successful New Zealand educational leaders, with many of the stories drawn from the cases studies of the ISSPP in New Zealand.

For *Leading Schools Successfully: Stories from the Field*, each research group from the ISSPP was asked to nominate principals whose stories could illustrate the findings from the first three books. The researchers went back to the principals and interviewed them, focusing on why they had become a principal and what the principalship meant to them; key accomplishments/contributions and their personal and professional satisfactions from the job; key challenges; how and why they had made a difference in their schools, school community, wider society, perhaps with a story illustrating this; their hopes/aspirations for the future. We believe that such narratives complement the multi-perspective data presented previously, though they do not replace them; and that readers who are principals themselves or principal educators may find resonance with their own work and experiences.

In constructing this book we have grouped the chapters into themes of school turnaround, leader formation, values and trust, and social justice as explained briefly here.

The first theme consists of four stories of schools in crisis which have been turned around by the leadership of a new principal and in which the turnaround has been sustained. There is one story from the USA (New York State), and one each from Israel, Mexico and Kenya. In each case, principals with passion, belief and knowledge have, over several years been able to move the schools from 'failing' to at least 'good'. In one case (Minor-Ragan & Jacobson), we know that this success has been sustained over more than a decade.

The next theme consists of four chapters which explore the formation of successful principals, drawing on cases from Denmark, USA, Australia and England. What is evident in these stories is that whilst serendipity plays a part, there is a deliberate sense of recently appointed principals searching for more from their work, in order to exert more influence over the quality of educational practices in their schools. Long ago, David Loader (1997) described successfully leading a school as requiring an inquiring mindset, always searching for new ideas and new possibilities. In each case we see the restlessness of these educators, they are not satisfied with the status quo and are always seeking to improve the schools they are working in and themselves. Networking, choice of career progression, high standards, conviction and a broad understanding of school success are features of the cases.

The role of values and developing trust are the themes of the next four chapters, with cases drawn from New Zealand, Cyprus, Sweden and Singapore. The impact of personal and professional values on principal work and how values support the development of successful schools is explored in the New Zealand and Swedish cases, whilst the focus on the Cyprus chapter is on how high levels of trust are developed and sustained and how trust impacts on school improvement. The Singapore chapter shows a reciprocal relationship between the principal and school community in terms of the values that are important to the school and the high level of mutual trust shown.

The final theme consists of three chapters which focus on social justice in stories from Norway, USA (Texas) and Indonesia of schools in challenging contexts. The Norwegian case describes the work of a principal committed to providing an outstanding education for all students through the active and continuing promotion by the principal of high expectations, valuing of diversity and difference, fostering equity and social justice as personal commitments, and collaboration within and without the school. From Texas there is the story of a principal who grew up in the challenging community that she now serves as principal, and who is passionate about providing outstanding leaning opportunities for young people in this area. The Indonesian case provides an example of a 'cultural outsider' who has succeeded in creating a successful school, through taking controversial paths to provide local students with a high expectation school environment.

Each chapter concludes with reflections for the reader to consider. In this way we hope that the stories will raise issues and themselves will promote in the readers a restlessness to seek and develop new understandings about leading schools at both personal and institutional levels. In the final chapter we attempt to make sense of the many stories by linking their messages with research knowledge about successful school leadership, suggesting further possibilities for research and practice.

References

Day, C., Jacobson, S., & Johansson, O. (2011). Leading organisational learning and capacity building, in R. Ylimaki & S. Jacobson (Eds.) *US and cross-national policies, practices and preparation: Implications for successful instructional leadership, organizational learning, and culturally responsive practices* (Dordrecht: Springer-Kluwer), pp. 29–50.

Drysdale, L., Goode, H., & Gurr, D. (2009). Successful school leadership: Moving from success to sustainability, *Journal of Educational Administration*, 47(6), pp. 697–708.

Duignan, P. & Gurr, D. (Eds) (2008a). *Leading Australia's schools* (Sydney: ACEL and DEST).

Duignan, P. & Gurr, D. (2008b). Hope for a better future, in P. Duignan & D. Gurr (Eds.) *Leading Australia's schools* (Sydney: ACEL and DEST), pp. 157–164.

Gurr, D. & Duignan, P. (2008). Leading Australia's schools, in P. Duignan & D. Gurr (Eds.) *Leading Australia's schools* (Sydney: ACEL and DEST), pp. 5–12.

Jacobson, S., Johnson, L., & Ylimaki, R. (2011). Sustaining school success: A case for governance change, in L. Moos, O. Johansson, & C. Day (Eds.) *How school principals sustain success over time: International perspectives* (Dordrecht: Springer-Kluwer), pp. 109–126.

Johnson, L., Moller, J., Pashiardis, P., Savvides, V., & Vedoy, G. (2011). Culturally responsive practices, in R. Ylimaki & S. Jacobson (Eds.), *US and cross-national policies, practices and preparation: Implications for successful instructional leadership, organizational learning, and culturally responsive practices perspectives* (Dordrecht: Springer-Kluwer), pp. 75–101.

Leithwood, K. & Day, C. (Eds) (2007a). *Successful school leadership in times of change perspectives* (Dordrecht: Springer-Kluwer).

Leithwood, K. & Day, C. (2007b). What we learned: A broad view, in K. Leithwood & C. Day (Eds.) *Successful school leadership in times of change perspectives* (Dordrecht: Springer-Kluwer), pp. 189–203.

Leithwood, K., Day, C., Sammons, P., Harris, A. & Hopkins, D. (2006). *Seven strong claims about successful school leadership, National College of School Leadership* (Nottingham: National College of School Leadership).

Leithwood, K. & Riehl, C. (2005). What we know about successful school leadership, in W. Firestone & C. Riehl (Eds.) *A new agenda: Directions for research on educational leadership* (New York: Teachers College Press) pp. 22-47.

Loader, D. (1997). *The inner principal* (London: The Falmer Press).

Moos, L., Johansson, O., & Day, C. (Eds.) (2011). *How school principals sustain success over time: International perspectives* (Dordrecht: Springer-Kluwer).

Notman, R. (Ed.) (2011). *Successful educational leadership in New Zealand: Case studies of schools and an early childhood centre* (Auckland, NZ: New Zealand Council for Educational Research).

Ylimaki, R. & Jacobson, S. (Eds.) (2011). *US and cross-national policies, practices and preparation: Implications for successful instructional leadership, organizational learning, and culturally responsive practices* (Dordrecht: Springer-Kluwer).

Part I

School improvement

Sustaining the "turnaround"
in schools serving challenging
communities

Chapter 2

USA

Her own words: turning around an under-performing school

Yvonne Minor-Ragan and Stephen Jacobson

Introduction and overview

Since 2001, a research team from the State University of New York at Buffalo has been studying a kindergarten through grade 8 school in the second largest, but poorest, school district in New York State. Specifically, the team has reported about the work of an exemplary principal, Dr. Yvonne Minor-Ragan who, since she first took over the leadership of the school in 1994, has managed to turn around student achievement and then sustain and continue the school's improved performance for 17 years and counting (for more information about Dr. Minor-Ragan's accomplishments see Giles *et al.*, 2005; Jacobson *et al.*, 2005; 2007 & 2009).

During her tenure at the school, which serves a predominantly low socio-economic student population, with over 90 percent receiving free or reduced lunch, Dr. Minor-Ragan has helped transform it from being one of the worst performing schools in the district to one of its best. In fact, the school has been recognized as being one of the most improved schools in the entire state of New York.

In this chapter, rather than reporting second-hand about the work Dr. Minor-Ragan has undertaken at Fraser (a pseudonym for the actual school), I asked her instead to describe in her words how she approaches her work and her responsibilities to the children in her charge. Among other key issues discussed, she offers insights about how she developed the skills needed to be a successful principal and recommendations to other school leaders struggling to turn around low performing schools.

In order to frame this discussion, the chapter is presented in an interview format with Dr. Minor-Ragan responding to questions about how she successfully turned around her school's performance, how she has sustained high levels of student achievement over the years and how she learned and developed her leadership skills.

How did you approach turning your school's performance around?

Making a difference

When we prepare for a career in teaching, we approach the mission with the desire and belief that we can make a difference in the lives of students. We want to be successful. Therefore, tapping into teachers' desire to be successful was one of the key motivating strategies I used to launch the plan of turning-around the performance of our school. This approach, along with recommendations from the Effective Schools Research (Edmonds, 1979), gave us a clear direction for identifying our vision, setting our goals and developing, implementing and assessing our strategic plans. From this research, we understood that five key elements had to be present if our school was going to improve: (1) high expectations held by all; (2) an orderly environment; (3) clear common goals understood by everyone; (4) a strong professional development program; and, (5) strong parent involvement.

Setting high expectations

Setting high expectations focused everyone on the strengths of their students, channeled their teaching to meet those expectations and challenged students to deeper levels of learning. Concurrently, creating a safe, orderly environment helped to organize the school's culture by establishing routines and defining expectations, all of which enhanced student learning. Articulating a set of clear, common goals was necessary so that everyone would be working toward the same mission and vision, and that all planning and activities would be implemented for the sole purpose of achieving those goals. A viable and relevant program of professional development was instituted to assist the staff in achieving and maintaining excellence in their teaching. This program was designed to reflect the evolving needs of the staff as they improved and refined their instructional skills and strategies to meet the needs of their students. Strong parental involvement completed the five key elements, whether it was strong support at home, being highly visible in the school, or simply being available by phone. These five elements enabled us to become a thriving, successful school rather than remaining an underperforming school that merely existed.

Shared decision-making

Based on these five elements, shared decision-making was introduced in the form of five school wide committees – School Beautification, Discipline, Student and Staff Morale, Curriculum and Staff Development, and Parent Involvement. Every member of the school's staff, along with parent volunteers, was required to join at least one committee. The work of the committees initially consisted of surveying the staff to determine how each committee could assist in positively impacting the school's goals. The committees then developed a plan of action, communicated those plans to the staff, processed input and suggestions, and then further refined the plan. After the final plan was presented, staff members then agreed to support and implement the committees' actions plans. We monitored change and adjusted the plans accordingly. Strong communication between and among the committees and parents was instrumental to the success of our plans.

The committees were interrelated and mutually supportive. For example, one of our goals was to increase parent involvement. We discussed the barriers to achieving this goal. The follow-up action plan included strategies to alleviate the barriers. We had to define parent involvement, particularly in regard to its role and purpose in the classroom. We then had to examine whether teachers really valued parent involvement. Next, we provided our staff with professional development about how to have positive, constructive conversations with parents, addressing such issues as which words to use or not use when discussing children. We also discussed one's tone of voice and how to develop a strong system of communication. But the Parent Involvement Committee could not be successful without collaborating with the other committees. For example, the Discipline committee had to gain parents' support for the school's discipline policies; Professional Development had to improve communication skills in the school; School Beautification needed to creatively display student work; and, the Student and Staff Morale committee needed to find ways to acknowledge and value students and parents for their contributions to the class and school community.

Shared decision-making through the use of committees proved to be a successful strategy because it required on-going communication among the staff and parents and developed strong buy-in from everyone. Team cohesiveness and trust among colleagues increased. Fear of change lessened and we experienced an increase in people's willingness to try new strategies and their colleagues' ideas. The staff felt empowered to make important decisions about their school and one key result was that their confidence of their own teaching abilities increased. My role, as the formal leader, became one of monitoring the momentum and insuring that all staff complied with the agreed upon policies. This strategy also allowed me to become more of an instructional leader, resulting in increased time in the classrooms observing students and teachers, monitoring instruction, giving specific verbal and written feedback, and participating in classroom activities and celebrations. By knowing what was occurring in the classrooms, I was in a better position to recommend and guide our Professional Development program, and further support the work of the committees.

Improvements in the school's performance certainly did not happen overnight. It was slow and steady, but together we created a culture of professionalism that supported staff planning, sharing and learning. Utilizing committees that engaged in shared decision-making was a strategy that successfully produced a highly committed, goal-oriented staff dedicated to doing what was necessary for our students to achieve. And, our students definitely achieve!

How have you managed to sustain and improve performance?

Over the years, we have been successful at maintaining high performance standards by making it an intentional school goal, just as we do student success. We have accomplished this by utilizing several strategies: establishing and maintaining strong lines of communication within the school community; building a school structure that supports collaboration; providing a relevant professional development program that readily responds to the needs of the students and staff; and, for my part, as the instructional leader and chief cheerleader, being visible throughout the building and readily accessible to the staff, students and parents.

Strong communication needs to go in all directions: from administration to staff, parents and students; from students to staff, parents, and the administration; and from staff and parents to all others as well. We all need to know that we are being heard, and that our input and suggestions are being given serious consideration. Concerns must be addressed in a timely manner. Through a sense of collective ownership, we all have to take responsibility for our school's successes and failures. The result is that we then feel validated and understand that each of us has a key role to play.

School structure

Our school structure has been organized to support and enhance collaboration at all levels. We have bi-weekly, 15-minute staff meetings that support conversations ranging from informational meetings, celebrations of success, forums for concerns, or simply a quick way to share curriculum content. The frequency of the gatherings strengthens the bonds between staff and supports team building. We also have weekly longitudinal grade level meetings at which primary, elementary and middle school teachers plan, learn and share ideas pertinent to their respective grade levels. In addition, teachers have opportunities to intensify their planning with grade level colleagues during weekly common planning periods. The administrative leadership team also has weekly planning meetings, Overarching this entire configuration is the composition of the five school-wide, site-based committees. This organizational structure allows everyone to monitor, assess, and support our common goals. Our Professional Development program also serves as a venue for staff to demonstrate their leadership skills and creativity. The result has been increased self-confidence and motivation to continue to raise the bar for student performance.

Presence

Inherent in this entire plan of ongoing sustainability is my responsibility to be highly visible and accessible to my staff, my students and my parents. I feel that I must be in and around the classrooms throughout the day. This allows me to assess the instructional program and to keep my hand on the pulse of morale within the building. I can give informal encouragement and suggestions. I can make note of any concerns in need of follow up. I am also able to maintain a "connection" with each staff member and become closer to my students. Parents appreciate having an easy access to me, either by phone, or in my office. I greet parents in the morning when they bring their children to school and at the end of the day when they are picking them up. My policy is to return all calls in a timely manner. Being an accessible principal has enabled our school community to build a strong foundation of trust, which is central to the maintenance of our standards.

Sustainability of high standards and a successful school community must be intentional. It must be planned, monitored, and nurtured at all levels.

How did you learn about and develop your leadership skills?

The influence of biography

Informal experiences dating back to childhood, through college and up to and including my present professional career have shaped my personality and style of operation. These experiences also played a key role in the development of my educational philosophy. Being a sensitive leader who is highly visible is very important to me. I work to build and maintain a high level of trust among my staff, parents and students. I also believe that it is necessary for every member of our school community to be actively involved so we may realize our vision and achieve our common goals. Each member must have input in decision-making, take ownership of the tasks at hand, and be accountable for the success of student achievement.

As a child I was extremely shy, very sensitive and insecure. It took perceptive teachers to draw me out of my shell to respond to questions in class. Even then, I would cry as I was responding. The crying embarrassed me. My solution was to cry even more! Over my elementary school years, I began to slowly respond to my teachers' encouragements to participate, to share my correct answers and to offer my opinions. My crying stopped during my middle school years. I slowly began to emerge as a leader in my class. When I see children today who are shy and reluctant to participate in class, I understand. They, too, need teachers who are perceptive and sensitive to their needs. These are two of the characteristics I look for when interviewing and hiring staff. My staff must be kind, respect our children, strive to understand our children and demonstrate empathy, not sympathy. By empathy I mean concern for the personal issues of our students, while still being firm, fair and holding to high standards. When sympathy replaces empathy, there are built in excuses for the lack of student success, such as "these students cannot achieve because they are poor," or "these students cannot achieve because they come from broken homes." Expecting high student achievement, despite a child's personal issues remains a must.

I graduated from a high school with a 100 percent minority population. I attended a university that had a minority population of less than 2 percent. This was a classic case of complete culture shock! The totally alien environment threw me back into my shyness and insecurity. Once again I was reluctant to participate in class discussions. It took professors who sensed my uneasiness and anxieties to coax me out of my newfound dilemma. Slowly I found my voice and, as a result of these experiences, I value a multiethnic staff in my school and a curriculum taught from a multicultural perspective. In our school, we also provide many opportunities for students to build self-assurance through research-based, project-learning that culminates in oral presentations and numerous public presentations. We intentionally build their self-confidence so they may feel secure when in "unfamiliar territory."

While completing my university studies, both undergraduate and graduate, I learned the value of listening, collaborating and studying in groups. I gained new insights into problem solving and learned to appreciate the perspectives of others. My understanding of issues deepened and I fully recognized the power of a "think tank." My grades soared! Similar strategies are currently being used at my school as a professional development tool and as a process in our shared decision-making model. Our staff is organized into groups based on their interests, skill levels, grades and/or issues of concern. The impact of staff learning and solving problems together has been exponential. Not only does it enhance team building, it also builds school pride and ownership of issues and solutions. Everyone feels personally responsible for the success or failure of a plan of action.

The influence of others

Thomas Sergiovanni, a leader in the field of educational research, had a powerful impact on my professional training and shaping of my educational philosophy. He recognized the benefits of shared-decision making, collaboration and mentoring. In 1984, he stated, "shared leadership is where much of the true work of building a school's vision happens." In the process of becoming what Sergiovanni refers to as a "community of leaders," teachers, administrators, parents, students and others become collectively responsible for envisioning and implementing school reform. This thinking virtually duplicated my style of operation. Sergiovanni's research helped to organize my thoughts and my plan of action. No matter how great the leader, positive and effective change is impossible without teamwork. As the leader of my school, I saw one of my key roles as creating an environment that would support collaboration – one that would support flexibility and positive change, and value the contributions of others.

I also see my role as being chief motivator. After the planning is done, then what? When things seem to be moving slowly, or not at all – who motivates the staff to keep going? When parents do not understand the process, whose role is it to clarify the plan? My role is to keep everyone focused, to keep them moving and help them when they are "stuck" in a process. An additional role is chief communicator. Everyone must be kept abreast of the school's plans, and of its progress or lack thereof. When committees and groups are working together, I provide the "glue" to keep everyone on track and aligned with our vision, goals and mission. Committee work and shared decision-making can easily become compartmentalized. My role is to assure that we all understand how each group's piece of the puzzle helps to create the larger picture.

In my role as leader, some situations must be solved with quick decision-making and do not allow for collaboration. My staff knows, understands and accepts that I reserve this right. There is no resistance to following top-down decisions when they occur, because we have been careful to build a foundation of trust and respect.

It is through this accumulation of lifelong experiences and professional training that I have evolved into who I am today. Because of my sensitive nature, I understand and respect the shyness and sensitivity of others, whether child or adult. Because of my upbringing in a totally segregated minority environment, which left me unprepared to face the culture shock of being the true minority in a much larger majority environment, I highly value the merits of a multiracial-multiethnic staff that teaches the curriculum through a multicultural perspective. I know that to be an effective leader, the entire school community must be involved in key decisions. In successful schools, I know that everyone shares the responsibility for student learning, thus increasing everyone's accountability and positively impacting student achievement.

I believe the essence of my leadership style and personality are now interwoven throughout our building. The school's climate is one that values individuality, nurtures the shy, builds self-esteem, invites collaboration and challenges and expects the best of our staff, students and parents. We have a strong foundation of trust, we are not afraid of hard work and we expect to be successful.

Conclusions: success is more than test results

Successful school leadership requires a level of consistency between one's personal espoused values and beliefs and the leadership practices exhibited in the school workplace. Dr. Minor-Ragan's responses reveal an individual whose approach to leadership is an embodiment of her beliefs and lived experiences. I have spent over a decade documenting the transformation of her school from an underperforming, often dangerous site – where it felt that the only reason students and teachers were in attendance was because they had no other options – into a high performing school that has the feel of an extended family committed to the proposition that everyone in the family will work to improve the life chances of everyone else in the family. This is a student-friendly, staff-friendly, parent-friendly, community-friendly organization that, as Dr. Minor-Ragan notes, has interwoven the essence of her leadership style and personality. When I interviewed a group of parents and asked why they to come to the school whenever needed, to a person they responded that they didn't want to disappoint Dr. Minor-Ragan. I saw this as the ultimate compliment a school leader could ever receive. The community had internalized their principal's mission and recognized that the high performance expectations she'd established for her staff, their children and, most importantly, for her, also applied to them and they would not let her down.

The most often-used measure of school success is student performance on standardized tests and by this measure, Dr. Minor-Ragan's school has exhibited remarkable improvement over the course of her tenure. But improved student test scores alone don't do justice to the extent to which her school has turned-around. In our publications, my colleagues and I have tried to capture the positive changes in the school's climate that have occurred, but I think the best way for me to express my own observations is to note that when I first visited the school, it was not a place I would have sent my own children unless I had absolutely no other choice. But today I wish my children (who are now grown) had been lucky enough to attend this school and experience what I think a true learning community for children and adults feels like.

Reflections

Ultimately, the utility of these memoirs is the extent to which they can influence, inform and improve the practices of others. Dr. Minor-Ragan's story is one of commitment, service and persistence. There are those in society we call "first-responders." These are the people, such as firemen and emergency medical technicians, who resist the natural impulse to seek safety, but instead run towards dangerous situations in order to help and save others. While schools that serve predominantly low socio-economic communities may not be equivalent to burning buildings, they are challenging educational environments and often times the youngsters they enroll are at risk in terms of fulfilling their full potential. Dr. Minor-Ragan is a first-responder of sorts, one who has made it her life's mission to serve these youngsters. But no less important than her own effort has been her ability to engage others in this important work. She has given a whole community confidence in their ability to provide their children with the quality of education that will give them a chance at a brighter future.

How does she do it? Clearly, leading by example has been the unstated, but most symbolic aspect of her approach. She embodies the values and behaviors she wants others to incorporate, such as holding high expectations for everyone – and mostly importantly herself; by maintaining an orderly environment in which all children and adults are treated respectfully; and by being very clear in the goals established for the school, which are developed collaboratively by everyone with a key stake in the enterprise – especially her educational professionals and parents. Moreover, with 17 years of service to the school and community, she has left her mark on several generations of families.

In the Leadership Initiative For Tomorrow's Schools (LIFTS) preparation program at the University at Buffalo, the first reading we use is a marvelous motivational book called *The Right Mountain: Lessons from Everest on the Real Meaning of Success* (Hayhurst, 1997), that tracks the efforts of a Canadian expedition team's efforts to climb Mount Everest. Ultimately, the team fails to summit Everest, but all make it home alive – unlike a team of expert Alpine climbers from France who die on the mountain because they were unprepared for the effects of climbing at Everest's altitude. The story drives home the point that regardless of how technically competent one is, those skills can come to naught in the wrong environment. How many technically proficient school leaders have lost their bearings when placed in the wrong educational setting? There is a temptation to encourage the reader to just do what Dr. Minor-Ragan did in her school and that all will turn out well. Certainly there are important lessons to be learned from her work that can cross contexts, but just as I remind students throughout the two-year LIFTS program to seek their "Right Mountain," so too must I remind those who happen upon this book. Dr. Minor-Ragan has employed her talents and energy on what is the Right Mountain for her. She knew she had the skills to be successful and she knew they could be utilized to best advantage in a school serving a low socio-economic community. The key lesson to be learned from her story is to develop and hone your technical competence and skills set; commit, serve and persist, and then make sure you have found a place where you can experience the true meaning of personal and professional success.

As you reflect upon your own practice, especially if presented with the opportunity to take over the leadership of a school that has a long history of under-performing, here are three questions we think you ought to consider:

1 *What are your personal and professional values, beliefs and goals?* Can you clearly articulate what it is that you stand for both as an individual and as an educator? If you can, then you can probably articulate clearly the direction and goals you hope to set for yourself and your school. You also need to be confident that upon reflection your actual practices align with your espoused beliefs, because there is no better way to lose the trust of those you are supposed to lead than to say one thing, but do another. As a school leader, you are always on public view and therefore are held accountable for modeling the actions and behaviors you expect of others.

2 *Do you have the persistence, resilience and commitment to service needed to take on the leadership of a school confronting challenging circumstances?* Turning around a school that has had a history of under-performing, especially if it is located in a community that is struggling economically, is not something that tends to happen quickly or without setbacks. Such an endeavor requires an understanding that success and its resulting gratification may come slowly. Therefore, a key role that you will play is to constantly buoy the spirits of those around you, even at times when you yourself feel a bit discouraged. It is during these darkest of times when leadership counts the most, because you will be the one who needs to keep the light of hope shining for the sake of those in your charge.

3 *Is this your Right Mountain?* Even if you feel confident that you can address the first two questions, you still need to reflect on the specific undertaking and whether it is the right place and the right time for you as a leader. You may

in fact be able to articulately assert and model your beliefs. You may feel confident that you possess the requisite skills and disposition to take on the role of leading a school that has to start turning around. Nevertheless, take a moment to reflect upon whether you will still want to be on this particular mountain perhaps five or six years from now, or however long it may take to lead the school to success and then feel confident that its success will sustain after you leave.

This internal checklist of personal reflections is offered as a guide, not an assurance. We cannot guarantee that simply because you feel confident in addressing these questions, you will in fact be successful. But what we can say as a caution is that if you don't seriously consider these simple reflections, you are probably diminishing your chances of success and the consequences of continued failure will be borne by more people than just yourself.

References

Edmonds, R. (1979). Effective schools for the urban poor. *Educational Leadership*, 37(1), pp. 15–27

Giles, C., Johnson, L., Brooks, S. & Jacobson, S. (2005). Building bridges, building community: Transformational leadership in a challenging urban context. *Journal of School Leadership*, 15(5), pp. 519–545.

Hayhurst, J. (1997). *The Right Mountain: Lessons from Everest on the Real Meaning of Success.* Toronto: John Wiley & Sons.

Jacobson, S., Johnson, L., Giles, C. & Ylimaki, R. (2005). Successful leadership in U.S. schools: Enabling principles, enabling schools. *Journal of Educational Administration*, 43(6), pp. 607–618.

Jacobson, S., Johnson, L., Ylimaki, R. & Giles, C. (2009). Sustaining school success: A case for governance change. *Journal of Educational Administration*, 47(6), pp. 753–764.

Jacobson, S., Brooks, S., Giles, C., Johnson, L. & Ylimaki, R. (2007). Successful leadership in three high poverty urban elementary schools. *Leadership and Policy in Schools*, 6(4), pp. 1–27.

Sergiovanni, T. (1984). Leadership and excellence in schooling. *Educational Leadership*, 41(5), pp. 4–13.

Chapter 3

Israel

The evolution of success

Ora Bar Yaakov and Dorit Tubin

Introduction

Oftentimes, just as it takes a village to raise a child (Clinton, 1996) it takes a school to raise a principal. Whereas educational leadership literature often deals with successful school leaders (Day & Leithwood, 2007; Day *et al.*, 2010), the journey to success is discussed less, and Ora's story reveals how long and winding this road can be.

When she was accepted to the position of principal, Ora possessed all the necessary requirements: qualifications including a master's degree in biology; experience including 18 years of preparing students for matriculation examinations and teaching students with learning disabilities; leadership opportunities including coordinating a biology curriculum and serving as a deputy principal; appropriate personal qualities including striving to succeed, and to learn from mistakes; and a supportive family. Still, success did not come immediately. The way in which Ora's leadership evolved with the success of her school is the subject of this chapter. It is organized around four parallel aspects, all of which affect a school's success: Ora's leadership career, the physical environment, the educational staff, and the educational vision. But first, we shall briefly present the school as it is today.

Rabin High School (named after the former Israeli Prime Minister, Yitzhak Rabin) is a public high school comprising a junior high (seventh–ninth grades, 13–15 years old) and an upper-secondary school (tenth–twelfth grades 16–18 years old). In 2010 the school had 1,350 students, 105 teachers, and 30 administration and maintenance staff.

The school is located in a town in southern Israel and caters for students from the nearby neighborhood, which has a medium to low socio-economic status. Despite the desert climate and the neglected surrounding environment, the school buildings and yard are well-tended, clean, and pleasant. Green lawns, blossoming gardens, and colorful murals welcome you on your arrival. The diverse student population consists of 35 percent new immigrants from the former USSR, 15 percent new immigrants from Ethiopia, and the remainder are Israeli-born from different ethnic groups. The teacher population is also diverse, with one-third of it comprised of newcomers from the former USSR. This diversity influences the school's vision, which seeks to create a caring and supportive environment for advancing and empowering teachers and students alike.

The school's success is evident in its high matriculation eligibility (81 percent compared to the national average of 46 percent), a low dropout rate (4 percent), the high degree of partnership the teachers feel for the school, its low rate of vandalism and violence, and the well-tended school building and yard. Many factors contribute to success such as this, and we shall begin with Ora.

Ora's career

When Ora was a research assistant in the biology department at the Weizmann Institute of Science (a world leading multidisciplinary research institute) she was sure about her academic career, and saw her future as a professor of molecular biology. But as a result of an accidental encounter with teaching, she discovered how satisfying and meaningful educational work could be.

At the age of 27 she started work as a biology teacher, and only later realized that she wanted to become a principal. After 18 years' experience in various positions as a teacher, coordinator and deputy, Ora felt ready to lead a school better than anyone she knew, based on her strength of character, professionalism, and knowledge of how to create a good and supportive educational place for students and teachers alike.

In 1995, she was selected to establish a new high school. She was the founding principal, and this was to be her work until she retired at the end of 2010. She realized from the start that her mission was not going to be easy. The school was under construction in both the physical and human aspects. In the first year, 400 seventh grade students (starting junior high) and tenth grade students (starting upper high school) attended the school. The teaching staff included 40 teachers, one-third of whom were newcomers from the former USSR who had lived in Israel for about five years, with only partial fluency in Hebrew. The entire teaching staff was somewhat haphazardly composed: some came from elementary schools, others from high schools, and some were new to the profession. The municipality provided the maintenance staff, with most being inexperienced newcomers from the former USSR. The administrative staff were under-qualified, and the administrator in charge lacked organizational knowledge. At the same time, part of the schoolyard was closed for ongoing construction that lasted for an additional two years. The municipality believed that "if there are students, chalk and blackboards, there are classrooms and a school."

To accomplish the daunting task of consolidating all of the above into a coherent school with a unique "personality," Ora acted in three directions: developing the physical environment, integrating staff, and developing the educational vision and curriculum.

Physical environment

The school was planned according to high standards and a unique architectural concept, and initially was a beautiful, pleasant, glass-filled building, open to the surroundings. The imprudence of this planning haunted the school in its early years. Pergolas leaked, the yard was disorganized, and on weekends the open corridors became a leisure center for the neighborhood's alcoholics, prostitutes, and vandals. Windows were smashed, classrooms were burgled, and dirt and filth reigned in the open corridors. When a ceremony or celebration took place in the schoolyard or auditorium, all the neighborhood's hooligans were in attendance, interrupting, throwing stones, and harassing the students and teachers.

These events evoked deep frustration amongst the school community, and Ora began to take systematic action to address the issues through fundraising, involving the municipality, and finding practical solutions such as metal grilles, replacing the glass doors with more solid ones, and so forth. Slowly, there was a transformation. The maintenance team invested a great deal of effort in nurturing the school, and everything that was destroyed was repaired immediately. Graffiti was erased from the desks and dirty classrooms were constantly cleaned. The teachers understood the importance of the learning environment for the school's pride, and the maintenance team developed an esprit de corps and identified with and nurtured the school.

Ora maintained the school's appearance in additional ways. She employed a painter, who had been sentenced to community service because of the graffiti he spray-painted all over the town, to decorate some of the school's walls. The outcome was that his graffiti and paintings were not only colorful and lively, but also prevented further defacement. In addition, Ora invested in irrigating the grass and keeping the schoolyard green, as part of the message of nurturing and beauty. All of these efforts bore fruit. The rich and nurturing environment, the students' and community's feeling that the school was working for them, and the high achievements, have all led to a low rate of vandalism, a good reputation, and the bullying and harassment that characterized the early years has stopped.

These processes emphasized for Ora the importance of the physical environment, not only for creating a good image but also as a meaningful educational act. Especially in a low-income neighborhood, a nurtured and clean environment is a necessary condition for high achievements. Despite Ora's educational vision, she realized that first she needed to attend to creating a safe physical environment. The educational and physical steps are interlocked, and serve as a setting for any further development (Tubin, 2008).

Staff development

From the beginning, Ora knew that she was going to lead according to the good examples of educational leadership she had encountered, while trying to avoid the bad ones. Poor behaviors included principals without a clear direction, principals who allowed the development of cliques, mutual mudslinging amongst staff, lack of backup by and for the teachers, and burned out principals who lacked authority and creativity. She promised herself to avoid such behaviors and stay with the good examples, some of which are described below.

On appointment, Ora initiated steps to present the high standards she aimed at. She introduced a computerized reporting system; established four computer laboratories; received the first staff of computer engineers in town; and conducted "open days" that included students' presentations for positioning the school as innovative, progressive, and offering a new option for the town's students.

In the years that followed, by which time the school had 1,500 students and more than 100 teachers, Ora realized she could not lead the school alone. She began to define areas of responsibility, appointed coordinators, created cooperation, and "infected" the staff with the school's ideology and her commitment. Ora was involved all the time in every tiny detail, admonishing teachers for lateness and inappropriate dress, maintaining strict discipline and a proper schedule, showing everybody what a ceremony should look like, participating in endless staff meetings, analyzing, clarifying, and modeling how things should be done. As one teacher relates: "I have never heard 'Do it yourself.' She (Ora) asked me many times: 'Do you need help? Let's call the parents together and talk to them.' there is a lot of support from the principal." At the same time she tried to understand teachers' needs and supported them with various experts on disciplinary matters, and national and social issues. Concerned for her school to thrive, Ora constantly monitored the school and the work of teachers, like a mother checking if her baby is still alive.

The challenge was not easy. The first senior staff she appointed did not last, and collapsed under her stringent demands. Fortunately, these teachers did not remain in the school, which could have been potentially destructive. Ora is willing to fight to maintain the high standards of her staff and school. For example, there was the case of a school administrator who was forced upon Ora and introduced norms of corruption and dishonesty. For a year and a half Ora fought the relevant authorities until she succeeded in having him removed. This move was important, as she believes that good administration is a prerequisite for a school's success. In a school that offers well-ordered financial management, copy-print-stenciling services for learning material, organized storage and stocking, and a professional administrative service, the teachers have the time to focus on teaching and learning.

During those early days, the administration and maintenance staff was also consolidated. Some left, and as the municipality realized the importance of the school's needs, the new people that arrived were more skilled and integrated fully with the school's spirit. As the years went by, and as positive relations based on trust were slowly formed with the school staff, Ora changed her leadership style in several ways.

Open and direct information flow

The audit and control approach Ora employed in the beginning, developed into an information-informed style of management. Instead of looking for people to check their activities, Ora realized that for effective management she had to receive valid information not only from the management team (deputy and coordinators), but also directly from teachers, students and parents. Thus, she established open discussions with everybody. In addition to the open-door policy, which enables anyone to come in and talk to her, Ora never hesitates to ask for information if she needs it. Every teacher and staff member knows that at any time they can be asked to provide information about their actions and achievements. As one of the teachers said: "I've got to have answers. Having no answers is not an option." This is not for the sake of control or inspection, but rather a process of inquiry and learning about how the school is progressing. It obviously relies on the development of an environment of trust as indicated elsewhere in this chapter.

This approach is widespread throughout the school and is reflected in the teamwork evident. Ora understood that the most important organizational unit is the intimate team within which teachers work, obtain support, share knowledge and experience, and gain the confidence and courage to innovate and explore new avenues. Through teamwork Ora has distributed her educational leadership to numerous partners, transferred the decisions to the place and people who can implement them, and allowed them take over part of Ora's work of managing a large school.

Succeeding with the current staff

The turnover of teachers who did not accept Ora's way on the one hand, and the limited authority of the Israeli principal regarding staff recruitment (which is usually done by the Ministry of Education and the municipality) on the other, led Ora to the conclusion that she had to succeed with her current staff, accepting their strengths as well as their limitations; this is an example of the contemporary need to manage the talent within a school (Davies & Davies, 2011). She learned to obtain the maximum from her staff in the following ways:

- *High demand and high support* – in addition to clarifying the roles and expectations required from each member of staff, Ora provides support and care. She creates personal working space for teachers, provides time for preparation of learning materials, is responsive to their various needs, and praises initiative and investment, usually in front of others. At the same time, Ora maintains an open and transparent environment by discouraging cliques, avoiding the creation of favored circles of staff, and shunning the use of flamboyant events.
- *Teacher involvement in school responsibilities* – Ora has learned that given appropriate opportunities and experiences, teachers are perfectly capable

of sharing the leadership and management of the school. Thus, she offers numerous positions for shared leadership and teacher involvement in school management responsibilities. Today, half of the teachers serve in different positions of responsibility.

- *Full backing* – over the years Ora has learned that to achieve teachers' trust and commitment, she has to back them against the pressure and demands of various actors inside and outside the school. Even when such backing required confrontation with different authorities, Ora used it for delineating borders that respect teachers' professional autonomy, and allowed them a professionally safe space for trying new ideas, thinking creatively, and occasionally making mistakes.

These methods bore fruit, and a committed, professional, and responsible staff was created in the school. The teachers trust Ora, they are involved in initiating changes and implementing them, critiquing new ideas, and increasingly contributing to the school's success. As one of the teachers said: "Despite my long years of experience I still enjoy coming to the school … I know I am appreciated here and get full backup. I love the students, the cooperation with the parents, and the wonderful staff."

Educational vision and the curriculum

Since the early years, Ora has declared that the school's organizational focus is "achievement promotion." This element, which prima facie seems fully instrumental, helped to set a clear direction for the diverse student and teacher population, and conveyed the ideology whereby the school commits to allowing every student to achieve to their maximum, more than could be expected from his/her family background, and thus enabling greater opportunities and choices in their future. This element was universally accepted and enhanced the school's image as "The Best."

Such a declaration leads the teachers to start checking the students' actual achievements. On inspection of the proficiency examination taken by all the seventh graders when entering the school, a low level of skills and knowledge, especially in language, was found. As a result, the staff developed a special curriculum, "Language Milestones," which has operated since 2003. The curriculum's aim is twofold: the first goal is to establish and strengthen language foundation (reading, writing, learning strategies, reading comprehension, and wording), and the second is to connect the students and teachers, many of whom are immigrants, to the Hebrew language and the Zionist ethos (that Israel is the country of all Jews). Dealing with the strata of the Hebrew language, Bible stories, and Zionist history, connects the students to the Israeli time, habitat, and heritage.

The "Language Milestones" curriculum is implemented at the seventh and eighth grades by "cluster teachers," who are responsible for one class and teach it 16 hours a week in humanistic subjects (such as language, literature, history).

In addition, these teachers meet their class every morning for the good morning blessing, checking of attendance, and engaging in conversation on topical and student matters. In this way the teacher becomes deeply acquainted with each student's strengths and weakness, and manages to create a stable environment, a sense of belonging, and good learning habits. Additionally, the school holds morning assembly for all students to inculcate important events like November 29 (the date in 1947 on which the United Nations General Assembly adopted its Partition Plan for Palestine and the establishment of the State of Israel). The "Language Milestones" curriculum worked well from the first year: the number of disturbance and obedience problems was reduced, and student achievements increased.

For responding to the learning needs of students across all grades, the school offers diverse programs in areas such as the sciences, social sciences, management, arts, music, sport, theater, communications, cinema studies, electrical practical engineering, and computer programming. In addition, to enable every student to advance at his/her own pace, the school offers several levels of study: empowerment classes in small groups, and for longer hours for students experiencing difficulties, regular classes, and excellence classes. The request for excellence classes came from students and parents, and Ora was willing to try this. It has been a success with achievement and satisfaction of students in the excellence classes increasing, and achievement of good students in the regular classes also improving. Parents of these students have also shown increased satisfaction with the school.

But success has not blinded Ora. She discovered that despite her confidence and ambitions, she does not have all the answers, and her current theory of action was constructed over a long process of trial and error. Failures are part of the process of knowledge acquisition, and each new failure is needed for creating new hypotheses. Realizing this, Ora encouraged open discussion and polyphony of views, believing that from many voices some will always have the right answer for the problem at hand. Open discussion has been institutionalized at the school in several ways:

- *Open door* – Ora's door is open not only as a policy, but also physically. Any student or staff member can enter the principal's office at any time, and any problem is dealt with in a relevant and participative manner, aiming towards a constructive solution.
- *Students Day* – one day every trimester no regular classes take place. This day is devoted to a personal meeting between the teachers and each of their students, to ask them how they are doing, set targets for the next trimester, and discuss ways of achieving these targets. Students love these days, and none miss them.
- *Relations with parents* – according to Ora, a school is obliged to listen to the parents, explain itself to them, and learn from them. She has managed to transform the parents committee (in Israel there is an annually elected parents committee) into a leading group that works hand-in-hand with

the leadership team to promote the school and to fundraise. A transparent discussion process was created in which the parents committee ask for explanations and accountability from the school, cooperate in developing school policy, and become ambassadors for marketing the school. This process with the parents committee gives the school confidence that what the school is doing is worthwhile, maintains its high regard in the community, and builds its reputation as a successful school.

- *Cooperation with the students committee* – Ora considers the students committee as an important partner for open discussion in many ways. The discussions reveal students' needs and difficulties, and are a forum for developing mutual solutions to the issues that arise (such as the need to replace the cafeteria contractor, or to change to healthy food). The student group helps market the school inside and outside, and they help on open days for students from the feeder elementary schools.
- *Professional authority* – one reason teachers consult with Ora and share their thoughts and difficulties, is her professional authority. While according to Ora there is no necessity for a principal to teach in a class (she has important matters to attend to that nobody else can do for her), teaching experience and pedagogical expertise is a mandatory requirement for having professional authority with the teachers, gaining their trust, and creating an environment of openness.

Insights and lessons

Ora's first years in the principalship were years in which the school developed Ora no less than she developed the school. Her basic confidence, the leading team she chose and developed over the years, the development of collaborative thinking, real time reporting, and everyday encounters, facilitated constant improvement of the school. Reflecting as she approaches her retirement at the end of 2010, Ora can see that the school is a success and that it is in good shape for her successor. She is grateful for the wonderful privilege of establishing the school, seeing it flourish, and she summarizes this personal process with several insights and lessons:

- *It takes time to succeed* – it is very difficult, if at all possible, to succeed immediately in the first years (Tubin & Regev-Ofek, 2010). It takes time to get to know the school, its members, and also yourself as principal. Leaders of successful school need to be there long enough to create sustainable management – a key for an effective school. It took Ora seven years! Only then did she feel she was on the right road to decoding the complicated system of leading a successful school.
- *Nothing succeeds like success* – the principal's capable, positive and high expectation attitudes were evident in the school from the beginning. When there is vision, commitment, motivation and the right direction, this helps the staff to trust the principal. When this leads to success, success itself

becomes a key ingredient in the school's progress, and enables dealing efficiently with numerous factors inside and outside the school, while maintaining autonomy and professional space.

- *Success has its price* – leading a school is a very demanding job that requires endless patience, long hours and a great deal of energy. Personal circumstances can help sustain this type of work. Ora is lucky that she has a supportive family. While raising her children, her husband always provided a secure and supportive place to discuss experiences and distress. Her family's wonderful acceptance, her ability to travel abroad with her husband to recharge her energy, and engaging in regular physical activity (working, gym, and swimming), all supported Ora and allowed her to devote herself fully to her school.

Ora sums up her rich and long experience in the following working principles:

1 *Choosing a clear and agreed direction* – choosing the direction of "achievement promotion" defined a curriculum development pathway, and it enabled the constant clarification of basic school values such as integrity, transparency, credibility, caring, commitment, ambition, and partnership.
2 *Building a positive reputation* – wanting to be "the best" and to be regarded as "innovative" meant setting high standards throughout the school in physical and human resources, in teaching and learning, and in the symbolic and cultural elements (Sergiovanni, 1984). For example, wanting to be involved in a high status program like the experimental school network confirmed the school's innovative image and contributed to its good reputation.
3 *Developing the school staff* – in a culture of partnership and trust, staff are allowed space for trial and error, and to try new experiences. Trust can be enhanced by providing opportunities for discussion, by being selective about which programs are introduced into the school, through repelling unreasonable initiatives enforced on the school, and by enhancing the social collegiality of staff.
4 *Management flexibility* – use of information to inform decisions means that policy and practice decisions can be made according to school needs and successes.
5 *Creating operating partnerships* – to gather funds, resources and legitimacy, partnerships inside and outside the school can be cultivated. Examples include creating cooperation with the parent and student committees, community representatives, and stakeholders for fundraising, and with universities and external professionals for new pedagogical ideas and innovations.

For Ora, there is no job as powerful and multifaceted as the principalship. Not because it necessarily presents the optimal career, but because of the meaningful effects it has on so many people, and most importantly, on students. No other position as a supervisor or in management seems as attractive in the same way.

Reflections

Ora's story about her path through principalship is a *thread* of several interlaced narratives. One is about the importance of the teachers as partners, more than about their strengths and weakness. Principalship is not about leading a school – it is about leading the teachers to motivate every one of their students. Another narrative is about patience: patience for mistakes that promote learning, for failures that sharpen goals and their indicators, and for a process that takes time until it bears fruit. But the most salient narrative is about promoting each student's achievements so that his/her origins no longer matter; to give them all the chances necessary for fulfilling their potential and enhancing their social mobility prospects. According to Ora, this focused target sets high expectations and brings the school staff together around a shared goal. Believing in the educational goals, students' abilities and her staff, Ora navigated her school past obstacles such as students' low SES background, neglected neighborhoods, and a heterogeneous staff, toward high achievements for all.

To promote achievements, at least in the Israeli context, it was found that a principal has to set high achievements as the school's main goal, actively search for students' data, institutionalize professional teams for data analysis, provide resources for personalized education, and maintain a proper work environment (Tubin, 2011). The main idea in Rabin High School is that the teacher should focus on teaching and learning, follow each student constantly, listen to the students' voices, learn their needs, and provide them with proper answers. The basic practices that implemented this idea are open communication channels and data-based decisions. The professional teachers along with the committed administration and maintenance staff combined their efforts in the strenuous work of providing supportive educational environment for each student.

The story in this chapter reveals the school's road to success from the principal's perspective. For her, principalship is about making a difference and touching people in a way that improves their life. Leading a school is not one-woman show, and it is well known that teachers, administration staff, and stakeholders all have a significant role in bringing the school to success and maintaining its position there. In the middle of this flurry of activity there is a principal, and Ora's story shows how interactive the two are: the more she changed and promoted the school, the more she herself was affected and changed.

Ora's narrative is based on a "sample of one" and by no means is it representative of the best way to run a school. It can, however, give some good examples and provide inspiration. It seems that the main challenge is to take a direction and stick to it while checking yourself constantly, adjusting practices, and never abusing the leader's position. It is also about giving school members the time and space to learn and institutionalize their lessons in the school's organizational structure, thereby enhancing the ability to decode internal and external signs, and to better cope with opportunity and threat.

Based on Ora's narrative about leadership for high achievement, four areas for reflection are suggested:

1 *What are the pulling and driving forces that affect your practices as leader?* People not only operate toward goals, but are also motivated by the right and proper way to behave (Van de Ven & Poole, 2005). These two causes are not identical and can lead to inhibition. For example, if a principal believes that she shouldn't divulge the direction and let everybody choose for themselves (driving force), it will stand in her way toward setting a goal of high standards for all (pulling force).

2 *By what criteria do you set your priorities? How do you know that these priorities meet school needs?* As a leader, you may face many challenges that all need your immediate attention: physical problems (leaks, damages, dirt), interpersonal relationship issues (inside the school among the staff, parents and students, and with stakeholders outside the school) and pedagogical matters (unsuitable curriculum, low achievement). Difficulties attract attention, but they are often only a symptom indicating a far more severe and basic problem. Thus, constant diagnosis is required, according to the school's hierarchy of needs, contextual expectations, and the principal's strategies (Tyack & Cuban, 1995). In this case we can see that in the beginning Ora had to pay special attention to the physical environment, but her priorities have changed over time, as was also found in the case of layering leadership strategies (Day *et al.*, 2010).

3 *How do you manage unexpected failure or success? How would you diffuse and implement change in the school?* When Ora became principal, she discovered that student achievement was low. Instead of blaming the students' background, she, based on her values and clear vision, established a sense of urgency (Kotter, 1995) and initiated innovative change to improve academic outcomes. Not everybody followed in her footsteps, especially when introducing innovative change. But Ora managed to enlist the innovators and early adopters (Rogers, 1995) to diffuse the innovation around the school.

4 *How does your leadership in your school create a culture of trust and transparency? How can you avoid mixing trust with flattery?* Trust is one of the most important adhesives in successful teamwork, but for achieving trust, you sometimes have to give up your own goals to back up the other. Trust and integrity are connected. For building trust a principal should back teachers that share the school's vision, and judge teachers by their actions, not their words. When teachers act to implement the vision, they deserve the principal's backing against outside partners and stakeholders who disagree (Day & Leithwood, 2007).

Striving for high academic achievement does not necessarily mean compliance with standard movement and inequality. In the Israeli case, achievement promotion becomes the main tool for empowering the students, provides them with experience of success and bolsters their self-esteem and competency. It is not an easy task, and the principal should be aware of the many traps lying ahead, such as arrogance and dominance. Reflection can help in avoiding such traps: while leading the school, the principal should check herself again and again and use the mutual journey for evolving with her school.

References

Clinton, H. (1996). *It Takes a Village: And Other Lessons Children Teach Us* (New York: Simon & Schuster).

Davies, B. & Davies, B.J. (2011). *Talent Management in Education* (London: Sage).

Day, C. & Leithwood, K. (2007). *Successful Principal Leadership in Times of Change* (Dordrecht Netherlands: Springer-Kluwer).

Day, C., Sammons, P., Hopkins, D., Harris, A., Leithwood. K., Gu, Q., & Brown, E. (2010). *10 Strong Claims about Successful School Leadership.* (Nottingham: National College for Leadership of Schools and Children's Services).

Kotter, J.P. (1995). Leading change: why transformation efforts fail, *Harvard Business Review*, March–April, pp. 59–67.

Rogers, E.M. (1995). *Diffusion of Innovations* (New York: Free Press).

Sergiovanni, T. (1984). Leadership and excellence in schooling, *Educational Leadership*, 41(5), pp. 4–13.

Tubin, D. (2008). Establishment of a new school and an innovative school: lessons from two Israeli case studies, *International Journal of Educational Management*, 22(7), pp. 651–663.

Tubin, D. (2011). From principals' actions to students' outcome: an explanatory narrative approach to successful Israeli schools. *Leadership and Policy in Schools*, *10*(4), 1–17.

Tubin D. & Regev-Ofek, N. (2010). Can a school change its spots? The first year of transforming to an innovative school, *The Journal of Educational Change*, 11(2), pp. 95–109.

Tyack, D. & Cuban, L. (1995). *Tinkering Toward Utopia* (Cambridge, MA: Harvard University Press).

Van de Ven, A.H. & Poole, M.S. (2005). Alternative approaches for studying organizational change. *Organization Studies*, *26*(9), pp. 1377–1404.

Chapter 4

Mexico

From fragmentation to community: a journey of change

Celina Torres-Arcadia and
Eduardo Flores-Kastanis

Introduction

Education in Mexico is faced with many challenges and amongst these is the challenge to have successful 'Secundaria' (secondary) schools (grades 7 through 9) (INEE, 2005; 2006; INEE and Fundación Nuestro País, 2004). Since the mid-1990s when Mexico (and many Latin American countries) decided to include education above the seventh grade as 'basic' education, the provision of good secondary schools on a wide scale has been difficult. What is immediate by decree is not immediate in real life. The unexpected and unplanned demand for education above the seventh grade once it passed from optional to compulsory education generated a number of problems due to the shortage of teachers, facilities and materials that had had a negative impact on the academic performance of students. However, there are examples of principals who have been successful in developing excellent secondary schools, and in this chapter we report on one of these outstanding principals, Irene Villafuerte-Elizondo. The chapter includes discussion of the school's context, the principal's professional trajectory, her main personal and professional traits, and the practices she has engaged in to create and sustain a successful school recognized by the community for its achievements and participation in national and international projects. This case is the first of 27 case studies funded through a grant from the National Science and Technology Council and the National Ministry of Education (CONACyT and SEP, respectively their acronyms in Spanish).

Secundaria No. 50

Public Secondary School No. 50 'José Vasconcelos' (PSS 50) is a school on the south side of Monterrey, in the state of Nuevo León. Monterrey is Mexico's third largest city, second in terms of economic development only to Mexico City. Monterrey is characterized by its industrial tradition, combined with high numbers of professionals from all parts of Mexico and abroad. The school is located in an urban middle-class area. But as is common in most large Mexican cities, the neighbourhood also includes several areas that house families below the poverty line. PSS 50 has 900 students in 19 groups, with 50 teachers and seven administrative staff (including custodians). In Mexico a 'Secundaria' includes grades 7 through 9. Education in Mexico is compulsory up to grade 9.

Most of the student population comes from middle-class families. Both parents work, mostly in white-collar and professional jobs. The school also accepts students with special needs as part of the national inclusion program developed by Mexico's National Ministry of Education (SEP is its acronym in Spanish). The school has an infrastructure and facilities similar to most private schools in the area despite being a public school. All classrooms have multimedia equipment. All sports areas are under cover. Laboratories are well equipped and always have material for students to work with. Access to the school is restricted to provide a safe environment for students and faculty.

This may be common to many schools in other contexts. But it is important to note that PSS 50 is not, by any standard, a typical public school. Despite receiving the same funding as any other public school, PSS 50's facilities are the result of good management, parent involvement, and the idea that public schools are the best kind of school and that it should show from the building up. And it does. In a country, and especially in a city like Monterrey where most parents would prefer to send their children to a private school, PSS 50 is their first choice for their children's education. The building is only the half of it. The school is recognized throughout the city as an excellent school as far as academics are concerned, having received the citywide 'School Excellence' Award five years in a row, and the State 'School Merit' Award and the State National Quality Prize twice. It is also recognized internationally through, for example, being part of the UNESCO Associated Schools Project Network (www.unesco.org/new/en/education/networks/global-networks/aspnet/).

In nine years this school has been transformed. When Irene Villafuerte arrived at PSS 50 it was a school taken over by local gangs and students weren't even safe in their own classrooms. When she talks about her first week in PSS 50, she says:

> What we had to do before anything else was to do something about the gangs. During the first week we had one student a day beaten up inside their classroom by people that weren't even students! We had constant fights, friction all the time among students and teachers, students and students, teachers and teachers. Mondays and Fridays we would have half the student population in class. Some would even jump the fence as if they were breaking out of prison! That is how it felt. I almost didn't come back to PSS 50 after that first week.

To understand how a school goes from almost a prison to one of the best schools of Monterrey we need to know how Irene Villafuerte got to PSS 50.

Irene's road to the principalship at PSS 50

Irene Villafuerte-Elizondo started her career as an educator 34 years ago, as a teacher in Francisco Garza Sada, a public elementary school in Monterrey, the city where she was born and where she attended the local teacher's college. Five years later she applied for a position as a maths teacher at PSS No. 8 while she worked on her certification, and three years later she was given tenure in PSS No. 19. Irene was an excellent teacher. She was recognized as such by students, parents and teachers alike. Yet she wanted to do more for students, so she decided to apply for a principalship.

She was granted a temporary position at a school no one wanted to work at because it was in a semi-rural area outside of Monterrey – PSS Francisco Pruneda Alanís in El Cercado, Nuevo León. It was at El Cercado, faced with a dilapidated school in a very poor area, that the kind of leadership that characterizes Irene was developed first. Her first strategy as the new principal was to improve the school building, and to do so with the Mayor's support. This is easier said than done because it implied hours and hours of waiting for the Mayor to see her, and to look for different opportunities and spaces in the community.

> I am not the kind of person that sits down and waits for things to happen. I go out looking for solutions, not problems. I don't sit on the side of the road crying. If the road doesn't lead to a solution I take another road.

At that time Irene's highest priority was to have a school building fit for her 760 students. 'Definitely, when you have a school where students can work, a nice school that students like to be in, the kids' attitude changes. It is amazing!'

Her second challenge as a principal was at PSS 19. Teachers at the school were seriously divided. Conflict was the order of the day, to the extent that the faculty was more engaged in 'beating' the other side instead of working for and with their students. Dialogue and clarity of goals was the antidote to conflict, and without losing any teachers.

> Everyone has something to share. Listening to teachers helps me know what they are willing to share, and that is what I expect them to do – nothing more, but nothing less.

Six years later, PSS 19 started winning awards that the faculty thought impossible when Irene arrived: the Award for Schools of Excellence; a nomination as a Quality School; first place in different citywide competitions (school band, school choir, dance, flag-bearers).

> At PSS 19 I was able to unite the faculty working together for our students, and students with a different mind-set and attitudes.

Irene is now the principal at PSS 50, José Vasconcelos Secondary School. She has been the principal for nine years. She arrived at a school plagued by gangs, with a divided and very aggressive faculty, who even tried to oust her during her first week of tenure. That school is today the most sought-out public school in Monterrey. It is more highly regarded than many private schools, and is more successful, especially in academic terms. Irene herself received the 2010 award given by the Mayor of Monterrey as an outstanding principal. And only one of the original faculty members has left PSS 50 since Irene arrived. She is the second newest member at José Vasconcelos.

Once may be an accident. Twice is a coincidence. But three times in a row leading a successful school is more than that and so we now turn to exploring Irene's leadership in more detail.

Planning for success

Irene seems to think that there is no recipe for success when she says, 'the needs and priorities of each school are different.' So the first step she takes as a principal is to find out what those needs and priorities are. She tries to understand, with the help of the staff, the peculiarities of each school and how the faculty as a whole can address issues. But her idea of a 'whole' is taking as much advantage as possible from the individual strengths and interests of all members of the school.

> Each one of us has a particular role. Each can contribute in his or her own way to meet the school's goals. So what we need is a plan with clear goals known to all, so each one of us can know how we can contribute to achieve those goals. And a clear set of measures so that each one of us knows if we are contributing. Then each one simply does what s/he is willing to do and knows if s/he is contributing or not.

Seeing Irene at work with the faculty is the best example of what Senge (2006) calls Personal Mastery as one of the five disciplines of a learning organization. She knows every teacher. She knows what each teacher is really good at, and also what they really like to do; and these are what Irene asks them to do for the school. She then finds someone else (parents, local authorities, even students) to do what her teachers don't do well, or don't like to do. Like an orchestra conductor, she brings them all together. To be able to work this way the principal needs to plan.

'Being organised is making sure everything is clear', says Irene. 'As the principal you have to be very clear about what is going to happen that month, during the day, every day'. One faculty member comments:

> Irene leads by example. She is in early, she's the last to leave, she is always there for you, she knows what she is talking about. She has a plan for each thing, she will give it to you in writing, she'll remind you what is next. You know exactly what you should and should not do.

This detailed planning that Irene does with the group (faculty, administrative staff, and parents) is given to each student for the first day of classes. It is PSS 50 Planner, a hardbound printed organizer where students and parents can follow-up on all school activities, as well as each student's performance. At any given time someone can open a student's planner and know what projects the school is working on that day, as well as the student's academic performance to date. Irene believes that planning without follow-up is not effective.

> Here we follow-up on everything so we can really understand what we are doing and why we are doing it. I can tell you what our opportunities or threats are, which are our strengths and which are our weaknesses, but these are just ideas. When we follow-up we have information that lets us know if what we think is an opportunity is really an opportunity we are taking advantage of. Or if we think we have a weakness if we are really overcoming it or not. We can't really know this without follow-up.

This very detailed and on-going planning and evaluation process that Irene and her faculty engage in is not a just a private, 'administrative' matter. Each student and each parent are constantly informed on how things are going.

> Principal Villafuerte is always talking to my parents about the school. Teachers meet regularly and talk about everything, and then tell us how things are going. We are all informed about the school projects, and we can then inform others.
>
> (Eighth grade student)

This is how Irene sustains a school environment that favours good working relations among teachers, creating a climate of collective work based on respect and trust for everyone that works at PSS 50. With only one teacher having left since Irene became principal, it is no surprise that there is a high degree of continuity when it comes to school-wide initiatives. Irene considers that the school environment at PSS 50 is a result of the 'Principal-Faculty' bond, based on a relationship of collaboration and solidarity between each member of the group with all other members of the group. 'This bond allows us to be a cohesive unit in spite of our differences. It helps us communicate quickly and clearly, and enables each one of us to actively participate in having a better school for all'.

Developing community and collective effort

One of the teachers at PSS 50 tells us:

> Teaching has become a new profession, because now it demands new competencies that I didn't have or didn't use or didn't need before to do my job. So we have to develop them now. We have to be competent using

new technologies. We have to be competent in English and other second-languages. We need to be able to work competently as a team. We can't really teach anymore if we aren't able to use technology, understand English, or work as a team.

The need for teachers to incorporate new competencies and skills in their daily work undoubtedly impacts on the principal's job in terms of her capacity to recognize the talent of the faculty and put it to use for the common good of the school.

What a principal has to do is discover the skills each one of us has, to detect what each teacher is good at. For example, if a teacher likes to talk a lot and does it well, he is a perfect master of ceremonies. If another teacher is good with arts and crafts, we will ask her to help out with the mural paper and to decorate the gym when we have an academic competition. This way we benefit from what people do and know well and align it to what needs to be done to benefit the school. If all of us principals value our teachers, if we let them be themselves, if we believe in their work, we can identify their strengths, and this makes working as a team easier. They get better and better at what they do, and each one has something to offer.

In this same line of thought, Irene believes in developing a strong sense of community in which all contribute to school success. The development of the school's yearly plan mentioned previously is an example of how Irene translates this idea into action. Irene drafts an outline of the school's yearly plan following guidelines set by the State Department of Education. She then calls a meeting with the faculty and representatives of the school's parent association. Irene lets the group know what the local authority wants from its schools, and then opens the session so that all can participate and propose projects where the school can distinguish itself, or projects aimed at solving specific problems that need everyone's efforts to be successful. At this meeting, committees are created and each chooses a leader for their project. Finally the plan is included in a hardbound daily organizer that every student, faculty member and parent receive on the first day of the academic year. This way the entire school community knows what is to be done, what is expected, and how to judge if the community is on-track or not.

Having a sense of community, of collective effort is, according to Irene, important for school success:

If there is a teacher that does a great job teaching his or her children whatever the program requires but doesn't want to collaborate – to share – to say to other teachers, "Look, this is what I do, what works for me", I feel that we wont achieve what we want. We want successful students, in and out of school, and because we want successful students we need to work as a team, we need to function harmoniously. Harmony is achieved when teachers, parents and students make an effort to provide and achieve an education of excellence for all the school. Not just for one student or another, one family or another, one teacher or another.

To reinforce this idea of the teacher committed to the important task of education, Irene tells her teachers:

We all want the best teacher for our children. Let's think that our students are our children, and let's be for them as we would want our children's teachers to be. And then when tomorrow comes along, as it will sooner than later, our students will be grateful for the love, trust and dedication we gave them when they were here.

Creating other leaders

A crucial part of Irene's work is that she recognizes that every teacher is a leader:

You all are leader teachers. You are the leaders in your classrooms, with your groups. You are responsible for what goes on in class. Whatever you tell these children to do, they will do. Whatever you ask them to give, they will give. And it is up to each and every one of you what you do with your leadership.

A teacher elaborates:

The Principal only knows two kinds of teachers: ordinary and extraordinary ones. If you want to be an ordinary teacher, well you'll be remembered as an ordinary teacher. You will give your students ordinary things and at best what life needs now, what society needs from its people now … If we already live in a very competitive city we have to take on a new role, and to take on the new role the city means we can't just expect our students to hear us and agree with our ideas. They have to see us, their teachers, in the new role. We have to be a living example of competence and competitiveness. We have to strive to be extraordinary so that our students, one day, will try to do the same.

When someone asks Irene which trait does she consider the most important for a leader, she doesn't hesitate at all:

I believe that one of the main points of thinking about leadership is teaching teachers to be leaders, because it isn't easy. A good leader is firm and decisive, creative, likes innovation, is positive and knows how to motivate.

A teacher that is a leader assumes responsibility to motivate the students they lead. Irene asks the teachers to focus attention in the time and space they share with their students, knowing that they have a most important influence not only on learning but on the whole development of their students. More than knowledge, what a secondary school teacher can instil in students is an attitude to excel and to help others succeed.

> Let's not look for culprits. 'His mother doesn't help, her father won't collaborate'. None of that! We are their teachers. How are you going to sell her the idea? How are you going to motivate him? How are you going to let them know that they are champions, that they can do it?

Teachers at PSS 50 know and agree with Irene's position. They accept and are proud of their commitment to give their students more than what is ordinarily expected of teachers as these quotes from teachers illustrate:

> Follow-through with what you do with and what you promise students. It isn't only clocking-in and clocking-out. You have to look for ways for students to do more, to achieve more. They should be out-standing, because they are out-standing.
>
> We are always in the top-three of any competition or contest we participate in, and that is also a challenge we have to meet all the time.
>
> This is a high demand school. It has a reputation, and because it has a reputation I feel more committed to do more. So we can continue living up to our reputation.

Motivating teachers and students

Motivation is the key, says Irene. She is the first to admit how important it has been for her to be motivated to achieve the best for her students. In her case a sense of achievement has always accompanied her in her career as a teacher and principal. But Irene knows that motivation doesn't come from educational authorities. She recalls one of her early experiences as a first-year elementary school teacher:

> I remember reading somewhere that there was going to be a citywide contest. Each school was supposed to design and execute an original tableau that included music and a choreography. So I decided to do something related to Star Wars, which had the kids in a rage since that summer when it opened. Sixty kids of all grades decided to participate so we worked on that for over a month, and we won! And I was expecting my principal to say something: "Congratulations! It was really nice!" At the very least I expected him to ask me how did it go. Didn't happen. However, what did happen was that most of the children's mothers were really happy and really proud of their children and they let me know that. And what really made me cry with happiness were the children. Our students were happy, exhilarant, yelling and jumping and clapping, "We did it! We did it!" I have been carrying those three words in my heart for over 30 years. We did it! What more motivation can you wish for?

This may be one of Irene's most distinctive characteristics; the feeling of shared accomplishment that is found in every school she has been a principal in, a feeling that remains even when she has left for another school. It is visible when she talks to teachers, students, or parents at PSS 50. Her positive attitude is contagious. Because she knows, and everyone in PSS 50 knows, that *they* collectively (not her, not a couple of teachers, not some parents) will achieve whatever *they* decide to achieve. Says Irene:

> It only takes one success for everyone to know what can be done. 'We did it!' also means 'We can do it again!' Leadership is motivating everyone, convincing all, telling everyone we have the skills, we have the knowledge, we have the will, we have all it takes to win. Leadership for me is to participate and see results, knowing that sooner or later success will be here.

However, it is not clear sailing all the way. Rough patches are present every day for an innovative and very competitive principal like Irene. This doesn't worry her. She believes that all problems include a solution just waiting to be found. She also knows that succeeding is much more meaningful for her school when the going gets tough. It is a good time to focus everyone's efforts to meet the goals they have all agreed on.

> I am not the kind of person that says, "This won't work, or this can't be done." Maybe we need to do things differently, but it will work! It can be done! I try to see options because there are always a wide variety of needs, many different ways of doing things. I won't throw the towel in. I will never say, "We can't do it!" Maybe we need to wait. Maybe we need to try something else. But it is my job as a principal to be the first one to say, "We can do it!" I can assure you that everything we have set our minds to, we have achieved.

Considering the track record of the three schools where Irene Villafuerte has been principal, we can only concur. Finally Irene reflects:

> When obstacles don't stop you from where you want to be, when you are continually discovering and taking advantage of new roads and ways of doing things, that is the true meaning of success. Life will always be full of what seem to be obstacles. What is great is that you, me, anyone, everyone can find a new path, and new paths must always be explored, regardless of where one ends up at. I really believe that we can do anything we set our mind to if we have a positive outlook on what we do, on who is around us, on why we are doing what we do. Education is a noble profession and if all of us, all of us educators, were committed to make our children successful, our country would be a very different place. There is no doubt in my mind that teachers are the key to all so half my job is done. The other half is simple: remind all my teachers, every day, that they are the key to all.

Thinking about the principal

In this section we reflect on what we have learnt from exploring the leadership of Irene Villafuerte.

The principal as promoter of a learning community

The teaching faculty is the principal's main resource to fulfil the school's vision and subsequent plans. It makes perfect sense that one of the most common practices of successful school principals is related to faculty development (Leithwood & Day, 2007). In Irene Villafuerte's case we find an interesting variation. She first recognizes each teacher's individual talents, and then builds on these individual talents to develop the talents of the group as a whole, aiming to meet the school goals. She believes that success comes from collective effort, and that to achieve this, each individual needs to be supported to do their best.

The principal as promoter of shared leadership

We can see in the Villafuerte case how leadership and administration are integrated and how leadership is shared. Irene is able to build a shared vision with all members of the school community, where all are informed and reminded of the school's goals and can follow what is being done and what needs to be done. Participatory planning empowers her faculty. Not only do they design the plan, but it publicly acknowledges how each teacher is working to make things happen for the benefit of the entire community, and lets everyone know what is to be done and the goals the school wants to meet, with an invitation for all to collaborate. Leadership and administration blend in the same practice as each member of the school responsibly assumes their role and recognizes the roles of others.

The principal as motivator

We have shown how the principal uses intrinsic motivation factors to help people be their best. She encourages teachers to continually develop in light of new requirements. Irene encourages teachers to realize they are leaders, who are able to motivate and help form other leaders. Irene models good behaviour in regard to positive internal motivation by, for example, showing how problems can be regarded as opportunities for success, and how teachers can overcome obstacles and focus their effort. She also encourages her staff to share success so that as a staff they can own the successes that come from their efforts and can claim, 'We did it!'

Reflections

We conclude with some final reflections. Irene's case exemplifies how a principal with a very clear idea of what it is to educate children can do extraordinary things. Her view of education is the 'glue' that binds together her professional experience, the courses and workshops she constantly participates in, her graduate degree in management, her conversations with people in the educational sector and from other walks of life, the books she reads, and the ideas she shares with the community. She is an educator first, and an administrator second. Irene is an *educational* administrator, and not an educational *administrator*. Since she began her career as an elementary schoolteacher she always distinguished herself as someone in search of excellence and enthusiasm, leading her students and staff to experience a feeling of accomplishment. As a principal she has taken on difficult posts. All the schools she has led have had challenges such as insufficient resources, a divided faculty, or undisciplined students. Irene views each of these challenges as an opportunity to show the school's community that despite obstacles and shortcomings, there are goals that are worth pursuing, that the community can reach and surpass these goals, and that in each challenge faced there is something to learn. Key to Irene's leadership is her ability to form leaders, to form 'successful people' as she calls them.

The lesson we learn from Irene's case in terms of how to form successful principals may be so obvious it is often overlooked in principal preparation programs.

> It is of the utmost importance that principals have a clear idea of how they contribute to the education of children.

In Irene's case she contributes by forming leaders, fostering internal motivation, and developing a strong sense of community through collective effort. Other principals may decide to contribute in different ways. What is important is that anyone leading a school should be clear of the *educational* contribution they want to make. Our attempts to prepare principals will be worthwhile if it opens up a few more spaces to think and decide about this personal contribution.

Fullan (2001) considers that school leadership is complex, mainly because of the inherent dilemma involved in prioritizing what to do. Irene's life as a principal is full of deciding moments where this dilemma is faced over and over again. Especially in an educational context where resources are extremely limited, and where the main (and at times the *only*) resource available are people from the educational community (faculty, students, parents, community members): people that have to take on responsibilities and accept challenges. Schools need leaders who are willing not only to share leadership but to also prepare other leaders, what Sheppard *et al.* (2010) view as *distributed leadership*. Sheppard *et al.* present empirical evidence on how distributed leadership in schools develops leadership capacity among faculty and boosts their morale and enthusiasm.

This has happened over and over again in all schools where Irene has been principal. Once she decides on a course of action Irene opens up spaces so that other members of the school community can exercise leadership and take control over their actions, and they in turn replicate this form of distributed leadership with other people they work with in school projects. Organizations such as schools traditionally have a hierarchical structure where the principal assumes total command and responsibility for all school endeavours. Traditional or 'concentrated' (as opposed to 'distributed') leadership tries to shape new challenges to existing conditions set by the school's prevalent structure and organizational culture, thus limiting the potential to deal successfully with new complex issues faced by schools, which usually require a broader and multi-referential perspective. Distributed leadership, on the other hand, allows the principal to shape the school's structure and organizational culture to establish better conditions to face new complex issues successfully (Murphy *et al.*, 2009).

Leadership such as the one presented in this case begins with a very pragmatic vision: Which is my priority? Where should I start? This first set of questions leads to the deployment of the professional and personal resources that Irene has at her disposal: effective resource management, teamwork, and the ability to build a shared vision (Senge, 2006). Among Irene's resources is the ability to create a sense of shared accomplishment celebrating success with the entire school, letting people know that what they want is possible, and that a collective and sustained effort is what allows the school to achieve goals that seem unattainable if tried only by one individual. This positive environment is what allows the school to achieve its goals and face new challenges. It is the sum of these small gains that are known and celebrated by the school that allows a school to become a successful school. All members of the school contribute to that success, and all are responsible for maintaining such success. This is what Irene understands as the school's reputation: the community knows that a school is successful because it has a successful principal, but also successful teachers and successful students. In sum, this sense of belonging and accomplishment is the fuel that a school needs and uses every day when its community wants to continue being successful, because the school knows what they are capable of doing, and are reminded daily of what they can do.

Questions to ask

1   *What is your leadership approach as a principal? How does this approach promote or thwart that other members of the school community to assume responsibilities and exercise their own leadership?* Principals need to understand their leadership style and how their behaviours as a leader influence others in the school.

2   *How do you decide which challenges are worth taking on? What is your process to ensure that accepting these challenges engages those who will be involved and affected by the decision in ways that allow them visualize how important it is and assume their responsibility?* Undoubtedly a principal faces all kinds of challenges every day, but knowing that time and resources are limited, it is important to prioritize these demands. How these challenges are selected, and to what extent people are engaged is critical to achieve results (Senge, 2006).

3   *In what ways do you follow-up on your school's key projects?* Starting an initiative is very important, but following-up is crucial. Informing all people involved is

what lets individuals value their effort and to be aware of the impact their actions have to meet the school's goals. People respond better when they have feedback and are informed of what is happening.

4 *How do you recognize what people do and how do you celebrate success in your school when challenges are met?* Creating and maintaining different spaces and practices to acknowledge results allows individuals and the community as a whole (students, faculty, parents, educational authorities, etc.), to capitalize their efforts, and to learn form their experience to improve their performance in the future.

The principal's leadership is exercised successfully to the extent that it allows others to develop their own leadership capacities. This model helps the principal build a school that belongs to all and is improved and developed by all. A principal that shares the school's leadership contributes by building a shared vision, and this includes deciding which challenges to face all the way to following-up what results, and which goals are achieved. The Mexican case shows us that the main resource a principal has, and in many cases the *only* resource s/he has, is the school's human capital. This is why valuing and developing faculty, students and parents is crucial, especially in a society facing great challenges with scarce resources. Distributed leadership is a viable option, as Irene's case shows us time after time. In these times that look so grim, a leader that develops leaders is a promising alternative for a better and sustainable future.

References

Fullan, M. (2001). *Leading in a Culture of Change* (San Francisco: Jossey-Bass).

INEE (2005). Desafios Educativos: Reformar la secundaria. Breviario No. 3. México, D.F.: Autor.

INEE (2006). Desafios Educativos: Tendencia del rendimiento académico de alumnos de primaria y secundaria a lo largo de cinco años. Breviario No. 7. México, D.F.: Autor.

INEE & Fundación Nuestro País. (2004). La secundaria: principal reto del Sistema Educativo Mexicano. México, D.F.: INEE.

Murphy, J.J., Smylie, M.M., Mayrowetz, D.D., & Louis, K.S. (2009). The role of the principal in fostering the development of distributed leadership. *School Leadership and Management, 29*(2), 181–214.

Leithwood, K. & Day, C. (2007). What we learned: A broad view, in C. Day & K. Leithwood (Eds.), *Successful principal leadership in times of change: An international perspective* (Dordrecht: Springer-Kluwer), pp. 117–137. Sheppard, B., Hurley, N., & Dibbon, D. (2010). Distributed leadership, teacher morale, and teacher enthusiasm: unravelling the leadership pathways to school success. Paper presented at the annual meeting of the American Educational Research Association. Denver, CO, April 30 to May 4.

Senge, P. M. (2006). *The fifth discipline: The art and practice of the learning organization* (Revised ed.) (New York: Doubleday/Currency).

Chapter 5

Kenya

From perdition to performance

Teresa A. Wasonga

Introduction

Kiptai Primary School (KPS) is a public school for boys and girls ranging in age between six and fifteen. It was built in 1980 as a dispersal school to reduce congestion at a nearby school. It is located in the outskirts of a major industry but in a different district (administrative unit of government). The population served by this school was settled here by the government in 1965 after being displaced by floods. The natives of this locale are of a different ethnic group, and over time ethnic tensions have surfaced leading to clashes over land. The population around KPS has grown and evolved into a squatter community that has generationally become poorer as industrial jobs have disappeared, rains have failed, and the land becomes infertile through overuse. The majority of buildings of this primary school are temporary structures (mud/dirt walls), and it was not until 2007 that the school got its first permanent structure.

Primary education in Kenya is the first step in an education system that is structured in three parts, also known as 8:4:4 (eight years of primary; four years of secondary; and four years of university). It should be noted that there are also two- to three-year tertiary colleges that Kenyans can attend after secondary school. Both primary and secondary school education culminate with certificate awards to students – Kenya Certificate of Primary Education (KCPE) and Kenya Certificate of Secondary Education (KCSE) respectively. These certificates are awarded for completion of the approved eight- and four-year course work and national examinations. The national examination at the end of primary school determines the secondary school to which a student can go ranging from National schools (highest scores) to Provincial and District/Division schools (lower scores). The subjects examined at primary school level include math, English, Swahili, social studies (Kenyan history, civics), science, and religious studies (Christian, Islamic, Hindu). The quality of primary education is critical as it is the most likely factor that determines the educational trajectory of every Kenyan student. Those who attend high quality primary schools are more likely to achieve higher scores and therefore more likely to attend National secondary schools from where they are also most likely to proceed to subsidized public universities. The inverse is true for those attending poorly staffed, poorly managed, or rural primary schools. Because of the likely long-term effect of primary schools on the educational trajectory of Kenyans, this study focused on a primary school, Kiptai.

For over two decades, Kiptai Primary School (KPS) deteriorated from a well functioning school to one that was chaotic and non-performing (poor student achievement, lack of trained teachers, lack of community support, poor buildings, and no sanitary facilities). The school lost children to other schools, child labor, early pregnancy or marriage, alcohol, and the village streets. The situation was made worse by ethnic clashes that continued for ten years. The population of the school dropped from 600 students in 1988 to 80 in 2002. In 2003, standard eight (the last class of primary education) was discontinued because there were only two students enrolled. By this time, the school had lost all government paid trained teachers including the principal. The school community was at odds with the school principal because under his leadership, the school board had run down the school through incompetence, corruption, and lack of oversight. Government funds to the school could not be accounted for. Based on conversations with community members, it was apparent that the principal was often absent from school and contrary to rules from Ministry of Education, he handpicked members of the Board of Governors. The Board of Governors is the body that governs school affairs including financial management. Student achievement was low. In 2002 the average score on the national exam was much lower (36 percent) than the national average score of public schools (48 percent) and even lower than what is required to enter the lowest caliber of secondary schools (53 percent). School documents indicated that no student had joined a secondary school from KPS for six years prior to 2004.

However, in the last five years the school has experienced tremendous growth especially in physical facilities and human resources. By 2010 the enrollment had increased to 450, and the school has new buildings, 11 trained teachers, and a counselor. The community, teachers, and government officials attribute this turnaround to its leadership. Under the leadership of the principal, Mr. Chamuada, the school has secured two permanent buildings that house four classrooms, a staffroom for teachers and a unit of ten toilets for girls. The principal's office has been upgraded from a mud-walled structure to steel-walled structure. Besides inadequate physical facilities, social problems at this school were so extreme that the District Education Officer (DEO) demanded that a counselor be posted to the school by the government. At the time of this study, the school had a competent Board of Governors and an active Parent-Teacher Association (PTA). The current board members had received training in school management organized by the Ministry of Education and facilitated by the current principal. In terms of academic achievement in national examinations (the main measure of success in Kenya), the school average score increased to 51 percent in 2007. In the years 2007 and 2008, nine out of 31 and 8 out of 28 students respectively qualified to join secondary schools. Documents provided indicated that the school has a strategic plan that stipulates its vision (a place where children can learn safely), areas of need, current strategies for school improvement, and prospective funding agencies. The budget and financial reports are all available to the public.

Who is Mr. James Chamuada?

At 28, Mr. Chamuada was asked to lead KPS. Mr. Chamuada knew that the school was in crisis and that his work would be complicated by the fact that he came from a rival ethnic community. He was incensed by the chaos at KPS.

> I was so angry with what I saw in this community. I decided to channel my anger to work for these children who, I think, are paying for the sins of society. How could I turn my back on children?

He was familiar with the issues here, as they were similar to those in a previous school where he was the deputy principal. At this school he had collaborated with civic organizations to raise awareness and funds for people and children living with HIV, and with government and non-governmental agencies to provide for poor and orphaned children. He learned about the inner workings of government, politicians, community leaders, grant agencies, and government officials.

Mr. Chamuada trained as a primary school teacher and holds a certificate in teaching. At the time of this study, he was attending college to obtain a bachelor's degree in Education. Mr. Chamuada was driven not by passion to be a leader, but mostly by empathy for children. Empathy was demonstrated by constant reference to the fact that "I always imagine how I would feel if these were my children [referring to school children] and what I would want others to do." His hope was that "somebody else would do the same to my [his] children." A teacher, who is a member of the school community, narrated an incident when Mr. Chamuada invited her to his office after she had missed school for a couple of days. He told her,

> These are not my children, they are our children and it hurts me to know that you do not care about their future. I live very far from the school, but I make sure that I come to school everyday. If you care about these kids, show it by doing at least what the government pays you do. That is all I ask.

According to the teacher, Mr. Chamuada's consistency in focusing on children made her feel guilty about her actions. In her view, his appeal to personal altruism and social commitment won many hearts and minds in the community. Because of his focus, Mr. Chamuada has been able to navigate multiple and competing interests without controversy. He asked, "who would disagree with you if you tell and show them that what you are seeking for is for children? Many school leaders do not do that."

Turning around Kiptai Primary School

Mr. Chamuada embarked on a journey to turnaround KPS by starting to work on two things: first, developing a strategic plan that would be a road map to improving the school; and, second, engaging the community in a collective process to improve community involvement. He reasoned that the ineffective leadership and poor governance over the years had left the school and community without radar. While the community needed a plan for a way forward, Mr. Chamuada needed community leaders with whom to work. He identified and invited to the board people that either valued education or were influential in the community. He said to the group, "We need to create this school together." As a group, they worked on strategies to involve and gain back the trust of the community. He convinced the group that whilst he was a friend, he is "paid to do this job whether or not I help the school." According to the president of the board, this statement evoked instant reaction, a sense of "waste and loss for our children if we cannot benefit from the government." The government spends 97 percent of its education budget on teacher salaries and very little on infrastructure and textbooks. Local communities can only benefit from the government if they have government employees. In this case, Mr. Chamuada said in an interview,

> I needed to get them to think differently, … it is their problem if the children do not do well, and they do not take advantage of government employees. They should own the school and find ways to improve it, and keep it open.

From the beginning, Mr. Chamuada had to deal instantly with the problem of assimilating local culture and language while building internal capacity (teacher expertise) and creating a system for decision-making and actions. He spent a lot of time in the community. He needed immediate results to show the community that change was possible. With an anxious board, they approached the DEO with startling statistics on dropout rates, number of pregnancies among students, the extent of child labor, the level of poverty, and most importantly, that standard eight (the last year of school) was closed because of a lack of students. They also commented on the lack of female teachers at the school. The DEO visited the school and immediately convened an emergency meeting with other government officers. It was decided that a counselor and four trained teachers be posted to the school immediately. With this success, Mr. Chamuada won instant praise and trust of the community. As he said, "my work had just began and I was determined not to have this school remain the same."

In the following couple of years, Mr. Chamuada implored political leaders, government officers, and funding agencies to find money to improve the physical and human resources at the school. He wrote grant applications to agencies, community development funds, and the ministry of education. Four years later, the school had the first permanent building, toilets for girls, a full staff including two female teachers, and a counselor. The board organized for the community to raise funds to provide lunch for teachers. His greatest achievement was that "children are coming to school, they are learning and parents are supportive of what we are doing."

The principal encouraged sharing information among staff about the community and students as this increased sensitivity about the children and their community. He had noticed that intentional understanding of unique cultures of the community enabled teachers to reach out to students and their parents.

According to Mr. Chamuada, because he spends a lot of time working with outside entities, he has "ensured that school leadership is shared with teachers and parents." One of his major aspirations is to build a school community in which "leadership will outlive me." That means, building leadership capacity within the school and community. He realized that inadequate capacity (knowledge and skills) in the school and among the population in the community made it difficult for those willing to help their children and school to do so. Most lack secondary school education and it took a lot of effort to mobilize community "towards children support services in order to end child labor and early marriages." Most importantly, Mr. Chamuada hopes that at some point, the community can "establish a comprehensive school feeding program" so children do not go hungry because they are orphans or have parents who cannot afford to feed them.

In discussing significant achievements in the last five years as principal at this school, Mr. Chamuada was emphatic that what had been achieved were the efforts of many people, "I cannot do anything alone," he said. The achievements included:

- Creating an orderly and safe school environment.
- Improved student learning.
- Increased enrollment and retention.
- Reduced truancy and absenteeism of female students.
- Active engagement of the wider community
- Withdrawal of children from the worst forms of child labor, like loading of raw materials for the local industry, charcoal burning, and commercial sex.
- Supporting the Orphan Support Program, a local community initiative that was "assisting children whose parents died, mostly from HIV/AIDS."

Leadership philosophy at Kiptai Primary School

Although this chapter focuses on the story of Mr. Chamuada, this research revealed a complex web of activities initiated by Mr. Chamuada that perpetuated and sustained changes taking effect in the school. Mr. Chamuada's leadership is not a "one man show." He aspires to empower and stimulate the community, teachers, and even children to be "their own leaders" and to participate in school. This way, he said, "I do not have to police anybody." A parent proudly said,

We want the right hand to know what the left is doing and Mr. Chamuada has taught us that this is a good idea. Our school is very different now. As parents we feel that this school is our future now and we try to help. Many of us went to school here, and we left school with nothing, so we cannot help our children. Many of us had children when we were teenagers and now we are grandmothers at a very early age because our children also had children when they were teenagers. We did not go anywhere and if our children and grand children do not go to secondary school, they will not go anywhere also. The principal tells us that he cannot do it alone, so we come and he explains to us how we can work with him.

It was evident that Mr. Chamuada has led this school in a way that leadership is not invested in him only. Instead, he plays a supportive role in establishing a framework of co-creating leadership through: first, common purpose; two, context for co-creating with members of community, students, and teachers; three, social architecture; four, institutional designs for systemic decision-making and actions; and, five, dispositions that engage constituents.

Common purpose

Everybody in the school was cognizant of the purpose for which they were in this school. And for Mr Chamuada, that purpose was to "improve the learning and learning environment for children." He also stated that his leadership has a purpose, "to create order" because children cannot learn when there is no order. If children find school to be a safe and welcoming place, they will come despite their circumstances, and then "we can educate them as much as we can when they are here." The chair of board, said, "the Principal focuses more on what the school can do for children and their parents so that they can come to school." He uses stories, analogies, and experiences in everyday life to help people connect the purpose of school to their lives. For example, at a meeting with parents, he explained how a new statute – all Members of Parliament would need to have a college education and all ministers must have a bachelor's degree – would impact the community. He said, "the grumbles of a frog will not stop a cow from drinking water. If we continue this way, if our children cannot go to high school, we will never have a representative in parliament. Other communities will." A parent later told me that he could now figure out the purpose of school and its larger impact. He would encourage children to stay in school.

At another meeting, in which parents and teachers were discussing how to raise money to hire an "untrained teacher" to help tutor children who were not reading at grade level, Mr. Chamuada said, "we have to pull together, remember when two elephants fight, it is the grass that suffers, our children suffer if we keep going in different directions. Early intervention is better than waiting to see a witchdoctor." This seemed to instantly make sense to the parents who were not willing to compromise. He set direction by using familiar cultural language and practice. Unique to Mr. Chamuada is not just the ability to use language that appeals to traditional thoughts, but also analogies that have, and continue to shape, the people's consciousness.

Context for co-creating with members of community, students, and teachers

For Mr. Chamuada, a context needs to exist for people to work together for a common purpose. He described context as conditions of work at the school. He referenced genuine democratic practices and empowerment (evolving) as pillars of good context. Teachers specifically indicated that the main reason they are still in the school was the high trust work environment. Mr. Chamuada does not lock the principal's office when he is out of school. Even though this school has been designated as a "hardship area" by the government, the attrition rate among teachers has been very low since Mr. Chamuada took over. Eight of eleven teachers have been here for the last seven years and they credit their stay to supportive leadership. One teacher said, "We have an open school here, in which we discuss a lot of things that we do. Most importantly, we support each other, and the principal has given us freedom to be creative with time and teaching." Mr. Chamuada described his leadership as focused on creating "genuine opportunities to participate" which he described as "people being truly and respectfully engaged in everything we do in this school like taking turns to supervise sporting activities in the evenings, leading workshops, meeting with parents, visiting the community, preparing students for exams, and learning the local language." Mr. Chamuada himself had become proficient in the local language.

Mr. Chamuada believes in empowering people, from locals in the community, to teachers and students. Through shared governance, and rotations on various duties in the school including acting as deputy principal or principal, teachers have mastered the operations of the school. According to the deputy principal, "many of our teachers have evolved and they are leaders in their own rights. We do not worry when the Principal and I are both away from school, we have enough leaders here." The counselor noted that:

> Our teachers are empowered through constant conversations about teaching, learning, and the community around us. We all feel that we have enough information and knowledge about our school, students and parents. And even though sometimes we lack resources, we are happy that we do our best.

Social architecture

Social architecture can be thought of as the social networks, scheduling and communication systems created to enhance and sustain school improvement. Social architecture at KPS included leadership behaviors, communication systems, teacher knowledge and skills, and teacher professional development. Mr.

Chamuada supported collaboration by restructuring the schedules so that teachers had common planning time to engage each other. Teachers indicated that Mr. Chamuada consistently made explicit the fact that common purpose would not be achieved without the collective involvement of talents and expertise. To support this, a very simple communication structure was instituted. Mr. Chamuada established a phone tree called "three way." Three teachers have volunteered to create and lead a network of teachers and parents to whom they can easily and quickly communicate information from the principal or any other entity in the school. According to one teacher, continuous and consistent communication has increased transparency and clarity of expectations.

Mr. Chamuada has also set up organizational structures like the leadership team, curriculum committee, parent and teacher association, and social events like lunches that bring teachers and community leaders together with a hope to disrupt the hierarchical social status and enhance quality of relations. According to Mr. Chamuada, good relationships among teachers, parents, community and students enhance cooperation. He explained that when he first came to Kiptai, people only talked ill of each other. The students did the same. There was no trust. This situation, he said "had to change and it did." As a teachers explained, " I and my colleagues, we have a good relationship and we trust each other to do their best for the children."

Discussions with teachers and parents indicated that social hierarchy and authority are engrained in people. For this reason, Mr. Chamuada has had to work extraordinarily hard at Kiptai to convince his constituents that "it was OK to eat together, chat with each other, seek each other's opinions, laugh and joke with students and parents irrespective of their status." He encouraged constituents to do all these to enhance quality relations. He believes that quality relations enhanced participation, hence democracy. However, he said, "Peoples' loyalty to authority provided me the opportunity do a lot of things initially, but I knew I could not sustain progress if I continued doing everything because I am the principal." There was need for a social structure to engage others.

Professional development (PD) as conceptualized in western countries does not exist at Kiptai Primary School. Teachers and school leaders have no access to government organized or sponsored PD. Individuals find various workshops that they can attend at their expense. Mr. Chamuada intimated this as a major drawback for progress. Most teachers do not have any additional learning beyond teacher training and the further they are from the time they were in college, the lesser they know in terms of new knowledge and skills. Mr. Chamuada shared,

> At Kiptai, we have agreed that we will learn from any field and so I have invited my friends who are social workers, counselors, or government officers to come to our school and share with us what they are doing or learning out there …When the District Officer visited he emphasised learning and told us, "if children do not learn, it does not matter how much you teach." That was

one of the best PDs we have had, and since then we have focused on learning not just for students but for our families and us.

Teachers had organized themselves with the help of the principal and found grants to sponsor one or two teachers to a PD workshop. When they returned, they shared what they learned. This, they said, helped keep them up to date with new knowledge and skills.

Institutional designs for systemic decision-making and actions

Limited opportunities to fully engage in collective decision-making processes negatively impacted co-creation at Kiptai Primary School. So Mr. Chamuada developed mechanisms through which the common purpose would be achieved. These included a leadership team, also called School Management Committee (including school governors, teachers, and members of the community), curriculum committee (teachers, parents, and Ministry of Education representative), coaching group, and school and community partnership through PTA. He summed it up this way,

> I think everybody needs to be given an opportunity to use their skills. But also they need to be trained. When I first got here, there was no order, there was no rhyme or reason for how things were done, there was no system. If the principal was not in school, there was no leader. So we talked a lot about leadership, not leader, about leadership in your classroom and what those qualities are. We want our children to internalise the qualities also. You have to have those conversations for people to actually start thinking about the approach of stepping out and doing more. And it is not just about doing more, it is more of encouraging and attitude of doing that which I want to, and doing the best that I can do and bettering myself as a member of this school.

The curriculum committee was established to look at how teaching and learning would be done effectively, given the limited resources. This committee was intended to be creative in finding teaching aids that could be made using local materials. The collection of learning materials created has enhanced learning. Peer coaching among teachers was one of the latest ideas developed at the school. Initiated by the counselor, it was for children to work with other children, and teachers have supported it. And lastly, developing school-community partnership is one of Mr. Chamuada's significant achievements. The school has a very active parent-teacher association, an effective board of governors and the community has become an integral part of the school. Conversely, the school with its new buildings has become the pride of the community. The success of these mechanisms has allowed Mr. Chamuada to spend more time seeking outside help for the school without jeopardizing the operations inside the school.

Dispositional values that engage constituents

Values were the core of Mr. Chamuada's leadership. He is spiritual in nature and uses a lot of proverb analogies and biblical stories during interviews and conversations. To him, dispositional values were the radar for leadership emphasizing ethical purpose in life and profession. He explained that value orientations were important as they were the intuitive tendencies that motivate action and expected consequences. Tendencies that have been found to favor co-creating include humility, patience, collaboration, resilience, active listening, cultural anthropology, trust, and subtlety (Bruffee, 1993; Collins, 2001; Follette, 1927; Freire, 1990). Teachers, parents, and board members cited responsiveness, willingness, opportunities for collaboration, and trust as reasons they were able to work together. Mr. Chamuada noted that there were "continuous conversations that challenged assumptions" helped to build trust, and thus focus people on the core purposes of school. He explained that dispositions, "the attitudes that I bring to work," make it easier or difficult to work together. Mr. Chamuada was described as empathic, trustworthy, humble, a good listener, a collaborator, flexible, and persistent (resilient). He constantly reminded community leaders, parents, students, and especially teachers about value orientations. For example at a PTA meeting he said the he expects the teachers "to do to the children in this school as they would want others to do for their children." To him this was a simple test of one's values and commitment to the children.

Reaction

The story of Mr. Chamuada and Kiptai Primary school is in many respects congruent with what has been found to be the core of successful school leadership (setting direction, developing people, restructuring the organization, and focusing on teaching and learning; Leithwood et al., 2006). However, we can learn from Mr. Chamuada's success in what is a very challenging context. He was chosen for this study because of his resilience in creating stability and order. Unlike many other countries, in Kenya the government's input in education is dismal when it comes to physical development (Bold et al., 2009). In poor and rural areas, success (student achievement and physical development) in school, especially primary schools is more likely associated with or dependent upon individual's commitment, efforts and skills. Accountability, for the most part, is left to the moral obligation of the individual school leader. As Mr. Chamuada elaborated, he is paid whether or not he does anything. Like many others, he works in an environment in which there is hardly supervision, evaluation or tangible consequences for purposes of accountability from principals and BOGs that would deter malpractice. At the same time communities have minimal opportunities for legal or other recourse in case of mismanagement. The leadership choices that Mr. Chamuada has made in spite of the environment set him apart.

Mr. Chamuada has been in this school for eight years and the school has steadily improved. His school has not been the top school in the national exams, but it has been turned around from the edge of perdition to new heights of performance. For many people in Kenya, Kiptai Primary School is a success story. The success achieved so far in student achievement, is attributed to physical development, community engagement, and attendance. But these are indirectly the result of Mr. Chamuada's actions. Mr. Chamuada hopes that more will be achieved when they can focus on curriculum and learning.

In addition to setting direction, developing people, restructuring and focusing on teaching and learning, Mr. Chamuada used dispositional values and social architecture to sustain success. Dispositions, he said are the "glue, the lubricant, the oil" that keeps stakeholders creating together to sustain school improvement in an environment where common good is the least preferred, and apathy is entrenched. He also believes that social architecture, especially quality relations and communalization, has led to a complex web of interactions not only between internal and external entities, but also among different levels of power structures in the larger society. Managing and sustaining these interactions, "persisting even when it seemed fruitless has been the greatest challenge and reward."

Significant lessons from this story are: first, that it takes the commitment of an individual (the heart, the soul, the body, the time, the intellect, the energy, the passion, the person) to turnaround a school in the given circumstances; and, second, to sustain progress the individual must work on efforts to enhance collective capacity. In other words, initiating success may depend on individual competencies, but sustaining success depends on the collective capacity that is co-created. As is found in the old African adage, "it takes a village to educate a child." Mr. Chamuada's story is an example of how a leader can weave in and out of multiple identities and cultures (village) to position self and others to influence not just a school but a whole society. I asked Mr. Chamuada one last question: what do you hope your legacy will be when you are done at Kiptai Primary School? His response was,

> We have yet to take a student to a national school. However, my greatest hope is that the success in this school will outlive me. ... That many of the children I have here today will live better lives than their parents, and that this community will look back and be proud of what we have achieved together.

Discussion

Many leaders may be gifted in solving immediate problems within and outside their organizations; few leaders do turnaround and sustain success in organizations that have experienced destructive leadership and perdition. Creating and sustaining turnaround as was found in Kiptai Primary School highlights the significance of creating change by strengthening relationships and institutionalizing systems and processes by which stakeholders pose, solve, anticipate, and act on problems side by side. Without such systems and processes, sustaining gains and improving school outcomes, especially when the turnaround leader departs, may likely be a challenge. In recognizing this challenge, Mr. Chamuada acted deliberately in planning for future leadership by creating opportunities for others to experience leadership.

Co-creating and sustaining turnaround implies understanding one's unique context in order to engender, with others, solutions that are specific to their circumstances. Unlike Mr. Chamuada, other school leaders were found to undertake change by replicating actions and activities that were ongoing in high performing schools. Ideas were implemented without consideration of context. In schools where such efforts did not lead to positive change, there were hardly new efforts in seeking alternative solutions or critical questions about such actions. From this school, we learn, not only that solutions that are context-based are more likely to yield and sustain success; but also that leaders should be conscious about the impacts of context on capacity to be successful.

It was evident in Kiptai that co-creating solutions was contingent on dispositional values, the orientations with which the school leader, teachers, and members of the community approached school issues including their actions. The essential element that was utilized to get stakeholders to be part of the turnaround was dispositional values that bred evolving power. According to Short and Rinehart (1992) and Short and Greer (1997), evolving power increases stakeholder participation organically and may be achieved through broad base empowerment that includes both teachers and students. Evolving power emerged as key in sustaining and improving on gains as it broadened the leadership base. In many ways, the experiences of teachers at Kiptai Primary school reflected the six dimensions of empowerment expressed by Short and Rinehart (1992). They include:

- Decision-making: participation in critical decisions that directly affect their work.
- Professional growth: opportunities to learn, grow and develop professionally.
- Status: professional respect and admiration.
- Self-efficacy: perception of competence, skills and abilities to help students learn, or effect change.
- Autonomy: belief that they can control certain aspects of their work-life schedule, curriculum.
- Impact: perception of having effect and influence on school life.

Parallel to dimensions of teacher empowerment, Short and Greer (1997) also provide dimensions of student empowerment including:

- Early identification of a definition of student responsibility, successful experiences, competence, and choice.
- Intense focus on students including students as team members, students as workers.
- Flexibility and resourcefulness including expertise, funds, manpower and time to support innovation among students.
- Risk-taking and experimentation based on belief that one can make mistakes, take risks and experiment with new ideas.
- Principal as a facilitator with a leadership-management team and advocate for students and learner.

Although the experiences of students at Kiptai Primary School did not reflect the majority of dimensions identified by Short and Greer (1997), these may be the next steps in enhancing student achievement at Kiptai Primary School. This research noted that student empowerment has not been a focus at Kipatai Primary School as much as teacher empowerment.

Reflections

This chapter focused on turnaround of leadership in a primary school in Kenya. Based on qualitative analyses, it was evident that initiating and sustaining turnaround requires leadership that stimulates stakeholders' creativity in thinking up mutually benefiting solutions. Based on this finding, two areas of reflection are suggested: first, the role of context and second, dispositional values.

Context: in reflecting about context, stakeholders should consider factors that make them unique including questions like: How can a leader identify the strengths within the school to improve student achievement? How does a leader engage those strengths to mutually advantage students and themselves? How does a leader leverage strengths in the school and community without losing control?

Dispositional values: at Kipatai Primary School, values including trust, collaboration, resilience, and humility were evident in the practice of leadership by the school leader, teachers, and adults in the community. As a leader, how would you exemplify practices that generate interest in these practices? How would you go about developing and sustaining these practices among stakeholders? How would you use these practices to evolve power among teachers and especially students?

References

Begley, P. T. (2008). The nature and specialized purposes of educational leadership, in J. Lumby, G. Crow, & P. Pashiardis (Eds.). *International Handbook on the Preparation and Development of School Leaders* (New York: Routledge), pp. 21–42.

Bold, T., Kimenyi, M., Mwabu, G., & Sandefur, J. (2009). Free primary education in Kenya: Enrollment, achievement and local accountability. Paper presented at Annual

Conference of the Center for the Study of African Economies, Oxford University, UK, March, 2009.

Bruffee, K. A. (1993). *Collaborative Learning: Higher Education, Interdependence, and the Authority of Knowledge* (2nd ed.). (Baltimore: The John Hopkins University Press).

Collins, J. (2001). *Good to Great: Why Some Companies Make the Leap ... and Others Don't* (New York: HarperCollins Publishers).

Follette, M. P. (1927). Leader and expert, in H. C. Metcalf & L. Urwick (Eds.), *Dynamic Administration: The Collected Papers of Mary Parker Follett* (New York: Harper & Brothers Publishers), pp. 247–269.

Freire, P. (1990). *Pedagogy of the Oppressed* (New York: Continuum).

Fullan, M. (2006). *Turnaround Leadership* (San Francisco, CA: Jossey-Bass).

Lumby, J. & Foskett, N. (2008). Leadership and culture, in J. Lumby, G. Crow, & P. Pashiardis (Eds.). *International Handbook on the Preparation and Development of School Leaders* (New York: Routledge), pp. 43–60.

Leithwood, K. A. & Riehl, C. (2005). What do we already know about leadership?, in W. A. Firestone and C. Riehl (Eds.), *A New Agenda for Research in Educational Leadership* (New York: Teachers College), pp. 81–100.

Leithwood, K., Day, C., Sammons, P., Harris, A. & Hopkins, D. (2006), *Seven strong claims about successful school leadership, National College of School Leadership* (Nottingham: National College of School Leadership).

Prahalad, C. K. & Krishnan, M. S. (2008). *The New Age of Innovation: Driving Co-created Value Through Global Networks* (New York: McGraw Hill).

Reyes, P. & Wagstaff, L. (2005). How does leadership promote successful teaching and learning for diverse students?, in W. A. Firestone and C. Riehl (Eds.), *A New Agenda for Research in Educational Leadership* (New York: Teachers College), pp. 101–118.

Short, P. M. & Greer J. T. (1997). *Leadership in Empowered Schools: Themes from Innovative Efforts* (Columbia, OH: Merrill Prentice Hall.)

Short, P. M. & Rinehart, J. S. (1992). School participant empowerment scale: Assessment of level of empowerment within the school environment, *Educational and Psychological Measurement, 52*, pp. 951–961.

Part II

What new principals do

The first few years

Chapter 6

Denmark

A strength of purpose: building credibility and trust

Lejf Moos

Introduction

This is the story of the career of Tom Frandsen (not his real name) as he decides to become a teacher and then goes on to be deputy and then a principal. Part of this story has emerged from Life History Interviews that were conducted in 1999 and published in Moos (2005) The interviews were continued in the International Successful School Principalship Project, and the latest of those interviews took place in 2008 (Moos & Kasper, 2009). One could say I have followed this principal over a period of ten years.

From middle manager to teacher

Tom Frandsen was trained to be a professional industrial graphic worker in the 1970s. This was a time and an industry that was very focused on fighting for workers' rights through the trade unions, and which promoted workplace solidarity. Despite gaining a middle management position in a small private company with 8–10 employees, Tom was restless. Although he enjoyed the solidarity to be found in the industry, he found the focus on satisfying customers gave him little sense of long-term commitment. He also realized that the political discussions he had with his colleagues were very often about educational and social issues. The culture Tom heard was in schools, of dialogue that builds on respect and responsibility towards other people and which promotes democracy, increasingly appealed to him. So instead of standing outside looking in, he decided he wanted to be part of it himself – he wanted to be a teacher.

Looking back, he had always wanted to be a teacher. He liked going to school as a child. He was one of those students who attended to his duties, and who worked hard, even though he wasn't the most gifted. He liked the sense of community, the fellowship in school, and he thrived in being together with other people in situations where leisure time and working hours were interconnected.

In order to make the transition to school teaching, Tom, now in his mid-twenties, had to rearrange his life. He stopped paid employment in the daytime but went on working nights and weekends, and started at a teacher education college. So, even at this early stage he got used to having to work 'a full working 24 hours' and to living the life that he had dreamt about.

At teacher education college Tom joined the educational development committee and the executive committee. He didn't see it as a political activity, but rather as an organizational activity to improve the college. Together with several other students he formed a professional social forum where they discussed how to transform schools, and not just improve them.

Tom completed his teacher education programme in 1979 and was employed as a teacher in a social democratic governed local authority. He also took part in politically oriented tasks there, becoming a substitute for the shop steward, and chair of the teachers committee where he worked hard on the educational development of the school. He took part in school board activities and in the municipal joint teachers committee, and was thus entering a traditional career path for Danish school leaders. He was in these posts for seven years. At that stage he felt the need to move on in his career, so when a deputy principalship became vacant in his municipality Tom thought to himself that he would apply for it.

In and out of leadership

He was appointed to the deputy principalship of a 'Folkschool' (primary and lower secondary, students aged 6–16 years), and after a few months he was appointed temporarily as acting principal because the principal had been seconded to work for the local authority. He held this post for ten months and then was, 'Pushed back to the deputy post', he said. He didn't feel good about that, and felt disempowered in having to return to a position without the overview, the planning and the delegation to which he had become accustomed as part of his employment as acting principal. Serendipitously, as Tom was feeling frustrated in his deputy role, the politicians decided to close the school in a move to reduce public expenditure. Students and employees were dispersed to several schools, and Tom found himself placed in a transformation-minded school.

The local school system initiated a leadership education programme at that time with themes like 'educational development of the school system' and 'quality development'. At Tom's new school the staff started talking about these items. Tom implemented some of the ideas in collaboration with his colleague, the principal. The principal had arrived half a year earlier than Tom, and as they knew each other, they had a ready rapport to help improve the school. So they initiated an educational transformation that involved joint school development initiatives, which looked like the national initiatives that were to come in the late 1990s, such as developing teacher teams and emphasizing student project work. It worked perfectly in this school, Tom said, partly, because the two members of the leadership team inspired each other and partly because they were very diverse in their leadership approaches; the principal focused more on the administrative aspects of leadership, while Tom concentrated on the relations between teachers, and on the school development plan.

Losing one's footing

Tom was a deputy principal at that school for six years, involving himself deeply in school development. After that period of time he wanted to be a principal himself, and therefore in 1995 he applied for, and was appointed principal, at his current school. It is a school of 550 students and 40 teachers, plus 20 other staff, and is situated in a more conservative and wealthier suburban municipality than his previous school. Shortly after taking over the principalship he established an educational development committee with teacher-representatives in his school because he wanted to promote collaborative school development. When he took up his position, he cited the Danish philosopher Søren Kierkegaard who suggested that 'one might lose one's footing for a short moment, when moving, but if one doesn't move at all one risks losing it for the rest of life.' The teachers didn't think he meant it until he actually began 'moving' by talking about pedagogic change and using professional terms such as 'didactics', 'distribution' and 'cognition.' He demanded that everybody should understand and use these and other professional terms, arguing that they would not find a craftsmanship or professionally trained group without a language. A professional language was the basis for understanding each other:

> Professional discussions can only take place if you as a leader are alert and if you intervene in teacher's activities, if you show a profile at once, if you question things. You must have ideals, you must have things you stand for and teachers must very quickly be able to measure themselves against them. You must definitely not be pompous and you must be informal in dealings with the teachers. You must be careful not to create distance, and at the same time create distance. These are difficult mechanisms.

Tom's long-range objective, is to establish an educational credibility so the teachers don't have to hide from their school community, so that teachers know that what they do is acceptable, and for them to be proud of this so that they can gain the trust of the school community. This demands that they develop a profile with the parents, who, in this school's neighbourhood are very well educated and know precisely what they want for their children. The children need to be educated in a way that parents find meaningful and that is explained to them. Having good accountability to parents, therefore, is a major concern for Tom.

The changes that Tom instigated were regarded by many teachers as important and exciting challenges; these teachers had joined the transformation. Whilst sometimes teachers felt run-down and they protested vigorously, the small team that Tom had created around himself as an educational development committee understood his way of thinking and helped to spread the message and allay the concerns of staff. However, not all teachers lived up to the professional and educational demands of the school development that Tom expected. As an example, it was difficult for some of them to collaborate closely in teacher teams.

When leaders act, it has got to have an impact on staff, and it is often the case during major change that some teachers might not agree with the reforms and so move on to another school or retire if they are of an appropriate age and circumstance. At Tom's school, more than 40 per cent of the teachers left within the first four years of his principalship. Some retired from teaching, and some were asked to leave. These staff changes proved to be very important because, in dialogue with these new teachers, Tom could form a staff group that was aligned with the school development plans.

Tom now clearly leads the school, but he does so in a constant dialogue with others. He tries hard to be open-minded and outgoing, to be visible and involved in the school so staff can communicate directly with him. 'One has to be in dialogue with the fellow human beings and talk openly to them so they have confidence in the things you undertake', said Tom. Nevertheless, he was known to be a bit autocratic because, in practice, he didn't always find it necessary to discuss matters that he felt strongly must be enacted:

> You have to balance the fact that sometimes you as leader have decided upon something and you therefore can be action minded, and at the same time make sure that teachers feel they own things. This balance is very important in the everyday life of school and it is important for democracy in schools. It is important for each individual to be participating the whole way through. At the same time I have experienced as a leader that there is a tendency to much talk without action. When we have a dialogue then it's not for the sake of the dialogue itself. We have a dialogue in order that it leads to action. When the decision about action has been made, it has been made and should not be redone. Nobody should resume that discussion because then anarchy is close at hand.

Room for manoeuvre

Principals have to be attentive and ready all the time. They cannot relax because suddenly a problem pops-up that they need to take care of. It calls for a special type of mental energy. Tom gets his energy when he occupies himself with things that interest him as a human being and professional: being with other people, being in dialogue and constant communication with other people. When those situations occur, he sets energy free. He says that normally he needs the same amount of sleep and everything else as other people, but in some situations he finds it hard to be patient; for example, when a child needs special care and it is difficult to get the right sort of assistance from the authorities.

Situations can occur, however, where he loses power and feels insecure: 'My biggest problem, where I become uncertain as a leader, is when a criticism is brought forward that I'm unable to act on. That paralyses me.' An example Tom gave is when a teacher is perceived by parents to be not doing their job properly, and as a consequence the parents take their child out of school without consulting or telling Tom. This criticism troubles him because, in his view, it could produce unwarranted myths about the reputation of the school. This makes him feel terrible and he finds himself paralysed and unable to act. Tom indicated that this very example often happens in this school district because parents act very individualistically and sometimes go directly to the municipal authorities instead of addressing him on the first hand.

Tom is connected with his staff and with other educators. That Tom has been a teacher before becoming a principal has been good for his leadership career and for his relations with teachers. He also attends to his networks of peers and looks for inspiration in dialogue with fellow principals. He looks for inspiration whenever there is an in-service program at the school. Then he is very attentive to what's going on and, through his involvement, models to staff the importance of these activities; something that the research literature has found is important in improving student learning outcomes (Robinson, 2007). He also talks to friends from outside the school and reads professional journals. But a lot of what he does is self-taught: 'You have the feeling that this is right. You can feel in yourself, that this is the right way to proceed. It's about credibility. If you can feel that what you do is credible you don't compromise your values.'

Credibility is related to a readiness for action. When you have decided on something you have to be goal-directed, or else you are in a zigzag course that may lead nowhere. The predecessor to Tom suffered from a lack of goal-direction, in that, often when a decision was made by the educational committee, somebody would undermine it and then the school would have to reconsider the decision. As Tom explains, '…you have to be very strict: Once the decision has been made I act or I would lose my credibility.' (Refer to reflection 1.)

Manoeuvring with several accountabilities

Tom was not worried that many school development initiatives come from the national level. However, whilst these might get stagnant schools moving, the national school development programme from year 2000 annoyed him because it was introduced as if it was new and ground breaking, which it wasn't. It was something that Tom and his school had been doing for the past seven years. Tom thinks it is sheer nonsense if somebody from the national level comes to the school wanting to transform it, when the school is already developing as a quality school. For example, Tom argues that in terms of assessment the school already assesses literacy in all grades several times each year, 'We are in control.', and so does not need to be told to do this. Tom despairs at the political forces that are trying to make everything measureable and efficient. Thus, he believes that some of the national and local initiatives can hinder principals in their actions. They need to be able to create room for manoeuvre, or else they are not able to act:

> Principals are in the midst of the space created by the pressure from parents, teachers and politicians. It might be that one group prevents principals from

acting according to the wishes of another group. Then one has to make sure not to be so closely attached to one group that you are unable to act. As a leader you need room for manoeuvre, you need latitude. That in many ways turns it into a political job. It was much easier to be a middle manager in the business world telling people that this is the way it must be because I tell you.

Tom finds it disagreeable to have a political pressure placed on himself that he is convinced can change the school's credibility: 'If you act only to satisfy politicians or parents or whoever it may be, it is wrong. You need latitude as leader. If you don't, you will be tied to poor solutions.' His integrity must be sustained whilst he is at the same time a loyal civil servant. That's why he has to challenge his school board if he thinks they are wrong, and likewise he has to challenge the local authority. (Refer to reflection 2.)

An example of an initiative from outside the school which Tom supports is the local authority's request for schools to produce a work plan every year. Tom finds that preparing this plan is worthwhile because it encourages discussions within the school. The work plan can become part of developing the school into a learning organization. Some phases are difficult. When chaos occurs everybody wants to have somebody tell them 'that's what we do'. That is exactly the moment where Tom is not telling them what to do, but enables the processes to stay open because that's when people bring the frustrations, the conflicts into the processes of dialogue, and in that apparent hotchpotch something emerges. Something of which they then are able to say: 'Now we own it, it's part of our system.' It is in those situations that teachers are energetic and active, and that's the basis upon which the school must be developed. Teachers learn when they themselves are active, in the same way as students.

When Tom distributes leadership responsibilities to individual teachers and to teacher teams, it is in the form of a contract that in many respects is similar to contracts from ministry to local authorities and from local authorities to schools. Teacher teams have been a pivotal cornerstone of the work and have been given a lot of room for manoeuvre in the daily life and in planning for education and teaching, so they often have felt very autonomous. Thus the relations between teams and leadership have often been enacted through the annual negotiations of the contracts and in annual meetings between individual teachers and leaders. Tom and the deputy principal only attend teacher team meetings if they are invited because teachers feel the need to discuss issues or problems with them. They also don't visit classes uninvited. These relations demonstrate to all parties involved, that the leadership had trust in teachers and the work of teacher teams. Over the past few years however there is a rising demand or wish from teachers that Tom and the deputy should be more visible in the daily life of the school. They need, says Tom, someone to lean on and someone who can act as a supervisor. (Refer to reflection 3.)

The leadership team does its utmost to strike a balance between humanistic development and knowing at the same time that test results must be improved

That's the fundamental balance in school, says Tom, in educating students and in being with them and raising them: 'It's about finding the balance so they come out with a democratic weft that turns them into proper citizens and people that carry some subject knowledge with them.'

Tom talks about several kinds of accountabilities and the collisions and clashes between them: The 'traditional', educational and ethical accountability towards pupils, teachers and parents often clash with the 'new', managerial and administrative accountabilities towards local and national authorities. This can create a major dilemma: 'You put your professional credibility at risk if you simply try to satisfy politicians only.'

When looking back on his life history Tom sees:

> an image of a leader who must consider so many things in the everyday life. He must try to avoid becoming paralysed because of those considerations. It is a principal who is talking a lot about credibility. But you need to keep yourself in focus, because the way you act is important to staff, parents and students. It's never accidental and I think that is clear in my history. It is important that the system believes that no matter if it's a conflict or a success story you are in mental balance. It's about managing, it's about objectives, and it's about having an idea of what the purpose of the institution is. That's the important thing, that everybody knows that task.

(Refer to reflection 4.)

Reflections

Tom's narrative is a story about a young man, who had always dreamt about being a teacher. Nevertheless, he started out with a career in industry and as a middle manager in a private enterprise before he entered into teacher education. The reason for his change of life was that the horizon was too narrow in industry; he wanted to enter into long-term commitments with teachers, children and young people.

In teacher education, and as a teacher, Tom entered often into committee work in order to find new ways of teaching and leading that could transform schools. A basic assumption in his professional school leadership life was that teachers needed to be trusted because they have professional credibility. He worked as often as possible with small groups of colleagues, leadership teams, in order to pursue his vision of a good and successful school.

A main feature of Tom's leadership is the dialogue with teachers and all other stakeholders, because he sees deliberations as the basics of a democratic community. However, he also needs room for manoeuvre in order to make good, productive decisions. When this room is restricted, he gets very frustrated and restricted. Therefore he always tries to balance the external expectations with the internal culture and sense making.

This narrative illustrates many themes. Four of which are trust, navigating stakeholder expectations, influence, and balancing competing expectations.

- *Trust* (Day *et al.*, 2011). Many principals' decisions are based on being both legal and legitimate: teachers and other stakeholders comply with the decisions because they find that the argument for them and the person who makes the decision are credible. They trust them. There can be many reasons for people trusting, or not trusting, other people. In schools it is pivotal that people trust each other. Sometimes trust is based on tight, personal relations, like in friendship, and sometimes it is based on the strength of the arguments being used in dialogues.
- *Navigating stakeholder expectations* (Moos *et al.*, 2011). Principals often find themself in the midst of conflicting expectations from the many stakeholders involved in schools: teachers, students, parents, local and national politicians and administrators. It can be challenging to find out what the expectations are and what kind of logic is governing them. It is worth trying to figure out what kind of expectations are manifested in legislation, budgets, administrative procedures, public discourses, parental demands and wishes, teacher unions, teacher identities, student SES background and so on, and then trying to figure out what kind of thinking lies behind the expectations. This can help to both understand the various demands placed on schools, and to navigate a sensible way for schools to respond to these demands that both meets stakeholder expectations, and which fits in with school direction and purpose.
- *Influence* (Moos, 2011). Relations between principals and teachers take many forms including direct, strategic and reciprocal influence. The direct form of influence is typified by situations where the principal commands or outlines what needs to be done. Strategic influences may involve formal or informal contracts that contain frames and expectations set out by the principal and items that the team has set out itself, and the progress and outcomes are evaluated on an annual basis in dialogue between the principal and team. Reciprocal forms of influence are the negotiations and dialogues that principals enter into on a daily, one-to-one basis with teachers when making sense of school expectations.
- *Balancing competing expectations* (Moos, 2011). One very important aspect of the conflicting expectations about schools is, in many contexts, the differences between administrative/local and political/broad expectations that schools must produce better and better results on a national league table of student learning outcomes, or some other form of tight accountability measure. Whilst at an administrative level there is often a narrowing of perspective of what counts as successful schooling, principals often find that the national and local culture demand a more comprehensive perspective on students' outcome of schooling.

Questions to ask

These themes suggest four areas for personal reflection:

1 *How can you as a principal build teachers' trust in you – and how can you go on trusting teachers?* Both aspects of trust are important, as both teachers and leaders need to engage in decision-making and implementation of decisions. Is there room for dialogue and deliberation in the leadership in your school?
2 *How often is trust based on personal relations, and how often on professional arguments?* What kind of trust is more sustainable and maybe less stressful because one form consumes emotions while the other consumes thoughts and deliberations?
3 *Can you think of situations where you use direct, strategic or reciprocal influences?* Are the reasons for using those forms good or relevant for the situation at hand, or do you experience unexpected consequences?
4 *Are any of the formal, political expectations contradictory to your vision of good leadership and good education?* If this is the case, can you think of ways to mediate or translate the external expectations into internal sense that is acceptable to teachers in your school? Can Tom's experiences be of use to you?

References

Day, C., Johansson, O. & Møller, J. (2011). Sustaining improvements in student learning and achievement: the importance of resilience in leadership, in Moos, L., Johansson, O. & Day, C. (Eds.) *How School Principals Sustain Success Over Time: International Perspectives* (Dordrecht: Springer-Kluwer), pp. 167–182.

Moos, L (2005). Memberships and relationships in a changing context, in Sugrue C. (Ed.) *Passionate Principalship* (Abindgon: RoutledgeFalmer).

Moos, L. (2011). Sustaining leadership through self-renewing communication, in Moos, L., Johansson, O. & Day, C. (Eds.) *How School Principals Sustain Success Over Time: International Perspectives* (Dordrecht: Springer-Kluwer), pp. 127–150.

Moos, L. & Kasper Kofod (2009). Sustained successful school leadership in Denmark, *Journal of Educational Administration*, 47(6), pp. 709–718.

Moos, L., Day, C. & Johansson, O. (Eds.) (2011). *How School Principals Sustain Success Over Time: International Perspectives* (Dordrecht: Springer-Kluwer).

Moos, L., Skedsmo, G., Höög, J., Johansson, O. & Johnson L. (2011). The hurricane of accountabilities? Comparison of accountability comprehensions and practices, in Moos, L., Johansson, O. & Day, C. (Eds.) *How School Principals Sustain Success Over Time: International Perspectives* (Dordrecht: Springer-Kluwer), pp. 199–222.

Robinson, V. (2007). School leadership and student outcomes: Identifying what works and why, *Monograph*, 41 (Melbourne: Australian Council for Educational Leaders).

Chapter 7

USA

The story of new principals

Thad Dugan and Jeff Bennett

Introduction

Framing the context: a school and community in trouble

Juarez Elementary School is one of thirteen schools in the Southwest Unified School District, located in an urban environment in Southwestern Arizona. The school serves 700 students who are predominantly Hispanic of Mexican origin (95 percent). Juarez has a large number of English Language Learners (ELLs) and the school is a Title 1 school, meaning that the majority of the students qualify for free and reduced lunch. Many of the grandparents and parents in the neighborhood attended Juarez as children and many of the parents work in labor and minimum wage jobs. The average family income is below the poverty level. Most parents and students speak Spanish as a first language. The school is termed a neighborhood "walking" school because 650 of the students that attend the school live in the surrounding neighborhood. The other 50 students who are bused in are special education students or students that have enrolled at Juarez through open enrollment.

When Lute Ingalls was appointed the role of principal at Juarez Elementary by Superintendent Gomez, it came to him as a huge surprise. Previously, Lute had applied for five elementary school principal positions in the district and had been denied each time for various reasons including little elementary school experience, little understanding of elementary curriculum, and a lack of ability to speak Spanish. In a strange twist of fate, he had been turned down at Juarez on two previous occasions. Although he was surprised to be assigned to the position, he believed that he was up to the task. This would not be the first time that Lute entered a situation with uncertainty; in the past, he had been able to adapt and was successful.

Lute had developed a reputation in the Southwest School District as an effective leader who was able to develop meaningful relationships that pushed people beyond their limits to attain desired goals. This had not fallen on deaf ears as far as Dr. Gomez was concerned. She felt that Lute had the skills, knowledge, disposition, and reputation needed to turn around Juarez. She also knew that he had the ability to overcome the perceived deficiencies that had prevented him from attaining a principalship on his own. In her mind, he was the "right man for the job."

Despite his self-perceived limitations, Lute felt that he had a plan to turn around Juarez. He would build upon his knowledge of coaching athletics as he approached the situation. Utilizing the strengths of his staff (e.g. knowledge of elementary curriculum; understanding of Spanish), he approached Juarez from a situational leadership style. He knew his background in coaching allowed him to take a broader view of situations and look at the big picture, which in the case of Juarez, was identifying the needs and putting the right things into place to address them. He knew it was not something he could accomplish on his own, but he also knew that he would have to be the one to ultimately provide the leadership necessary to transform Juarez from one of the worst schools in the state to a consistently successful school.

Neighborhood and school climate

Prior to Lute's tenure at Juarez Elementary School, Juarez had a reputation for being a tough school to lead. It was classified as an underperforming school on the Arizona ratings for schools and was ranked last in the Southwest District. This means that it consistently failed to meet the statewide minimum standards in numeracy and literacy (other classifications include performing, performing plus, highly performing, and excelling). The school had three separate principals in a three-year time-span. Juarez was known to be unclean, unsafe, with the curriculum that children received largely dependent on the teacher with whom they were placed. The neighborhood surrounding the school was also known for the high rate of crime including murders, drive-by shootings, and home invasions. As one teacher, Mr. Powell, recalled,

> As I drove by in the middle of the day, at the house right across the street, there was a drive-by. There were also a couple of times that the kids found bodies in the alley. Over here, there was a shooting almost every weekend, no matter day or night, right on the corner.

Another teacher, Ms. Garcia also emphasized that the crime in the area had a negative impact on students, even if they were not directly impacted by it. She noted that there were many instances where students were tired in class because of police searches in the area. As she discussed one specific situation with a student who was not participating in class and did not have his homework, she noted, "He maybe didn't have enough sleep. Maybe the helicopter was running around all night." It was not unusual for the police helicopter and officers to be searching the area for criminals, often shining lights in houses and knocking on doors at all hours.

Often, basic safety was more of a priority than students' levels of achievement. A sense of despair enveloped parents who walked their children to school because they felt it too unsafe to allow their children out of the house on their own. This sense of despair also led to students being isolated from many activities that children often enjoy such as playing outside after school.

Mr. Gomez, a third-grade teacher, highlighted this point and acknowledged that safety, along with the low socio-economic status of many of the families, had a negative impact on student achievement:

> When they [students] go home, because this is not the safest place in the world, they go inside and they watch TV, a lot. They don't ride their bicycles around. They don't get a lot of vacation time. They are not taken to Washington D.C., or even San Diego. If you talked to them about the beach, some of them are not even aware of what a beach is. When they're taught about the standardized tests, there are some concepts in the standard tests that they have never experienced. So, their world-view is very confined.

Despite the crime and location in a highly impoverished area, homes around the school are well kept and parents value the education of their children. Parents want the best for their children, but the circumstances of living in poverty and the disconnect between the Spanish dominant language of the home and the English language requirements of the school, often compounded the safety issues that students experienced in their day-to-day lives. Many of the parents do not speak English and many of them did not receive a high school diploma. As many of the parents are functionally illiterate in English and they work long hours, assisting their children with homework is a daunting, if not impossible, task. Regardless of these circumstances, families looked to the school to provide opportunities for success for their children, but the school was in no shape to meet the needs of the students and their families.

The environment outside the school was not the only environment that could be considered toxic for students. The school climate was one of negativity and in-fighting. Teachers were fighting with one another, and the school/community relationship was antagonistic and distrustful. Teachers were able to teach whatever they wanted and a core group of teachers held the power in the school. These teachers made all school decisions and were able to outlast the principals that came and went with regular and depressing frequency. One of the previous principals was removed in the middle of the school year. Principals were not able to deal with instruction; rather, their focus was on negotiating conflicts within the school and the community. Ms. Garcia noted that "we [the teachers and staff] were not talking to each other and we were spending a lot of time on things people already taught. It was chaotic." It was this chaos and Juarez's reputation as a failing school that inevitably led to the hiring of Lute.

Lute's background

On paper, Lute seems an unlikely candidate to take over Juarez as principal. His background and experience were not what one would typically seek as qualifications for an elementary school principal and several factors made him an even more unlikely candidate to transform a low socio-economic, predominantly Hispanic, dysfunctional school into the best school in the district.

A White male, Lute, grew up in the Midwestern United States. As a student, he was involved in student government and participated in sports. Even though he was a good student, the only reason he wanted to work in education was that this would allow him to be actively involved in coaching basketball. Coaching basketball was his passion and he saw involvement in education as the only route to attain this goal. This passion led him to the Southwestern United States, where Lute attained a Bachelor of Science Degree in education with a minor in health. He immediately pursued a master's degree in counseling, which ended when Lute and a professor in the program had a disagreement that led Lute to withdraw from the program. Although he was unable to complete the master's degree, Lute had an experience within the program that provided him a foray into his educational career.

He had begun working on a counseling project in a local elementary school where his talents were noticed by the principal, who soon became his mentor. The principal offered Lute a job facilitating activities with students at lunch time and noticed that he was good at working with the students. Although his mentor did not have a position open, she called another principal and informed her that Lute would be an excellent teacher and she needed to hire him. Lute had his first interview and his first disappointment at this time. Due to a certification issue, Lute was unable to attain the position. However, his mentor was able to identify a school that was beginning a physical education position and Lute was hired. Lute only remained an elementary physical education teacher for one year. As he recalled the story of his first interview and teaching experience, he noted that he was not "cut out" to be an elementary school teacher.

> There was a fourth grade position open at the time. I finished the interview and she wanted to hire me. She asked "what is your certification?" It changed everything. Because I had a B.S. in education degree and a health minor with some social studies mixed in, she could not hire me. I said that is fine and went back to my mentor. She said "I have a friend at another elementary school who is thinking of starting a physical education program. You may want to interview over there." They hired me. I was the PE program and I stayed there for one year. I hated it. The kids were too young.

Despite his disappointment, the physical education position had given him an opportunity to pursue his passion of coaching. It was his abilities as a basketball coach that opened up an opportunity for him to move to the middle-school level.

At this time, Lute was an undefeated coach and had gained the respect of fellow coaches and parents. During one of his games, Lute was approached by the principal of a local middle school and he wanted Lute to both teach and coach. He took a position at the middle school where he taught physical education and coached several sports. During the five years that he taught and coached at the middle school, Lute lost his passion for coaching. Though he was undefeated and had attained several championships, he did not feel that his efforts were truly appreciated. According to Lute, he became tired of being yelled at by parents that their children were not playing enough. In spite of a perfect record, he walked away from coaching and decided that he would go into administration. Thus, he focused his energy on becoming a school administrator and never returned to coaching. Though he would never be a coach by position again, he would utilize the strategy and motivational techniques developed over his successful coaching career in his repertoire as a future school leader.

Lute gained his certification in Secondary School Administration and moved from the area to teach for a period of two years before a position opened in Southern Arizona where he became an assistant principal at a high school in his current district. He transitioned from high school after two years and became a middle-school assistant principal for several years. It was during this time that Lute developed a reputation as a good leader and was well respected by teachers and other principals. He was also respected by the community and felt that it was his time to take a position as a principal. Unfortunately, the district had little turnover at the middle- and high-school levels. Therefore, Lute began applying for positions at elementary schools that had openings. However, attaining a principal position was more difficult than he expected. Until Superintendent Gomez called, Lute was resigned to remaining in his position as a middle school assistant principal, a position he thoroughly enjoyed. Upon receiving the appointment from Dr. Gomez, Lute at first felt apprehension because the Juarez staff and parents had passed on him on two prior occasions. After speaking with Dr. Gomez, Lute felt that he was ready to be the principal and any lingering questions from his prior interviews were displaced as the Superintendent assured him that he was right for the position. Lute knew that Juarez would be the biggest challenge of his life, but he felt that he was resilient and could adapt his coaching and leadership style to meet the needs of the school. He approached the position as a coach and viewed the turnaround of Juarez was an all-important game to play where the outcomes would significantly impact the lives of the players.

First steps

Lute's first step was to meet with teachers before the school year began. As a strategy, his focus during these meetings was simple and was to allow the teachers to tell him what was needed. Hearing from the teachers would allow him to formulate a plan to move Juarez forward. As he met with the teachers, active listening focused the conversation; "I want them to tell me what they want." The only thing I will say is "tell me what you want me to hear and ask the questions you want to ask me."' Only two teachers told Lute that they wanted him to run the school and only a few more reported that they wanted the school to be successful. Others focused their conversations on complaints about other teachers, the parents, and the community. As Lute recollected, "Everybody was telling about everybody else, this one and that one. Be careful of this one or that one." Throughout the meetings, Lute listened and did not interject his opinion.

Though most of the discussions focused on negative attitudes toward other staff and the community, several key themes arose. These themes, along with a review of the school's data confirmed that the school had no curriculum cohesion, that a small core group of teachers dictated everything that occurred in the school, and that student learning outcomes were low, especially in reading, although mathematics was stronger. This core group collaborated with the school's parent teacher organization (PTO) and decided how funds would be spent. The meetings confirmed the depth of dysfunction at the school, with teachers more concerned with themselves than with teaching and learning needed to provide a quality education for students. The next step for Lute was to meet with parents and the community to hear their needs.

Lute continued to focus on listening as he met with parents for the first time. He knew some of the families from his experiences at the middle school and felt that others were there to, "check me out to see who I am and what I would say." He asked one simple question and allowed the parents to respond, "What do you want from me?" He did not present what he was going to do, but wanted to know the community's expectations. Most of the parents echoed the same voice: "They wanted a safe and orderly environment." Beyond the environment, Lute also saw that parents wanted a quality education for their children, and that they deeply cared for them. When the meeting ended, Lute thanked the parents and began formulating a plan for improving the school.

Bottom-lines

After meeting with parents and teachers, Lute developed three "bottom-lines" or norms and values by which everybody in the school (parents and school staff) would have to adhere. These bottom-lines emphasized three themes, academic success, good behavior, and staff collaboration. First, every student at Juarez would learn to read and would be ready for sixth grade when they left the school. Second, all staff would view the students as their own children and would treat them as they would want their own children treated. This last point included student discipline, an area that Lute had found difficult to develop in his past work. His approach was not that of a disciplinarian as he had an expectation that both he and his teachers would coach students who were having discipline issues instead of using suspensions and other punitive measures. When asked to expound on his thoughts about discipline, Lute responded that he keeps a picture of his own family on his desk and uses the picture as a reminder to do "what I would want for my own children." He also had a strong belief that failure makes a person better, and behavior was one of the areas that failures are necessary. He noted,

> I can look a kid or adult in the eyes and say you are wrong and this is why. This is what we will do to correct the behavior. I think success and failure make a better person. We all want success, but if you don't ever feel failure then something is wrong.

The third bottom-line was that change at the school would be a collaborative effort. Everyone would utilize their strengths to accomplish agreed upon school goals, while working toward improving any deficits. Leadership responsibilities would be completed collaboratively and whilst decisions would be based on consensus, Lute retained the right of veto for all decisions. Leadership at Juarez would be distributed so that all staff and parents had a voice, but leadership was not shared. Lute would listen to all stakeholders and make decisions based on the last bottom-line which was having excellent student achievement. Lute was establishing a sense of urgency about improving the school, and whilst he was clearly involving the school community in this, there was a strong sense that Lute was in charge.

Setting the tone

Prior to the beginning of the school year, Lute held a staff meeting to discuss the direction of the school. Using information gathered from his individual meetings, Lute summarized his findings and informed the staff about his bottom-lines. He emphasized that everyone would have high expectations and work together to transform Juarez into a successful school. Success begets success and Lute told them the goal was to be an Excelling school (the highest accountability label in Arizona). He also informed the staff that the leadership structure at the school would be different from what they were used to. Leadership teams would be assigned and they would run staff meetings set on norms that were developed. He also stated that leadership teams would rotate so that everyone would get an opportunity to take on leadership responsibilities and ensure that everyone's voice was heard. Leadership team decisions would be based on data and consensus, which framed the goals to be reached.

His first leadership team meeting set the tone for the school. Though it did not start out well, the future direction and focus for the school were attained from this first meeting. As Lute recalls,

> My first leadership meeting, I found out the best way to run the meeting was from setting the norms and focus. But my first leadership team, we had a large table and I sat behind the table and brought one person from each team. For the first hour of the two hour meeting, I told them to talk. I wanted to hear

what they were thinking about the school. I had total chaos for the first hour. People were just upset with each other and told what they thought.

They were very negative but professional. I let it go for an hour and I jumped in. Everyone got two or three times to say their opinions. I said, "Now it is time to get to the business to set up an agenda." People saw what I was going to put up with. From that point forward, I did not run my leadership team meetings.

One of the outcomes of the first meeting was a focus on the need to develop a common curriculum for the school. Since mathematics scores were better than reading and many of the standardized assessment questions in mathematics were based on vocabulary, reading became the school's emphasis. Teaching all students to read would be the school's mission. The only problem was that Lute did not know how to teach students to read. This would be a challenge for Lute, and his job and reputation depended on how he responded.

The committee looked at me and said, "Lute, we need you to find us a reading program." That is how I knew what they were doing. I did not know much about reading programs and I was challenged. They were wondering what I was going to do and tried to run me off just as they did with the four principals within the last seven years. Maybe I would be the fifth, I don't know. I was very lucky that I had a very good program facilitator at that time.

Knowing that he did not understand elementary curriculum, Lute sought out assistance from a colleague he had known for several years. Lute recalled his conversation with the program facilitator and the beginning of a collaboration that would help transform Juarez.

The two of us sat down. My shortcoming is reading. I wonder why me. The committee said you were the leader. The thing I learned a long time ago is that you don't "fake" anything. I told the program facilitator I don't know anything about reading and you have to teach me. I also reminded her that I told the leadership team okay, you put me on the task and I will put the task on.

For the next six months, Lute and the program facilitator reviewed and analyzed different reading programs being used in the United States. They wanted the program to be research-based and Success for All was chosen. Success for All is a comprehensive reading program (e.g. structured time for instruction, remedial help, extended day tutoring) designed to ensure that every child will read at grade level or above. This literacy program includes intervention components for struggling readers, intensive professional development, peer coaching, and parental involvement.

Although Lute and the program facilitator chose Success for All, they knew that they needed teacher support. Teachers were sent to other schools to observe the program on several occasions and discussions were held. Weekly studies were held on the program. In the end, 35 of 37 teachers agreed that the program would work.

From this point forward, Success for All became the focus of the school's efforts. Time was dedicated to the program. This time was protected and all other activities at the school revolved around the block times dedicated to the program. Lute's efforts, as the principal who knew little about curriculum in the beginning of his tenure, were also focused.

Success for all

Because of the scripted nature of the Success for All program, Lute was able to monitor the curriculum and spent most of his time during the day in classrooms focused on implementation of the reading program. He was also able to focus on student specific data and work with teachers to improve specific student achievement. The program allowed him to monitor teaching and use data to drive discussions with teachers. Success for All bridged Lute's lack of curriculum knowledge and permitted him to utilize his greatest strengths– motivation and coaching.

> I like it because I can go in and guarantee the teacher is doing what he/she is supposed to be doing. Now, there is some flexibility built into it. I don't want to say it is that rigid and strict. There has to be a little. But the bottom line is that is I see that a scripted program helps. I am not here promoting a scripted program, but I am here promoting that this makes me better. This helps me as a principal and makes me a better principal because I know what the teachers are teaching.

Monitoring Success for All gave the school a focus on reading and allowed Lute to work with teachers to make them better, but this was only a part of Juarez's success. Other programmatic changes included an after-school program that highlighted interventions twice a week for students who needed additional support and extension activities for all students on other days. Ninety percent of students and teachers participated in the after-school programs. However, the real change at Juarez occurred through practices that facilitated learning and Success for All and the after-school programs gave the common ground for this to occur.

Practices that facilitated learning

Lute considers himself a strategist that identifies weaknesses and utilizes his coaching skills to improve them. His focus on coaching and building on both the strengths and weaknesses of parents and staff is what moved the school forward. Lute was realistic about the impact that parents had on improving their children's reading skills. Since most parents had limited English skills and many had little education, he utilized their desire to be involved in various ways. First, Lute did not rely on parents to teach students. He felt, and provided the motivation for teachers to feel that it was their responsibility. That being said, Lute set expectations for parents while emphasizing that their children would learn at high levels.

> I will tell you my success with parents has been more due to the school doing what it needed to do … I want the parent to support the school as they get their children in school every day and make sure they are well fed. Make sure they are on time. Make sure if they don't have something, let me know what they need … As a result, they get the kids in on time and they don't take the kids out of school for silly reasons. If you can help the children read, it's fine. If you cannot, make sure the kids get in the room and the child reads. If they are reading, learning is going on.

He also relied on parents for feedback and support. Utilizing parents to assist teachers with making photocopies of materials, for example, provided an opportunity to get them into the school and be involved. He was also the first principal to allow the parents to sell tamales at school, which forged deeper relationships and aided parents in providing income for their families. Lute also spent time meeting with parents as they brought their children to school and took them home at night.

Another aspect of the transformation at Juarez was the evolution of teacher involvement in the leadership and decision-making process. Lute promoted a *sense* of leadership in all staff and provided the opportunity for all teachers to take on leadership tasks. He encouraged input from his teachers and used their recommendations and feedback to make decisions. However, he maintained control over decisions. Ms. Smith, another teacher noted,

> He knows how to motivate students and teachers. He knows how to make you feel that when you are at your best, there is so much more to go … He is always pushing. Always pushing, pushing to do more.

Ms. Smith noted that this push was both in the classroom and in leadership. You were expected to be a leader and "support was provided to learn if you did not feel that you were ready."

Lute emphasized on-the-job learning, both his own and that of his staff. Mistakes were inevitable, but learning from mistakes was most important. He also held staff to the expectations that were set by his bottom-lines. Staff that did not adhere to the bottom-lines were removed. This only occurred on two occasions during his first year. Lute removed a custodian who did not keep the school clean and removed a cafeteria worker for treating students and parents in a negative way. Southwest District has consensus agreements with employees. The consensus agreement provides the structure for removing staff. This occurs through formal notices of needed improvement and specific goals. If goals are not met, the employee may be released.

Because decisions were made through a consensus process, teachers remained focused on the school's objectives and Lute held them accountable for their decisions. Once decisions were made, the expectation was that everyone worked to the best of their abilities to meet desired outcomes. As his assistant, Ms. Orion noted,

> If he had people complain, he would say wait a minute, on such and such a day you raised your hand and said you wanted it. Why are you complaining now? So he held people accountable and let them vote and choose and decide. He got buy-in all the time. That's huge.

Once consensus was reached, the decision held unless data dictated otherwise. Decisions that did not work were analyzed and modified or eliminated. Lute wanted people to "work smarter, not harder" and "did not stick with things that did not impact student achievement or staff growth." There was the Juarez way and it did not matter if the district wanted to go another direction. Ms. Gomez, a teacher that came to Juarez from another school recalled Lute's support and focus on the Juarez way:

> I have seen it only because I was on the same committee that he was on when I was at the other school and he would always stand up, stand up and fight for his teacher. 'No, my teachers would not do that, because that's going to take away time from the classroom.' So I would see this. Wow, why don't other principals stand up for their teachers like he does or give credit to their teachers or to their students. But he was always the fighter. And I think it just fits on the rest of us. We want to fight for our students the way he fights for us.

Sticking to the Juarez way allowed the school to move forward and the school has achieved the third of five highest ratings on school performance, Performing Plus, for many years. Performing Plus means that most students achieve above standards. Lute's support of staff and development of their leadership has led to many of his teachers taking administrative positions at other schools and the district office. Juarez has become the highest rated school in the district and parents, students, and teachers throughout the district refer to the Juarez way. Staff, students, and parents are so happy with the Juarez way that no member of staff has left the school after the first year except for retirements and administrative job placements. Students are happy and learning, and the school's attendance is the highest in the district.

If you were to ask Lute, he was just the coach. The teachers were the ones that made the Juarez way happen. According to Lute, what made him a good instructional leader was that he led by example. But, Juarez's transformation was due to his teachers. "They are the practitioners and I was not ... Every teacher is better than me at Juarez." In his opinion, his role was to coach people to be better. "I would tell teachers that they were better than me. But, I could tell them

what they were doing right and I could tell them what they needed to do better …
That's the Juarez way."

Stuck on being good

Juarez is still a Performing Plus school, however Lute is no longer the principal as
he has been tasked to lead failing schools in the district in a central office position.
Ms. Orion, his assistant principal, has taken the lead at the school. Although
Lute is not principal, he remains a fixture at Juarez and works with Ms. Orion
to maintain the Juarez way. When teachers and the new principal were asked
what changes would be made, they resoundingly responded that little would be
changed. The Juarez way remains, and this may be a problem in the long term as
we explain in this section.

When Lute first took charge of Juarez, the school was in crisis. It was the worst
school in the district and there seemed no way to improve it. Lute approached
the challenge of improving the school with a very directive and top-down style
of leadership that provided the direction, structure and supports necessary to
move the school forward. This directive style established high expectations in
regard to student learning and behavior (student, teacher, and parent), provided
teachers with the means to improve student learning outcomes in reading
(Success for All), and created a collaborative work environment. While Lute was
open to suggestions and feedback, and encouraged consensus decision-making,
he controlled the decision-making authority of the school. Lute understood the
importance of building relationships with parents and teachers, understanding
that their efforts would significantly impact on the level of student achievement.
But, these relationships were formed around *his* non-negotiable bottom-lines: high
student learning outcomes, good behavior, and teacher collaboration.

However, Lute's coaching centered and directive leadership created a condition
of charismatic leadership. Fullan (2001) noted that charismatic leadership may
inadvertently do more harm than good because episodic improvement can be
followed by frustrated or despondent dependency. In the case of Juarez, the initial
chaos and crisis required a directive approach (Fullan, 2006). Missing from the Juarez
case was a release of authority and development of distributed leadership or layered
leadership to promote leadership across the school community (Day, 2010). While
Lute promoted a sense of leadership amongst staff, he has yet to release control
over the Juarez way. This lack of releasing control has created a situation where
the Juarez way remains, yet the school is stuck in the status quo of being good and
not being able to move to great. In other research in the ISSPP, similar stories are
found. Most notably, are the Australian cases where differences in the ability of the
principals to continue improvement was linked to their attitude to change with some
principals able to continuously improve schools because they drove improvement
through promoting change (see Drysdale *et al.*, 2011, and Gurr *et al.*, 2009).

Juarez has gone from a school in chaos to a school that is now performing well
but which has stagnated in its growth. While Lute presents an interesting case for

turning around a low performing school, the steps taken to develop the school into a successful school may be limiting the school from moving from "good" to "great." The Juarez way is developed around their Success for All program and Lute's directive, coaching style of leadership that may diminish capacity of teachers, students, and parents to make independent decisions regarding the students. The focus on Success for All provides the school with clear direction for reading success, but this approach limits the view of "success" and focuses the attention of teachers and students on basic reading skills. While these skills have moved students forward, the school remains a performing plus school and has been unable to progress toward higher performance levels.

Lute's approach was consistent with the literature for turning around a school when the situation required a top-down, directive approach (e.g. Fullan, 2006; Minthrop, 2004). However, recent research by Day (2010) suggests that more is needed for sustainable success. In the English context, Day (2010) identified a school which parallels this story of Lute. The school had similar levels of dysfunction (e.g. unsafe environment, conflict, and low-achievement) and the principal utilized a directive approach to move the school from the special measures that had been imposed on it. As this school came out of special measures, however, the school goals became more long-term in focus. Day (2010) noted that the school adopted a distributed approach that built capacity through visioning that utilized students, parents, and teachers. The school also developed a conception of becoming a thinking school. Though Lute listened to feedback and elicited thoughts from staff, he never truly allowed others to be decision makers and the Success for All focus is the opposite of the concept of a thinking school. Unfortunately, Lute's approach and reliance on Success for All may have become a crutch preventing the school from moving forward. Minthrop (2004) noted that an authoritative approach is necessary in the initial stages of chaos and remedying gross insufficiencies, but it also creates a situation where there is no basis for moving forward. In the case of Juarez, Lute Ingalls may have to move away from influencing Juarez in order for the school to move forward. While he remains ingrained in the culture and decision-making at the school, the ability for creativity and progress is likely to remain thwarted. Part of the problem may also be that the initial successes and maintained level of "being good" have created a situation where everyone is happy and students are achieving at a narrowly defined level of success. This success has defined the approach to success. But, this lack of push for excellence and creativity means Juarez will consistently remain just a good school, when it is well placed to move to the next level and become a truly great school.

Reflections

The Juarez case and the practices implemented by Lute provide several examples of practices that promote improving circumstances for underperforming schools. Using an authoritative and charismatic style of leadership, Lute was able to improve student achievement at Juarez by implementing several "bottom-lines" associated with academic success, good behavior, and staff collaboration. These bottom-lines became the basis for change and the development of the "Juarez way" which has moved the school from the lowest level of performance (Underperforming) in Arizona to one of the highest (Performing Plus). The emphasis on providing a safe and orderly environment, treating children as if they were your own, collaboration, and a focus on reading are hallmarks of the Juarez way. The purpose of this section is to reflect on themes from the case and how these themes interact with current practices or practices that you have experienced. Six reflection areas are presented:

1   When Lute began at Juarez, he found lack of cohesion in the curriculum. In what ways was he able to develop a common curriculum? How was the common curriculum (Success for All) utilized to leverage improvement at Juarez? In your own practice, have you developed consensus around a common curriculum, and if so what impact has this had on student achievement?

2   Success for All became the instructional emphasis at Juarez. How did Lute protect teachers' time and the fidelity of implementation of Success for All? What are the instructional emphases at your site, how are these protected, and what are the barriers that you experience in doing this?

3   When Lute began at Juarez, a core group of teachers controlled decision-making. How did Lute distribute leadership? In what ways do you promote shared leadership and collaboration amongst your school community? How might you promote Layered Leadership – release of control and responsibility to teachers, parents, and students (Day, 2010)? How is this different from the leadership presented in the Juarez case?

4   Through discussion and review of data, reading was identified as the largest area of academic need. What are the targeted areas of need at your school, and how did you identify them?

5   Whilst Lute promoted collaborative decision-making, he remained in control of the decisions and remains a presence at Juarez despite the school being led by a new principal. In what ways might this be helpful or limiting for the continued evolution of Juarez? What do you feel is needed for Juarez to move from "good" to "great"?

6   Lute had several bottom-lines or norms. What are your bottom-lines? How do you build consensus around these bottom-lines?

References

Day, C. (2010). Capacity building through layered leadership: Sustaining the turnaround, in A. Harris (Ed.) *Distributed leadership* (Dordrecht: Springer-Kluwer), pp. 121–138.

Drysdale, L., Goode, H. & Gurr, D. (2011). Sustaining school and leadership success in two Australian schools, in Moos, L., Johansson, O., & Day, C. (Eds.) (2011). *How school principals sustain success over time: International perspectives* (Dordrecht: Springer-Kluwer), pp. 25–38.

Fullan, M. (2001). *Leading in a culture of change* (San Francisco: Jossey-Bass).

Fullan, M. (2006). *Turnaround leadership* (San Francisco: Jossey-Bass).

Gurr, D., Drysdale, L. & Goode, H. (2010). Successful school leadership in Australia: A research agenda. *The International Journal of Learning, 17*(4), pp. 113–129.

Minthrop, H. (2004). *Schools on probation* (New York: Teachers College Press).

Chapter 8

Australia

The developing principal

Joy Doherty, David Gurr and Lawrie Drysdale

Preamble

We have worked with Rick Tudor for several years. Through an intensive multiple perspective case study of his leadership of a highly successful independent boys' school (Doherty, 2008), and through involvement in teaching in our postgraduate school leadership programs, we have come to some understanding of the work of this outstanding educator. This chapter draws on the research of Joy Doherty, our submission for Rick's Fellowship of the Australian Council for Educational Leaders, and our many conversations with Rick. One of our conversations was particularly memorable and epitomizes Rick's work as an exemplary school leader. We had arranged to meet with Rick to discuss this chapter and several other matters. The conversation began with Rick excitedly discussing some recent teaching he had been doing with year 5 boys about the basis for differentiation in plant growth. The conversation continued on to a consideration of what a future school library might look like. Throughout there was an infectious enthusiasm and high energy – Rick is an educator who remains passionate and excited about education and the work of developing students and staff.

Introduction

Rick Tudor is the Headmaster of Trinity Grammar School in Melbourne, Australia. This school, founded in 1902, is a high-fee, independent Anglican boys' school of more than 1300 students, operating programs from pre-school (age 3) to year 12 (age 18). The school is located in a high socio-economic suburb about 7km from the central business district of Melbourne. More than 80 percent of families are classified in the top quarter of the index of community socio-educational advantage. Student performance indicates that the school is one of the highest performing schools in Australia (www.myschool.edu.au). In this chapter we begin by exploring the formation of Rick's leadership, and then look at his influence on students' outcomes, and staff and school development.

The formation of an educational leader

In *The Making of Educational Leaders*, Gronn (1999) described how a career in educational leadership involves stages of formation, accession, incumbency and divestiture. Taking this view, observing a school leader requires a sense of what formed them as a person who is capable of leading a school, how they prepared for and gained the role, what they do once in the role, and how they prepare to leave the role. Such an approach can balance out the emphases on structures and systems typical of leadership research, and provide further understanding of the sources of principals' self-efficacy beliefs and how they develop over time through various leadership roles and school contexts (Leithwood *et al.*, 2006). In this section we reflect on Rick's career as an educational leader illustrating some of the influences on his current successful practice.

In the career pathway of development that he has taken, Rick has demonstrated the strategies of Gronn (1999) to attain formal recognition as a leader. Rick has spent all but one year working in independent schools. Commencing in 1974 as a science and biology teacher in a regional Victorian government school, Rick moved to the independent school sector with a teaching appointment in 1975 at Melbourne Grammar, one of the oldest and most elite schools in Australia. During his time at the school, he was appointed coordinator of middle-school biology and participated in a teacher exchange to King's School, Bruton, Somerset in the United Kingdom (1977–1978). There, he taught O- and A-level biology, was a boarding house tutor and travelled widely in the United Kingdom, visiting a large number and range of secondary schools and teacher training centers. In his time as a teacher at Melbourne Grammar School, Rick developed an integrated curriculum for the school's environmental studies camp that involved the co-ordination of staff participation from both preparatory and senior school sections. Rick was collecting a range of experiences that steeped him in the workings of independent schools, and he showed leadership ability through his work in curriculum and people development; clearly these were important experiences in his leadership formation.

Within the first decade of his career, Rick gained his first senior leadership role when in 1984 he was appointed Deputy Headmaster (Curriculum) of the Peninsula School, Mt. Eliza (a high-fee, independent school). This gave him important experience in policy development and management, and further enhanced his abilities in curriculum reform. It was the beginning of his ascent to being the head of a school, and five years later, Rick became the Headmaster of Beaconhills School, a middle-fee, ecumenical, non-denominational independent school established in 1980 on the outskirts of Melbourne. It was an excellent opportunity to use the leadership skills he had been developing in a relatively new school that had become established, but which now needed curriculum and pedagogical development. During his eight-year tenure, the school increased in size from 352 in 1989 to 950 in 1997. The school enjoyed a period of stability, growth and solid development that laid the foundations for the current three-campus school of more than 3000 students. The changes that Rick initiated were associated with: formulating school aims that were used to underpin the operation and future development of the College; establishing sound administration and general leadership; restructuring of senior staff positions; introducing new subjects appropriate to the abilities and aspirations of the students of the school; developing a new model of pastoral care based on a house system with multi-age tutor groups; and involving parents through establishing a Parent and Friends Association. Whilst not the subject of this chapter, his time at this school allowed him to develop his leadership (incumbency) and to also demonstrate how he could leave a school as head and for that school to continue to develop and succeed. His tenure at this school was regarded as being very successful and led directly to his next career change, a move away from the Principalship.

In 1997 Rick was invited by the Headmaster of Melbourne Grammar School to take up the position of Deputy Headmaster (Head of Senior School) at a time of rebuilding for the school. This was an interesting career move as it was a step-down from leading a school, and it was a role that he had undertaken previously, but it was in a very prestigious school undergoing significant transformation, and a school he was familiar with. It provided an excellent basis to then take over the development of another old and prestigious boys' school in Melbourne. In 1999, Rick became the Headmaster at Trinity Grammar School, a story we describe below. At the time of appointment, Rick was in the position (a) to be approached by the School Council of Trinity Grammar School to lead the school, and (b) to be able to accept the role of Headmaster of the school. He knew, as did the School Council, that he had the capabilities to fulfill that role and the future needs of the school. It was a timely appointment for both parties.

Looking at Rick's leadership career there are several observations. He was able and willing to assume leadership responsibilities early in his career. These responsibilities included developing people and developing teaching and learning, two of the four elements of successful school leadership identified by Leithwood and colleagues (see for example Leithwood et al. , 2006). His first deputy principal role allowed Rick to further develop his leadership of teaching and learning and also exposed him to the important managerial side of schools. His first principal role was in a newly created school, and he was able to provide direction for the school, to grow the school, to develop curriculum, pastoral care and leadership, and to promote engagement with parents. In this role he demonstrated the other two leadership dimensions of Leithwood and colleagues – setting direction and restructuring the organization. The move to Melbourne Grammar in a lower-level leadership role showed that he was able to lead within the demands of an elite independent school. The move to Trinity was a perfect match with this experience as it was a school that was being transformed into a contemporary independent school through the work of two previous Headmasters. It needed someone to guide these changes, to provide clear direction, develop the teaching and learning to meet contemporary demands, and to develop the staff to be able to do this. In terms of self-efficacy and preparedness for this role, Rick had already demonstrated that he could be a successful principal, and his considerable experience as a teacher and leader in elite independent schools meant he was well prepared to be the seventh principal in Trinity's 100-year history.

In terms of the development of his leadership, it is continually evolving and this was a feature shown in Doherty's (2008) research. Whilst Rick clearly influenced the school, this was a reciprocal relationship in that his experience at the school changed how he works:

> the principal's leadership characteristics and practices had influenced the school community strongly in the time that he had been Headmaster of Victoria [Trinity] Grammar School. The traditional culture and identity of the school was a strong contextual feature for both influencing and being influenced upon by the principal's behaviour as school leader … He had had opportunities to extend and grow himself, and his leadership capabilities, through his work in the school and in the wider community, locally and globally. At times, how he had implemented some of the changes he wanted to initiate, that is, the pace of change, and the strategies he used, had been shaped by such contextual factors as: members of staff who have been in the school for a number of years and how they would accommodate the change; how change would affect long-established traditions within the school; and, how change would be absorbed by the school so that it effectively supported the sustainability of the school.
>
> (Doherty, 2008, pp. 110–111)

An example, which we will explore further, was a change from four to eight houses. This might seem a relatively minor event, but the school had been operating four houses since 1917 and, in some cases, three generations of families had identified with these four houses. They were an integral part of the culture of the school. They were, however, too large to offer appropriate pastoral care now that the school was larger, and at the beginning of its second hundred years, symbolically a change was most likely appropriate. Rick was conscious of the need to change, but also respectful of the culture and history of the school, and so his leadership of this initiative proceeded at a slower pace than might otherwise have been the case. He learned through this, to gauge, through using what he terms an "emotional thermometer'," how people involved in change were traveling and whether the pace of change needed to be adjusted. It illustrates how leadership can be influenced by context.

The final element in the formation of leaders described by Gronn is divesture. Rick has a well-developed personal sense of this, and for him the time to move-on is when his energy and enthusiasm are no longer at an appropriate level, as he explains:

> As a principal, you need to keep renewing your energy, to be one step ahead, to be proactive never reactive, so you need mental energy and resilience,

while you can do that, people are happy with you and will come with you, otherwise dissatisfaction will set in and the school will run down, relationships will run down. People then start to question whether you have a role in this school or not. I have seen principals that stay in schools too long, energy levels go down, motivation, relations etc., go down. My wife is a fantastic help on that – asks if I need to go to that meeting, is there someone else who can go to that? Sustainable employment is most important, where you are constantly reviewing your energy levels – that is the most important thing you can do. ... If I start to run out of energy, I will respond inappropriately and it will take time to repair a relationship. No energy = time to move on.

(Doherty, 2008, p. 170)

Influence on student outcomes, staff and school development

Developing students

In a climate of increasing accountability, a focus on academic student learning outcomes is almost a necessity for a successful school principal. Rick does this but does it in a way that develops the whole student. Significantly, this school is very popular with waiting lists at all year levels, and outstanding student outcomes: in 2010, 28 percent of the school's year 12 students were in the top 5 percent nationwide, and the school's median ATAR was 86.85 (the ATAR score is a percentile rank of year 12 student performance across Australia). However, the success of the school is more than these statistics. As one senior staff member commented:

He wants [the school] to continue to improve and make sure that we don't just stand still but we are continuing to move forward. ... to make it a place where boys enjoy learning and want to learn and it's not just academic education, which is extremely important, but it's nurturing their whole life education. He has such a concern for every individual and he knows so many of them by name, and so he has a real care for them which defines where he wants things to go. He just wants to get the best out of every boy.

(Doherty, 2008, p. 128)

Rick believes in developing schools that allow students to find their place in the world:

we need to provide schools that give meaning to the lives of young people, where they are going to go and make a contribution, and to be valued. So I am pleased to see students who gain this. If we can find for each boy and girl something that is meaningful for them, something that they are good at, something that every kid can be affirmed in. I enjoy seeing young people do well, build relationships, contribute to other people, to achieve what they thought they couldn't achieve – it is not just about fulfilling potential, but going beyond that and looking over the horizon.

There is a strong emphasis on student leadership, involvement in the broader community, and encouraging students to strive for excellence in all that they do. Rick has a strong belief in the development of an affirming school culture, and the importance of challenging young people to embrace and act on issues of social justice. For example, a feature of Rick's work at Trinity in recent years has been the close links he has established with several indigenous communities in remote parts of Australia and the scholarship program for indigenous students.

As the Headmaster, Rick has been concerned to provide not only a rigorous and relevant academic program, but also a broad and rich co-curricular program conducted within a Christian foundation that provides for the development of students as whole people. It is a learning community in the richest sense of this term and part of the sense of community comes from the emphasis on leadership and service within and beyond the school from students, staff and the alumni.

Developing staff

Principals do not lead schools by themselves, and much of their work is focused on the development of staff, which we discuss in this section.

Members of the Trinity community perceive Rick as being a charismatic and inspirational leader and comfortable with his role as Headmaster in the school. His leadership style is underpinned by a humility that liberates others around him in their endeavors within the school (Doherty, 2008, p. 125). He is highly thought of as a person, and the high caliber of relationships within the school is strongly attributed to his personable qualities, as described by a student:

> He's open, he's welcoming and he's nice. He's really friendly and always interesting to talk to. He's also a really honourable guy. He doesn't promote himself. He tries to cater for everybody not just purely academic or purely sport. He tries to get a range of things and interests. He's genuinely interested in like everything that goes on, and he's always looking for ways to make things better, and he gets the respect of everyone.
>
> (Doherty, 2008, p. 121)

Staff members and students believe that his outlook is as much that of a teacher as a headmaster and that it is important to him to be seen as a teacher. Staff members commented that he leads instruction by example (Doherty, 2008, pp. 142–143) as illustrated in the following staff quotes:

> He is a great teacher, but I don't think he thinks he is a great teacher. He thinks he can teach better. He still prepares his lessons.

Since the council committed to the introduction of the interactive whiteboards the principal has gone out of his way to be part of the collegial classroom visit situation with staff who are using interactive whiteboards, and therefore is seen as a practitioner and a learner in adopting that technology to his purposes in the classroom environment. So, he sees himself as someone who needs to be in the classroom and working in the classroom.

He constantly focuses the school (staff and students) on the beliefs that through working with others, people achieve more and learn more effectively, and that people grow by being of service to others. Members of staff believe that they are supported in their work and what they want to do. They are confident in the caliber of his pedagogical leadership, knowing that he is an outstanding teacher who has done most of what he asks staff to do. He has an empathy with teachers.

He encourages teachers to grow as teachers and as school leaders by attending national and international conferences, presenting papers regarding the school, and visiting schools connected to Trinity Grammar School in its student exchange. As a result he is able to grow the school's capacity for teaching and learning. He sees globalization as a challenge facing the school and encourages the school to grow globally so that students and staff will have learning experiences in a variety of other countries. He wants all students to have the opportunity of an international experience of some kind, and by forming partnerships with other schools internationally he has kept the school outward-looking.

Rick has been acknowledged by his peers for his work with school leaders through being one of five Victorian principals awarded in 2010 the John Laing Professional Development Award from Principals Australia (the pre-eminent professional development group for principals). Principals Australia described this as an award given to school leaders who have made a significant and outstanding contribution to the professional learning of school leaders. It is a non-competitive, peer nominated celebration of school leadership and professional learning. Its aim is to celebrate leadership learning: for school leaders by school leaders.

Rick has contributed significantly to the professional learning of teachers beyond Trinity through his publications focused on curriculum in general, and the teaching of science and biology in particular.

Not only is Rick concerned for the development of others but he models this through his own lifelong learning as shown by his enthusiasm for our research, his concern to encourage students and staff to develop further, his sense of social justice and place in the world, his fostering of an extensive global network of schools, and his work on committees and membership of professional associations including: the Science Teachers' Association of Victoria, Association of Heads of Independent Schools, Incorporated Association of Registered Teachers of Victoria, Association of Independent Schools of Victoria, St Margaret's School Board, Anglican Coordinating Committee of Education, and the Board of Anglicare, This piece from the school newsletter of July 14, 2004 illustrates many of these aspects:

I return from a term of Study Leave ... My wife and I were fortunate to be able to visit remote areas in both Central Australia and Alaska ... to appreciate the art forms created by the traditional occupants of these areas, and to compare the challenges which confront both indigenous populations in a contemporary context ... I identified some common and overarching themes:

a. To seek a better understanding to the specific needs and strengths of young individuals; in particular those – with special learning needs; with emotional needs, e.g., depression, attention disorders; associated with marginalizing groups and communities.
b. To empower families and communities to support these young people.
c. To promote an increased appreciation and understanding of the natural environment, and to celebrate the ways that human beings record this and elements of their culture, through paintings and sculpture.

Doherty, 2008, p. 123)

He is concerned to continually develop himself and takes whatever opportunities arise to reflect on his work as demonstrated in this consideration of distributing leadership which arose from a conversation with an overseas principal.

a Canadian Principal from one of our brother schools ... said, "I have five people reporting to me, no principal should have more than five people reporting to them." I said, "Well, I have conversations with about 20." But, with many of them I might throw in some directions as to the way we might want to travel. I am not managing this person (a), (b), (c), (d) and ticking it all off. But I am delegating the responsibility of leadership, the privilege of leadership to other people. But therein lies quite an interesting tension when you get down to management theory, whether all people who come to see you should be managed by you or whether it is in the case in the way I do it, which is a sharing of the journey and the direction of the journey through a conversation.

Developing the school

Independent schools comprise less than 15 percent of all schools in Australia, and high-fee independent schools are a small part of this group. There are many challenges in leading these elite schools. Often they have long and proud histories of academic excellence, social reproduction for the dominant society groups, well organized and vocal alumni, and cherished symbols and traditions. Whilst these elements suggest conservatism, at the same time these schools are expected to be at the forefront of educational innovation due to the wealth and privilege that the high fees afford. The schools are labeled independent, but as all receive state and federal government funding, they are subject to a range of accountabilities. Whilst principals need to be educational leaders, the wealth of high-fee independent schools means that they also must act like CEOs of moderate to medium-sized business enterprises. Clearly, these schools need principals that can excel in an environment with many tensions and dilemmas, who can deal with accountability pressures, and shape and enrich the school community in what counts for good education for its students, and who can provide effective "leadership which leaves a legacy that lasts beyond the leader's professional lifetime" (Mulford & Moreno, 2006, p. 204).

A challenge for Rick at Trinity has been to continually energize the school community so that it does not plateau in its development as we observed in one of our successful schools (see Drysdale *et al.*, 2011) in which the school had developed to be good, but could not become great. This has been more of a challenge in his last four years as Headmaster than the first eight due to a range of imposed changes that schools have faced such as new teacher registration requirements, public reporting of school performance, and preparing for a national curriculum. The school needs to grow and develop, and it also needs to ensure that it meets any external requirements for change and accountability:

> I was asked to chair a meeting the other day and an educator asked the question about as we are being curtailed more and more by accountabilities are we therefore being caught up more and more by bureaucracy and being less able to influence our school? And I said, "Yes, we are being drawn to more and more accountabilities, but in the end it is not the accountabilities that make our schools tick". You have to do the accountabilities and they are taking more and more time. But what you have to do is continue to be the model for the other person, and the other person will take on the model, and then will go to other people. It is the modelling of being genuine people ... The accountabilities will drift back into the distance, over the horizon ...
>
> (Doherty, 2008, p. 173)

An increasing important feature of privileged high-fee independent schools are the schools' social responsibilities to the wider community through the caliber and capabilities of the future citizens it grows. The sense of growth evident in Trinity Grammar School is not only to meet the needs of the school itself, but also, to meet the needs of the greater society that it serves through education. It is in this area that Trinity, already one of Australia's highest performing schools in terms of student learning outcomes, has shown significant growth through such programs as student leadership development. It is a good school that has become great (Drysdale *et al.*, 2011).

In defining his role as Headmaster of the school, Rick said:

> My interpretation of Headmaster is that of a pastoral-centered mission within the school context. As Headmaster, I am the leader of the school community and that is the key thing, and people look to the Headmaster as being the

leader of the community in all senses. In every word that you say, you are judged and you are reacted to and so on.

(Doherty, 2008, pp. 131–132)

To the school community of Trinity, Rick is the key leader of the school, but he is also seen to be a follower and supporter as well. He is, as Sergiovanni (2001, p. 358) states, "at the same time a leader of leaders, follower of ideas, minister of values, and a servant to the followership."

Rick demonstrates strong emotional intelligence in his leadership behavior. Day and colleagues (2000, p. 174) found evidence that emotional intelligence contributed to effective leadership where head teachers demonstrated the ability to recognize the emotions of others and their needs at certain times, and to be able to handle relationships effectively. An example is how he leads change. Rick believes that people expect change, and that with any change there is an emotional thermometer, a lot of emotional material that can go with that. He says that he has learned to be highly sensitive to that emotional thermometer and to pace change so that the thermometer does not boil over and result in anger, disengagement to the point where people leave. Similarly, Rick is aware of his own emotions and needs. As indicated previously, he believes that energy is the vital component required to manage himself and others in his role of Headmaster of the school, and when he doesn't have this energy he either needs to find a way to renew it, or to leave for another position.

Reflections

The continuing development of a successful school leader is shown in the thought that has gone into the experiences that Rick accumulated as a teacher, and in the senior leadership roles he undertook. The move from headteacher to senior leader to headteacher was an unusual career path, but gave him the skills, attitudes and abilities to successfully lead one of the elite high-fee schools of Melbourne. There is more that could be told of Rick's formation. For example, the fact that his brother is also a highly regarded and successful principal begs consideration of the role of family in leadership formation, and adopting a life history approach to studying leadership (see, for example, the excellent 1997 study by Dimmock and O'Donoghue of innovative school principals). Nevertheless, for the purpose of this brief chapter it is enough to consider the fortuitous, yet planned pathway that Rick took. It is also worthwhile to consider how Rick has thought through the divesture phase of his career, noting signs that to him would indicate it is time to move to something else, and also the degree to which he has built the leadership capacity within the school.

Through Rick's story, we can see that personal attributes interlink with accumulating professional knowledge, competencies and experiences. The "person in the professional" (Day et al., 2000, p. 67) continues to grow. Rick is able to define and refine his own personal beliefs, values and vision regarding education, social issues, and societal change in conjunction with the values, beliefs and traditions of the school community. There exists a process of reciprocal influence between the on-going development of his capabilities as an educational leader and the context within which he works. As he actively develops his own understanding and appreciation of social challenges and issues within Australian and global societies, he openly invites others to do the same.

At the core, Rick is a teacher, quintessentially the headteacher of the school. He directly contributes to the teaching and learning in the school as a classroom teacher and as a member of a faculty. He said (and this is confirmed by others we spoke to) that it is important for him to teach and follow his own interest in learning and current developments in pedagogy:

> never lose sight of the teaching, of the student in the classroom, keep up with teaching methodology, yourself as a teacher … as to lose sight of that [classroom] is to lose sight of everything.
>
> (quote from Rick Tudor in Doherty, 2008, p. 143)

He has the emotional maturity to be able to balance life, finely hone his leadership capabilities, and strengthen his resilience (Day *et al.*, 2000). Through his accrued experience, and reflection on this, he has developed the intuition and wisdom of how, when and what to do in different educational contexts and situations, demonstrating well the balanced leadership described by Waters *et al.* (2003, p. 2):

> Effective leadership means more than simply knowing what to do – it's knowing when, how, and why to do it … They know when, how and why to create learning environments that support people, connect them with one another, and provide the knowledge, skills, and resources they need to succeed.

Rick has formed his own self-image as a leader and has gathered knowledge of how different school contexts affect his self-image as an educational leader. Consequently, he has deepened his understanding of the interaction that occurs between the self, the principal's role and the school context in which that role is carried out. Through Rick's story we see sustained and purposeful personal and professional development. Clearly, a conscious personal and professional growth by the individual occurs over time through relevant experiences, shrewd choices, and an underlying sense of knowing where one is going.

Rick's on-going journey as an educational leader significantly deepens our understanding of the nature and practices of successful school principals and outstanding educational leaders. His story shows us that successful school leaders need to be able to facilitate growth within themselves as they grow their schools, and to adjust their leadership to the context in which it is exercised. From this, we can consider the capabilities, capacity and independence that are needed by principals within their role to effectively cater for their own ongoing growth as well as that of their school.

For personal reflection we pose three considerations:

1   *How do you plan to develop your leadership qualities?* Educational jurisdictions differ in the degree to which they have mandatory (system requirements) and voluntary (individual responsibility) leadership preparation and development programs. In the Australian context it is heavily weighted to voluntary preparation and development. Evident in Rick's story is someone who has taken individual responsibility for their development as a successful school leader.

2   *Have you developed the leadership qualities and skills that allow you to adapt your leadership to different contexts and situations?* Rick's story illustrates how one's leadership can be adapted to different circumstances, and how circumstances can be influenced by one's leadership; what we have termed the reciprocal influence of leadership and context. Major views of leadership, such as Bass and Avolio's transformational leadership (see Bass & Avolio, 1997), acknowledge the developmental and situational nature of leadership; an individual's leadership develops over time and may change when exercised in different contexts.

3   *How will you balance the demands of school leadership with other aspects of your life?* Leadership roles in schools demand much from the people in them, with for example, long hours, fractured work, and great expectations (Gurr, 2008). Looking after yourself emotionally (Leithwood & Beatty, 2008), finding time for those important in your life, whilst still meeting the demands of your school, are important aspects to balance. In the stories of leaders such as Rick, we can see that this is possible.

References

Bass, B. & Avolio, B. (1997) *Manual for the Multifactor Leadership Questionnaire* (California: Mind Gardens).

Day, C., Harris, A., Hadfield, M., Tolley, H. and Beresford, J. (2000) *Leading Schools in Times of Change* (Buckingham: Open University Press).

Dimmock, C. and O'Donoghue, T. (1997) *Innovative School Principals and Restructuring* (London: Routledge Falmer).

Doherty, J. (2008) Successful leadership in an independent school in Victoria, Australia. Doctor of Education thesis, University of Melbourne.

Drysdale, L., Goode, H. & Gurr, D. (2011) Sustaining school and leadership success in two Australian schools, in Moos, L., Johansson, O., & Day, C. (Eds.) (2011) *How School Principals Sustain Success Over Time: International Perspectives* (Dordrecht: Springer-Kluwer), pp. 25–38.

Gronn, P. (1999) *The Making of Educational Leaders*. (London: Cassell).

Gurr, D. (2008) Principal leadership: What does it do, what does it look like, and how might it evolve? *Monograph*, 42 (Melbourne: Australian Council for Educational Leaders).

Leithwood, K. & Beatty, B. (2008) *Leading with Teacher Emotions in Mind*, (Thousand Oaks, CA: Corwin Press).

Leithwood, K., Day, C., Sammons, P., Harris, A. & Hopkins, D. (2006) *Seven Strong Claims about Successful School Leadership* (Nottingham: National College of School Leadership).

Mulford, B. and Moreno, J.M. (2006) Sinking ships, emerging leadership: A true story of sustainability (or the lake thereof), *Education Forum*, 70, pp. 204–214.

Sergiovanni, T. (2001) *Leadership: What's in it for Schools?* (London: Routledge Falmer).

Waters, T., Marzano, R.J. and McNulty, B. (2003) *Balanced leadership: What 30 years of research tells us about the effect of leadership on student achievement.* (Aurora, CO: Mid-continent Research for Educational Learning).

Chapter 9

England

Identity challenge: the courage of conviction

Christopher Day

The best way of driving change is through people.

David has been at this 11 to 18 school for three years and it is his second headship. Previously, he was principal of a secondary school which he had developed into an all-through school (for pupils aged 5 to 18). His present school is one of a growing number of 'Academies' in England. These are schools which are funded directly by central government and given more financial and curriculum autonomy than schools which are funded through the local authority (district). Academies are also more directly accountable to central government for the progress and attainment of their pupils. In David's case the Academy was the first to be jointly sponsored by business and the local university. During his three years as principal, the school roll had grown from 300 to 800 pupils. As we shall see later, this provided unique opportunities for learning to staff and students.

David's story will be told through the presentation of extensive selections from interviews with him and interpretation is informed through an existing relationship between the author and David which began when he was appointed, one year before he took over the Academy. This unusually early appointment was in order to enable him to take a leading role in the planning of a 'new build' school, funded by national government and the sponsors. His story, like many others in this book, speaks to the tremendous challenges faced by new principals, however experienced they may be, especially when they take over a school which has suffered long-term decline in the quality of education, a loss of trust in education by a significant section of pupils, parents and the community at large and, in this case, a deterioration in the physical environments in which pupils learn and teachers teach.

Changing the teaching and learning environment

Much recent empirical research on successful school principals notes that one of the cluster of tasks to which they give priority is doing what they can to improve the physical conditions for teaching and learning (e.g. Day *et al.*, 2011). So it was with David. When he took over the school:

It was in probably one of the most unpleasant and most unfit for business buildings that I've ever seen, in one of the most deprived communities in the UK. There were weeds and mould running down the walls of the corridors ... it literally was hideous, I personally couldn't understand how any head could put up with it for more than two minutes.

It is worth providing a little of the history which David had inherited when he began at the school. When it had first opened more than fifty years previously, its focus had been for pupils, 'to plan their lives and prepare themselves to make a positive contribution to family, neighbourhood and society.' According to David, this emphasis on welfare, as against academic achievement, had led to, 'a diminishing cycle of external involvement' and the school had, 'slipped into an unproductive, almost caustic relationship with the local authority' (school district). As well as decline in the physical environment (grime, burnt light fittings, peeling paint), the school now was the lowest quintile for percentage of girls on roll; the highest quintile for free school meals (a proxy poverty indicator) and special educational needs; the highest quintile for school deprivation; and set in a community with significantly low literacy levels.

As with many new heads, David recognised that, even for the final year before the new school building had been completed, the teaching and learning environment of the existing school had to be changed. He painted and brightened the school classrooms and corridors so that they became better environments for teaching and learning. The following year the new school was completed and, on reflection, David had been pleased to be able to prepare the teachers and pupils for the move:

It's now in a 25 million pound building which even now three years, or two and a half years on, looks as fabulous as it did when we moved into it.

The community which feeds the Academy is, however, the same as before, with very low literacy levels, high levels of poverty, high levels of unemployment, high levels of drug abuse, high levels of teenage pregnancy and very small numbers of people involved in higher education.

People change

In common with other principals' stories and supported by research on transformational leadership (Leithwood and Jantzi, 2006), David believed in the power of many rather than the power of a few in improving the attainments and life chances of pupils:

I think your best way of driving change is through people. It is useful occasionally to just be able to know that I can do things my way if I want to, but it's amazing how often I don't think I would lead a normal state secondary school in a very different way.

His educational philosophy is that:

> People have to be believed in ... you can't say I believe that these kids are not beyond hope and that they can change, if you then make that same judgement on everybody who's teaching.

Thus, whilst he had the opportunity to appoint new staff in place of those who, at least on paper, had struggled to educate many pupils to the standard required by government, in the short term he had resisted. He met with the staff early on and identified that, although there were many positives, especially in terms of their sense of care for the pupils, they were also poor in their management of visitors to the school, and the image they presented to the world beyond the school gates.

> We'd have been very foolish to have immediately got rid of staff, in my view. And some of ... you know there are some people who weren't prepared to make the effort needed, as I said there's nobody that's working against me, but each year there's one or two who are being made to move on or are having to move on because they can't cope with the pace.

Meeting the challenges of context: the importance of history

In taking this approach he was taking a risk that, no matter what he did to support them, not all would or could be 'turned around'. He was also demonstrating his humanity and, in doing so, making a statement of intent to all those who had been connected with the school. Turning around staff is not always easy and the process is generally under-reported in accounts of turnaround leadership. The school had experienced a succession of three head teachers over the previous five years, was widely judged to be failing its pupils and most of its pupils and teachers were imprinted with the old habits, beliefs, attitudes and the old way of doing things. They were mistrustful of change. For David, this knowledge was to influence his initial approach to the work of leading change which he saw as being:

> as much about changing perceptions as about changing actions. Much as my experience had pushed me to develop distributed leadership styles, it was clear to me that I would need to place myself at the centre of change and tie my own character and credibility into the process, allowing the staff to personify the Academy.

So from the beginning he worked to turn staff around in their thinking and practices through sharing his vision for the school. The result was that:

> Everybody turned in the direction I outlined and said yes we want to be part of this; they all wanted to be part of a success, in a community that many of

them had worked in for years. And what's great is that some of the leading staff now, and some of the most enthusiastic and the most effective, are some of those who would have been lost by a policy of right we'll get rid of anybody who's been here before. They've been given a second chance and they're very grateful for being part of a new beginning ... we've got a nice blend now and where I think very soon with all the new staff we've appointed, about 50% who are from the old school and about 50% who aren't.

Setting the direction is not enough: injecting pace and energy

I asked David to talk more about how he had achieved change in his first few years. He spoke not only about setting new directions (another key element for success identified in the research on transformational leadership) but also about injecting energy and pace:

> You have to offer that kind of energy in to an organisation because I think what struck me about somewhere like the predecessor school was that there was a lack of any discernible direction or pace about it if people recognise what they've got to do, they will actually row very very fast, they will move ... it's only those that don't have the direction who are going to sit in the middle of the lake paddling away while the boat sinks. And so I think pace is an important part, but it's also an essential part of being a leader's work in a tough community like this. Staff have to realise that this is not and never will be a place where you can sit with your feet up in the staff room having a good natter.

Building the pride, spreading the belonging

Less well reported in the leadership research literature are what might be called the affective elements, less easily able to be measured but vital in the process of school improvement. Apart from the sheer physical and intellectual energy needed to turn the school around, David had also invested an immense amount of emotional energy in re-establishing the long lost sense of pride, both internally among staff and students and externally in the community:

> in general, they're very positive about what we're doing and about how we've made things happen and the kids most definitely are, I mean when the kids speak to visitors you can actually see them puff their chests out as they talk about it, and they WEREN'T proud of going to the previous school but they are VERY proud of going to this one, and they've told Ofsted and a variety of other people that they feel much safer and much happier and it's where they want to be.

He also spoke of the 'discernible pride' of the staff about being part of a positive change, and his own part in fashioning that, initially from the front, but, as time went by, more from the back as staff had become more confident in their own abilities to lead change further:

> to empower others to believe they'd rather change is how real meaningful long term change can be made. The person who's been doing that driving and creating the pace has to slowly disappear into the background because the pace has to be driven by themselves. It's a far better long term strategy to have the staff all driven internally and really wanting to be part of it and really proud of what they're doing than it is to be forcing them down a route, whether contractually or with fear.

One discernible measure of growing pride was the sense of belonging among students and parents. This was illustrated, on the one hand, by the increase in pupil attendance from just over 80 per cent, one of the worst in England, to 94 per cent in just two years, and, on the other, a 300 per cent increase in the number of 'first choice' applications from parents (in England, parents can choose the school, provided that there are enough available places). However, this also was causing some frustration in the community:

> We had over 40 appeals last year for places in year 7, which is local people desperate to ensure that they've got a place here.

Control and facilitation: the principal's role as 'head gardener'

David likened himself to a head gardener:

> in the early stages the head gardener has to play a huge part in putting the vision onto the area, using the skills to decide what works where, what doesn't, to move things when they're needed and to really look at the whole landscaping and how it is. There's then a very frenetic bit where there's preparing the ground the moving the seeding the propagating all those kinds of things. When eventually you look at the garden and you say wow isn't this amazing, the actual gardener's hand should be disappearing and not the first thing you notice.

This analogy speaks to the changing roles which successful principals play as they move their schools forward. In David's case, whilst he was very publicly at the centre of improvement efforts in the first two years of his tenure, often talking to groups of parents in the community, persuading them and others of his vision for the school, working closely with staff and students to raise expectations and improve teaching and learning practices, using, 'tools that a politician might use' and 'talking with passion about what I believed we could do', he claimed that he no longer did the day-to-day driving.

> In those early stages I was the vision, now, I think if you listen to the way staff talk to kids, the way kids talk to adults, that they are clear about our direction. To use the gardening metaphor, they propagate, they're actually now growing it, doing it, taking things on. The garden has a kind of energy of its own where things are happening and there's a dialogue. Whereas I, as the head gardener, am now able to look a little bit more from a distance almost once removed, suggesting to people they need to grow things in a slightly different way, or that they need to look at if there's some other way of doing their current situation.

When I questioned the usefulness of the gardening analogy in terms of the development of his staff, he spoke of growing teams of gardeners:

> You need to have a team of people who do prune, maintain, you have people who are going to be watching and looking. The head gardener doesn't need to be involved in the day to day. I'm clearer now that I could go away for a bit of time and the garden will still function, I am whispering very heavily in the ears of my new staff, particularly my one new vice principal, shaping him, because I see he's got the potential to be very good. I am hopeful that if I've made the right calls and the right judgements then over the next months and years I don't have to visit the garden as much, or I could even take on another couple of gardens at the same time. I have tried to become self- perpetuating, but at the moment yes I do have to be involved in a level of checking what's going on. I think it's bad leadership if you're still needing to be involved in the day to day maintenance of your garden, still essential to the running of your school four years into your principalship. You must be doing something wrong, because part of your role has to be looking at the whole picture and how things are with the community and being able to nuance the things that are already set up and happening.

Presence and visibility

Although he is now stepping back from leading the everyday life of the school, he maintains a high profile presence in other ways. He spoke of himself as being visible to staff, students and pupils and of his presence as part of a team:

> I don't want to sit in this office going I wonder what they're doing, because I actually do my strategic observation by seeing what's happening, by interacting with the kids to see where we are. But I'm not always there, I don't organise the duties, I do the duty that I'm given by one of my colleagues … I am not the controlling person in the team, the system I set up traces back to me, now I'm just part of the system …

He met with most of his senior team just once a week, 'just to catch up' on what they're doing, 'because that's where really the leadership happens now'. He gave an example of an initiative taken by a teacher, who had responsibility for equality:

> she wanted to make it live and breathe in this exciting way, she could have got away with doing a couple of worksheets and sending it round with a here you are, here are some materials, but she didn't. She did this exciting vibrant event and that's when I think it shows me that my leadership is having an effect on the life of the school. That's just one of hundreds of examples; it's like I start fires and I should see them raging around. All I occasionally have to do now is to watch the fires don't get out of hand!

The importance of leadership learning: enriching staff and pupils' experiences

David spoke of his own love of learning (he was already the author of two books and had enrolled in a doctoral programme). He had also passed this on to his staff:

> All the leadership team have been part of the Masters programme and PhDs and we have about well over half the teaching staff involved in some form of extra study. That's been a very positive process and one I'm very positive about modelling. The moment you stop learning is the moment you stop breathing in my view, and that's what I love about the job. We're going through change and for us we're going into a stage where we need to be a little bit more ordered. It becomes a little less exciting because it's about producing and going through it, but, you asked about the role of the heart, to me the driving force behind it is that excitement about what we're doing and what I love is that the staff share this. You know when we've had the residential for the Masters, we've had them on a frequency of roughly once every four weeks. They all turn up to all of them, they've always been there, they've always smiled, whatever they're doing. The fact that the staff want to do that, is a real demonstration of the heart they have, in and it points back to the passion and the faith they have for the academy. That's a fundamental part of encouraging sharing and learning, but where possible people learning together, means that they actually learn from each other.

So, as with other transformational and instructional principals (Day *et al.*, 2011; Robinson *et al.*, 2009) at the centre of David's priorities was always the quality of the pupils' learning experiences and the motivation and engagement of the teachers in this, and their own enthusiasm for learning. His own love of learning and the school's close association with the local university assisted him in this:

> In the work I did ages ago while doing my Masters degree it was very clear to me that there is a really strong link between your attitude, your engagement,

your aspiration and the outcome you have from your learning because, for example, if you've got a negative attitude to what you're going to do it doesn't matter how fantastic any technique of teaching may be, if you're not in the right mental space you are never going to make use of it ... So, some staff development activities are really just about putting the enthusiasm and the self- belief back in. Some of the work we've done with the university has been stunning. We've had, for example, a variety of projects around year 8 pupil literacy, where the staff and pupils have gone off to do something at different parts of the university. In some cases it was the security in some cases it was the eco houses, in some cases it was the veterinary school, and as a result of those experiences their engagement with literacy was many times improved.

Trust and trustworthiness: key factors in leadership success

Trust has been found to be key elements of successful leadership in all countries (Moos *et al.*, 2012; Tschannen-Moran, 2004). David was critical of mechanistic models of management and leadership. He believed that successful leadership would be achieved not through complying to an exhaustive set of rules, but from a few simple principles adhered to by all in an atmosphere of mutual trust. These were contained at the front of a Staff Handbook:

- Staff behaviour guidelines
- Intolerance of negativity
- Challenge the issue and not the person
- Find solutions and problems
- No back biting, moaning or tale-telling
- Leadership is something we all do

He had established a strategic leadership team which was fit for purpose and based upon a notion of organisational development cycle designed by Graves (2005).

Clare Graves, who was a social scientist in the 1940s/50s, talked about what's been called later 'spiral dynamics' and she recognised that every organisation went through certain phases. I have the phases on my wall), they go from 'self' through 'tribal' and through 'order', from order then into entrepreneuring. She says that no organisation on its own can skip more than one phase, but the reality is that you have to lead yourself in different ways through each. So when I first started the leadership the most important thing to me was to get the energy and the enthusiasm and to create the climate. For that we needed a much looser structure ... so I had much vaguer lines of responsibility between everybody. I was there in the middle with a group of people and I was finding out who wanted to really join me. Then, over time, we developed that into a kind of circle, so I could start to develop new relationships. At the start I had to really fight the term 'line management' because I hate that term. I didn't get rid of line management but I said it's not that simplistic. What I don't want is you as a classroom teacher to say I've got to go and ask him, who has then got to go and ask her, who's going to go and ask him, and finally they're going to ask the head. I just think that is why organisations don't change. That is why there were weeds growing out of the stairs, because nobody wanted to battle up the hierarchy.

So I said you're in charge. You empower people. That worked, but then you very quickly realise that there's one or two for whom it isn't working so well for, and you need a line management, more a line coaching or mentoring approach. So we then had some responsibilities which I started to structure more hierarchically, but not, certainly not pyramidal ... and I still keep the vice principal at that point almost out of day to day things because his main job was to liaise with the university, to keep the exciting and interesting things happening and coming in.

We've now shifted, we've lost a number of staff mainly for positive reasons and others and retirements, and the current structure is slightly more traditional in as much as I now have two vice principals, who do lead in a lot of the day to day things and there is more of a traditional feel to the structure in this precise moment, and in my mind I'm not worried about that, it's because going through the phase of what Clare Graves would refer to as 'order'. As we move through that phase of order we consolidate success and then self-perpetuating ... the leadership has to change again, so in other words what I believe is that leadership should not be handed from on high. It is just the way we do it now! I often say to staff this is how we're doing it this year, and I think that's the key to looking at it, what kind of leadership are you in in this exact moment, rather than what is the best way to lead an academy?

Professional identity: the courage, vulnerability (and fatigue) of leaders in challenging communities

The next section in this account of successful principalship focuses upon David's strong sense of professional identity, and the values which formed the rock on which this was built. At the core of David's way of leading are three words which represent his professional identity: courage, vulnerability and fatigue.

Leadership means not only having answers (to problems of the changing curriculum, staffing structures, building management, pastoral systems) but also having the courage to stand by them when they are questioned. It also means being prepared to hear these questions and change your mind if you need to, without losing the strength of those original convictions or confidence in yourself. It's a fine line, like everything else in leadership. The brave leader must show a positive face, an unstinting outward belief that not only is the battle eminently winnable but that it is practically won.

Like many successful principals, this statement reveals the depth of strength that David had in his own educational beliefs and professional identity. This strength had enabled him to remain resilient in the face of sustained challenges, not only at the beginning of his leadership in the school but also now, in his leadership three years later. Every day still felt like a battle, every aspect of the job was an ordeal, despite having produced the most improved GCSE (15+ national examination) results in the UK and a good Ofsted inspection report:

I felt that each step I took was being scrutinised by so many people who were all expecting me to do what, in their minds at least, they thought I should be doing … I can't look my pay cheque in the eye, let alone the children, staff and my own family, if I do things that I know, deep down, are fundamentally… the wrong things to do, even if everyone is telling me to do them … It is about being constantly vigilant to the fact that it is easy to let your internal well-being slip as you start the slide down towards negativity … I believe the quickest route to meeting the government's imposed targets of 50% for pupil examination attainment is not to tell them they need to, and to put them in a classroom where you try to force them to behave and learn … you've actually got to do things that actually change the way they approach their learning so you have be brave enough sometimes to do the slightly 'off-piste' thing to enable you to focus the kids back on to their learning.

He found it 'hard to remain calm' when explaining to government officials that the 'can do' attitude of staff and pupils, their willingness to make learning fun, their focus on 'wonder' and their relentless need to increase the self-belief of pupils and teachers and the school's imaginative links to the university were all part of the improvement picture:

Bravery isn't the absence of fear, it's actually knowing fear and coping with it. It takes a certain amount of bravery to say to the government and other officials, yeah we fully agree that these kids need literacy, but giving them 22 hours of literacy each week, is not the answer to switching their lives around … I just think there's some fundamental areas of education that governments really Don't *understand. They use KPIs, key performance indicators, to try and drive change, and that's what I* believe is totally and utterly ineffectual in causing the changes they want.

I asked David how much of his professional and perhaps personal identity was wrapped up in his work and how much that had been challenged. He spoke first of his sense of vulnerability:

> I recognised very early on that vulnerability is actually quite an interesting tool to be used, and I think some leaders use this in quite an unpleasant way. It's interesting because vulnerability is part of the armour and certainly when I started as a principal in my first school ... when I had to amalgamate an infant's, junior's and secondary school together ... I remember one of the strongest things I was able to do was to stand there and to say, I haven't a clue how we're going to do this, I really don't know ... can we do this together? In other words, I said I am not offering you an expert view of where we're going, I am actually merely going to try and channel your ideas. I think that vulnerable is something that I'm telling my leadership team to be. I'm saying, don't blame the head of house, blame yourself. Take responsibility that you've not got it right, that you're fallible ... that you haven't got everything under control, because people come and they look to leaders to provide them with the answers.

The work by Alan Flintham in, 'Reservoirs of Hope', finding out why so many head teachers left the profession or died of stress and his follow up work, 'When Reservoirs Run Dry', he argued every day you get people draining your reservoir. That has never happened to me faster than when I first started this job because everybody is taking out of the reservoir, everybody wants immediate results, everybody wants success at a snap of the finger. There's a kind of mass hysteria that suddenly these kids with immense problems, suddenly ... the kind of disadvantage they have by a little bit of good teaching and everything, can suddenly transform their lives.

David spoke passionately of his commitment to the education of all the pupils in this high need community. It was a key part of his sense of professional identity:

> I'm the first to think they have the right to good teaching, more than other kids, and I believe totally that we have to achieve to be believed in, but the problem is it's a kind of either or thing in society, it's a kind of, if you don't believe that every kid can succeed irrespective of their background, then somehow that's a negative. You're not actually saying these kids can't achieve because of their background. Those are two things that are nowhere near connected, and the problem is that I think governments ... and a variety of other people, there is a lack of understanding of how difficult it is to make a relevant and exciting education for kids from very deprived areas; because the reality is they don't want it, their families don't aspire to it, so this is not something that can easily be done. We're very proud we've only permanently excluded one child. We've worked with so many to keep them in education. I've always said this is a long term change. If we're truly serious about changing this community in the

way that everyone seems to want us to, you need to take 5, 10 years look at a minimum, at how you're going to do it.

He spoke, also, of the energy, long term commitment and resilience needed as a leader of change, together with some of his frustrations with the lack of understandings by some of those outside schools:

> You don't make changes to a community that's scarred overnight, and their lack of reality that some people have really challenges, it challenges you, makes you feel whether it's worthwhile what you're doing and I think I go through massive times when I guess my reservoir's empty, I go through times when I doubt whether it's worth it all, I go through times when I think that I would stop it all at a drop of a hat. I sometimes get frustrated that some others don't recognise the job we're doing because they don't understand the job itself. And people don't understand the amount of effort that's been to get us to a position where we've got hundreds of kids, from a tough area, who are in school and wanting to go to school in most cases, who are learning in their lessons and who are advancing. But even in achieving that, we are always going to be behind the middle class and middle upper class kids that they have to compete with together in examinations.

And there's time when you just feel tired, that you feel that you've banged your head against a brick wall for long enough and you actually say why am I doing this? And that's when I think I question what I'm in it for and why am I doing it. Then other times, when I'm with the kids, you just bounce back in and it's a bit like being a gardener and you just go 'hey yeah I'm doing this again' but I think if you're a gardener, it's when you take the long term view that it can become very silly ... because you know if as a head gardener, if I walk away, 200 years from now, there'll be no evidence of my gardening at all, there may be an odd tree, there may be ... but there's very little clear evidence of what I did. That's the reality here, I'm fascinated by archaeology, and I see echoes in the sand of people from generations ago in my own garden. I've got rows of stuff in my garden, that's the fragment we leave and ... I think that nobody understands how lonely being a principal is and how much weight there is.

Conclusion: the battle continues

I asked David what motivated him to carry on tending the garden in different ways and nurturing it when there were so many barriers to success. He spoke with feeling about what Stephen Ball once described as the 'terrors of performativity' (Ball, 2003):

> I suppose you could say that I see the kind of changes that government make and the long term proposals just fill me full of horror. The plans for key

stage 4 testing, just scare me, doing away with coursework and making it all final test. The reality is that all of the things that disadvantage the kind of kids that I've always served are always there. So to go back to the garden, it's a bit like somebody suddenly saying, yeah ok, that's very nice but over the next five years we're going to phase out fertilisers we're going to phase out this stock plant that you've always used. So it's not as if I can feel we're getting to the top of the glorious mountain where I can see the plane on the other side ... all I just see is another mountain just behind it. Most people see me, as the driving force of the energy; and that's what I am. I need to out there. I'm in at half past seven every morning, and I rarely leave here before half past five. Then I always do a couple of hours at home. It's very much that you've got to produce the results. I don't believe that for one minute that education is doomed, but ...

At this point, David, himself an author, read these words from Edward Tring, the head teacher of a school in the nineteenth century and Parkin, a Canadian who researched his life:

Sometimes the ways an atmosphere of responsibility works seems almost more than I can bear, I feel like a bird in a cage beating against the bars, longing to be free, a battle everywhere.

He dreamed of breaking through the monotony and grind of teachers lives the treadmill of constant preparation and ceaseless evaluation, which is so apt to dryer and narrow minded of spirit.

He described education as always being, a 'political football', always one of those things that politicians think they can change in a 4/5 year cycle:

The battle is just ceaseless. I've always done the hardest I can, I've always worked as hard as I can I always did the best I can for the kids ... we set up the academy to change young people's lives, and to make a difference in long term in the community, anybody who doesn't see that now is really blind as to what we're actually doing. Governors asked me to do a job, I've delivered it in the way I said I would, with even better results than I thought we'd get in the timescale we've done, and yet ... there is that kind of feeling that the government and others are changing the goal posts as you're playing the match. They're actually changing the game we're playing and the method by which that game is rewarded, and it just means that your own personal identity becomes questioned, and to me, the one thing I do need, just occasionally, is a feeling that I am being valued ... you need somebody who's there muttering in your ear in a positive way and when you need it, putting their hand on your shoulder, not putting their hand on your shoulder when your kids just happen to have done well.

I reminded David that, although he had been knocked, he did not appear to have changed his values, to have compromised his principles or his practices:

> I think I've got wise, I think I just see the world and the people in it with a greater clarity, which in some ways means I've got more to offer now than I've ever had, but, I still believe more strongly than ever in what we're doing, and I am very proud of what we've done. I've enjoyed that process when I look at it back in time. It's just that the kind of daily energy needed to create it is sometimes not appreciated. I felt with both the schools where I have been principal that they fitted me, yet I still did feel there were times when my beliefs have been utterly challenged. If I was in an environment where I actually felt my ethos and my heart were in a different direction, I would have been incredibly unhappy. Because the reality is you can't do it alone. So I think you have to get that match as a new principal.
>
> You've got to always have that passion for making a difference and, whatever decision you make, always bring it back to the kids, how does what are we doing benefit the kids. Where possible don't follow the instructions that you feel are expected of you by government, take your decisions because you believe it is best for the kids, and the community. Be brave that you can do it in another way. But doing it in another way is phenomenally hard work. But also don't be frightened to make mistakes. Somebody once said to me, "Don't you worry that if people are following you like lemmings that you're going to lead them off the edge of cliff?", and I said, "If you live your life assuming you're walking off the edge of a cliff, well what does that say about yourself? You have to have the confidence to say, this is my route and your heart and your gut feeling is something you should really rely on." If you feel strongly about something, if something is churning your guts up that this is wrong, then it probably is wrong, and you just have to find ways you can, and one of the best ways to achieve targets is not to aim directly at them, because the moment you aim directly at a specific target is the moment you lose the ability to see anything but that. That's where I think some heads go wrong. They look at what their targets are and their whole life becomes about meeting that target, as if that's the only thing that matters, I think that's where you've got to, to be successful in the job, you have to work to make a much bigger change than that.

Finally, I asked David if being a principal for the second time made the job any easier:

> I think there is a general belief that if you are an experienced head, you will know how to do it next time, that you will have developed a road map that you can simply follow in your next role. I guess that's fine if you are one of those heads who believes in the 'chain manual' approach to leadership. But if you have a more organic approach like my own, I feel the second time around

you are even more aware of what you don't know rather than what you do. I am even more convinced of the gardener analogy for my style of leadership – in this case a very successful head gardener from one town appointed by another to replicate his success would not simply copy his planting plans from his first to his new surroundings. He would study the soil, the aspect and the setting of his new patch – his experience would show in how he manages the growth of the garden – knowing when to intervene and when to leave it alone – knowing when a new feature plant was needed and when to remove an established fixture.

Reflections

As you reflect upon this principal's leadership journey, please consider the following seven areas of focus and challenge:

1 If you were newly appointed and planning your journey of school improvement, how would you go about deciding on and implementing your first priorities so that others felt a sense of ownership and belonging?
2 What cluster of core values do you hold?
3 How would you demonstrate these through the strategies you use to influence others?
4 What interpersonal qualities do you have, what do you need more of and how would you go about acquiring them?
5 How would you nurture trust and trustworthiness?
6 Identify the phases of improvement of a school as you have experienced them and reflect upon what caused them to contribute or to detract from the growing success of the pupils.
7 How will you use professional learning and development to grow a capacity for resilience in yourself and others?

References

Ball, S. (2003) The teacher's soul and the terrors of performativity, *Journal of Education Policy*, 18 (2): 215–228.

Day, C., Sammons, P., Leithwood, K., Hopkins, D., Gu, Q., Brown, E. & Ahtaridou, E. (2011) *Successful School Leadership: Linking with Learning.* Maidenhead: Open University Press.

Flintham A.J. (2003a) *Reservoirs of Hope: Spiritual and Moral Leadership in Headteachers*, National College for School Leadership, Nottingham.

Flintham A.J. (2003b) *When Reservoirs Run Dry: Why Some Headteachers Leave Headship Early*, National College for School Leadership, Nottingham.

Graves, Clare W. (2005) *The Never-ending Quest: Clare W. Graves Explores Human Nature* (C. Cowan & N. Todorovic, Eds.). Santa Barbara, CA: ECLET Publishing.

Leithwood, K. & Jantzi, D. (2005) A review of transformational leadership research 1996–2005. *Leadership and Policy in Schools*, *4*(3), 177–199.

Leithwood, K. & Jantzi, D. (2006) Transformational school leadership for large-scale reform: Effects on students, teachers, and their classroom practices. *School Effectiveness and School Improvement*, *17*(2), 201–227.

Moos, L., Johansson, O. & Day, C. (Eds.) (2011) *How School Principals Sustain Success Over Time: International Perspectives*. Dordrecht: Springer.

Robinson, V., Hohepa, M. & Lloyd, C. (2009) *School Leadership and Student Outcomes: Identifying What Works and Why*. Best Evidence Syntheses Iteration (BES), Ministry of Education, New Zealand. Available from http://educationcounts.govt.nz/goto/BES

Tschannen-Moran, M. (2004) *Trust Matters: Leadership for Successful Schools*. San Francisco, CA: Jossey-Bass.

Part III

Values and trust

Chapter 10

New Zealand

A values-led principalship: the person within the professional

Ross Notman

Setting the scene

Nestled within the afternoon shade of a church and overlooking Otago Harbour and its rugged southern coastline, Otago Girls' High School has provided secondary education for girls in Dunedin since 1871. Its neo-classical brick buildings reflect a strong sense of tradition and a healthy regard for a 'good education' on the part of the city's Scottish ancestors, characteristics which are shared by its principal, Jan Anderson.

Otago Girls' High School is a year 9–13 girls' secondary school (ages 13–18) in a medium to high socio-economic area. Situated in the South Island city of Dunedin, this state school has a roll of 800 students of whom 35 are international students, and a staff in excess of 60 teachers. The ethnic mix of the student population is predominantly European/Pakeha (85 per cent) with a small number from Asian, Maori and Pacific Island backgrounds.

The school prides itself on its sense of tradition as the oldest girls' secondary school in New Zealand. The broad-based curriculum covers a variety of academic, sporting and cultural pursuits. At year 9 entry, the students are offered a choice of six languages, as well as a range of technology and performing arts subjects including music, drama and dance. Intensive learning support programs are used to assist academic achievement and are regarded as a particular feature of the school. The aim of the curriculum structure is to enable every girl to develop self-confidence and to explore learning, leisure and sports skills, all of which are underpinned by a goal of personal excellence.

The school presently enjoys a very good reputation at local and national levels. The latest school inspection report by the Education Review Office describes the professional leadership of the principal and senior team as 'strong, dedicated and committed to providing high quality education for the girls.' This leadership performance is mirrored in the confident attitudes of the students who are said to demonstrate 'a love of learning and a self-belief that they can achieve in whatever area they choose.'

Since assuming leadership of Otago Girls' High School in 1995, Jan Anderson's contribution to her school has been immense, as have her accomplishments at a national education level. She has been the recipient of a Woolf Fisher Principals' Fellowship in 2002 to study schools in Canada and the UK, and an executive member of the Secondary Principals' Association of New Zealand and their nominated advisor to the New Zealand Literacy Reference Group and the New Zealand Retirement Commission. However, it is within the person of the principal and her school leadership role that the success of Jan's principalship can be gauged.

An early portrait of a leader

Jan's recollections of early influences that affected her values and views on life were typical of a 1950s style of upbringing in urban New Zealand: Sunday School, Brownies, organised sport, a range of club activities. In addition, school life and a series of significant teachers were to have a profound formative effect on shaping her personal and later professional development. Among a group of women with progressive outlooks whom Jan encountered in her secondary schooling, there was a senior English teacher whom she described as a Shakespearean enthusiast and essentially responsible for her studying for a Master's degree in English; a vibrant History teacher; and her French teacher who was also the tennis coach. She found the approval, confidence and personal interest from these female teachers had a lasting influence on her.

The sporting world also had an important bearing on Jan's development as a young woman: ten years as a member of a surf club; training daily at 6 am for national surf life saving competitions; and playing tennis at representative level for several years. In her sporting activities, Jan noted a key common factor: she discovered that her strong academic work ethic at school, which had seen her achieve first place in a Physics class one year, would lead to similar success in the sporting arena.

Jan's career path to principalship was not a straightforward one. In the process of completing her Master's degree, the prospect of a publishing career or doctoral research gained increasing prominence for her. However, she never got around to applying for jobs until a teaching position in English became available at a local urban secondary school. She casually applied for the post in a state of mind that was less than enthusiastic. However, the realities of teacher responsibility, leadership and sense of ownership were such that her first teaching position became a very positive experience.

When her husband secured a job in another city, Jan reluctantly relinquished her English position and careers adviser's role, and took up a similar combination of subject areas in her adopted city. In her third year of teaching here, she became pregnant. The next seven years were spent raising two children and working part-time for approximately 12 hours per week. A move then followed to a girls' secondary school teaching English and assuming the pastoral care responsibility of a year level dean. Under a new principal, Jan was appointed to the post of Head of the Junior School (years 9 and 10) before winning the position of Deputy Principal at Otago Girls' High School.

Interestingly, Jan's decision to apply for a principal's job was never part of a pre-determined career path or the result of any long-held ambition. She had enjoyed aspects of educational administration but had regarded her deputy principalship as a job for life until retirement. There were parts of the principal's job in which she did have an interest, such as working with the students and staff as a collective educational entity. There was, however, a much deeper force that motivated her to apply for, and win, the leadership position in the school she had attended as a pupil:

> I would have an absolute mission that the school will never be like it was in past days. And, hence, a lot more liberal, [interaction with] boys, much more open, being much of the future, not locked in the past. It was shocking. I also didn't like the view of Otago Girls that I saw when we came on interschools. Shocking discipline, kids all over the place, answering back. Rough as. That's my old school.

At the time of her appointment as principal in 1995, she still believed the school was not particularly academic and that the students' general behaviour was not under control. This prompted a key internal motivation for her and she was determined to 'pull it back to a classy girls' school.' Jan confided that maintaining this process of transformation remained a powerful influence, fuelled by a fear of the school returning to its former state – hence her search for continuous academic improvement.

Style of leadership

Jan's leadership of the school is premised by her collaborative way of working, as evidenced by her use of the committee structure involving staff participation in change decision-making. She summarises her collaborative style of leadership in this way:

> Basically, I see it as an upside down triangle. I'm the one underneath supporting and helping. And if I'm doing it really well, the staff actually think it's their bright idea and their initiative and they have ownership. It's not a top-down, stand and pontificate [model]. I've probably got to watch that, just occasionally, I don't give away too much authority. I think that could be a risk I run sometimes.

This is a fine balancing act that Jan continually faces: how much authority to maintain as leader of the school and how much to delegate to others. It is, she observed, a better balance to work than simply holding all the power to herself at the top of the school hierarchy and have everyone else underneath reacting and being angry.

Her major method of empowering her staff is by means of informal conversation: in her office, outside in the corridor, at the school gate or over a drink during a staff social gathering. She believes it is a non-threatening way to get staff motivated and moving in agreed directions rather than by a series of written requests placed in staffroom pigeonholes. It is a personalised approach that is reinforced repeatedly in subsequent observations of Jan at work in her office.

Strategies of successful leadership

Following her appointment, Jan had faced the challenge of transforming what she believed to be a partially dysfunctional school that produced average examination results and failed to successfully control student behaviour. Her strategies to address this situation were first reported in Notman (2009) and focus on three key areas: a well-rounded education; a school culture that engendered trust and an ethic of care; and attention to the quality of teaching resources.

Well-rounded education

In Jan's eyes, a balanced curriculum is reflected in student success across a range of academic, sporting and cultural activities, and an increased student participation rate. There is a holistic flavour to this strategy in that it attends to the overall well-being of students 'so that they are learning to deal with other people; they are learning to work in teams; they are getting success in their own personal life as well as academic success' (Deputy principal). Parents note that this had been achieved while also being inclusive of special needs students and students from 'less fortunate backgrounds'.

With regard to academic activity, Jan plays a role in this successful strategy by participating in the curriculum committee, visiting classrooms, and advising on classroom pedagogy and the co-ordination of a school-wide thinking skills program. Similarly, she also contributes through her committed support for sporting activities, for which her students remain appreciative as one student noted: 'She's willing to come down in her own time, just to see how the team's going ... knowing we're doing well with our sporting achievement as well as academic.'

Jan meets the particular challenge of raising student levels of achievement through a number of interrelated strategies. She insists on employing properly trained and qualified staff: '[Teacher quality is] crucial. It's getting the right person in the first place, and then getting them to believe in themselves and getting the professional development.' Together with her high expectations of success, Jan is focused on continuous improvement through high expectations and celebrating success: 'She definitely pushes a high level of performance, whether it's sporting or academic. She always seems very proud of people when they do achieve' (Student).

School culture

Jan is adamant that a key factor in the school's success is the positive relationship that has developed between teachers and students, and the trust and confidence in each other that resulted from this. Similarly, another influential factor is the relationship between school and parent groups which is based on establishing effective community links between school and home: 'Communication is a strength of this school. It's up to date, it's modern but it's also very informative' (Parent).

A third factor contributing to the school culture is the degree to which the principal shares leadership and decision making power within the school. Jan adheres strongly to a power sharing model and to staff participating in committee structures, as 'listening to them is the secret of your success so you're getting all that change coming from underneath and going with them as far as you can.'

Another factor is the integration of an ethically and socially diverse student population, as Jan explains:

> Oh, so careful to like and relate and connect to the groups in your school: your Pacific Island students, your Maori students ... and connect with your so-called solo mums, your deprived parents, so that they're not scared to come to school, happy to talk about having assistance. But they're all about relationships – hugely important.

A final factor is the establishment of a supportive school culture through the pastoral care of students. An ethic of care is integrated throughout the school: 'The girls have been led or taught by very caring teachers. Like they care about the girl as a whole, not just a part of it' (parent). This sentiment is also reflected in one student's comment on the principal's personal interest in her girls:

> When we first came in for interviews, she wanted to know everyone's goals and where they wanted to end up in the future. So it's sort of that individual tracking of what you want to do. And that's quite nice because it's not just all generalised: it was one-on-one talking with everyone.
>
> (Student)

Quality of teaching resources

Jan is very keen to employ teachers who are well trained and qualified, who are committed to the girls' all-round education, and who will fit into the ethos of the school. In turn, staff are supported by up-to-date resources and technology, and a plentiful supply of professional development. The Board chairperson emphasised Jan's willingness to keep the school at the forefront of any changes in learning developments. Staff are also supported by a motivated senior leadership team who have utilised their relative strengths well.

All of these successful strategies are underlined and informed by Jan's vision for the school. This is summarised by one teacher's description of the direction and anticipatory nature of this vision:

Her passion is to keep up with the latest developments in education and making sure her school is equipped to take her students into the 21st century … looking forward all the time and looking for possible glitches along the way.

The person within the professional

Impact of personal and professional values

Jan identifies four personal values that she believes impact most on her principalship: honesty, self-respect, the courage to do what is right, and an ethic of care. The instrumental personal value of honesty is deep-seated and connects strongly to Jan's expectations for high standards of behaviour and performance from students and staff respectively, and to her exercise of moral leadership. She is professionally honest in her feedback on student and staff performance and in the clarity of her behavioural expectations. She exercises moral leadership with a strength of conviction in what is right for the school and respects honesty in her dealings with other people. Jan's value of self-respect is similarly linked to the two professional values above and is synonymous with honesty. Honesty, for Jan, is the major means of achieving self-respect and cementing her own image of what constitutes an effective principal. Her self-respect also connects to her keen sense of personal and professional pride in terms of giving her best in the job.

Jan sees her personal value of courage as clearly linked to setting high standards of behaviour and to her exercise of moral leadership. Jan also links her value of loving/caring as a foundation to her professional value of leading a student-centred school, where student learning and development is the focus. This value of care is evidenced in her often unassuming assistance for disadvantaged students. Her ethic of care extends to supporting staff to develop.

In terms of her professional values, Jan has a very strong student-centred focus. Students are very important to her and she holds strong convictions that she and the staff can make a positive difference to their lives. One senior teacher commented:

> I think Jan feels that and knows that as a principal, she can have a real impact and make a real difference to those kids; and I know that, in a lot of good work that we do at Otago Girls, the concept of value-added or making a difference is very important in her job.

Jan believes in providing a balanced well-rounded education for students, where the mix of sporting and cultural activities sits naturally with their academic pursuits. This underlines Jan's notion of what constitutes success for the girls, and is something she defends with vigour:

> I fight like crazy in the staffroom if anybody tries to push us off the well rounded [education] … I won't give up the 70 minutes I spend on 'Clubs' every Thursday. And I won't give up letting the kids go off to Wellington to

do something because I think they learn by doing and those things …We're not giving up a lot of those crucial things that make teenagers want to be at school, that makes them enjoy being here.

For Jan, another core value comes in the form of high standards of behaviour. For example, standards of behaviour on school trips are clearly outlined to students, as are standards to be maintained in wearing school uniform. While strict guidelines regarding school uniform may have reinforced the conservative image of the school and the traditional outlook of the principal, Jan reveals broader thinking behind the emphasis on uniform:

If you get rid of the uniform, that's a good one. Yes, I'd fight you on that one because it keeps all the kids the same, no matter what background they come from. It also makes them identifiable, improves behaviour. There's that corporate belonging, sense of pride. We can manage the kids so that they are presenting themselves decently and feeling good about themselves.

Jan is able to distinguish between right and wrong on a range of issues, be it staff problems or student misbehaviour. As a senior teacher indicated:

These days, when it's a kid, say, who's crossed a barrier, it can often mean confrontation with parents and things like that. She won't back off from that. If a kid's done wrong, then it's got consequences and that's it. There's no wishy-washy stuff there: it's pretty much black and white.

This raises the link between Jan's core values and the engagement of moral leadership within her principalship. A particular example of this was in relation to the school formal dance for senior students and the advent of 'after-parties'. In this area, Jan maintains a firm line that is consistent over the years but out of step with some secondary schools in the city. She comes from a very strong value viewpoint that the school has no role in encouraging or condoning the use of alcohol by under-age drinkers, despite its consumption by teenagers at weekends. Accordingly, prior to the school formal each year, students are asked to sign a contract stating they will not attend after-parties and agree to remain within the bounds of the school policy on alcoholic consumption. While Jan's strong moral standpoint does not attract universal agreement from students, staff and some parents, she nevertheless holds firm to her beliefs and the school policy, despite a vehement protest on one occasion from about 80 Year 13 students.

It is evident in Jan's daily working operation that her demand for excellence is another core professional value and one that is frequently referred to by those who work closely with her. This is reflected in above-average academic results in national examinations each year. In her own principalship, Jan is continually aware of doing her best for every student in the school, regardless of their ability or whether the pursuit is an academic, cultural or sporting one. As well as her own self-expectation, Jan strives to ensure that students do their best in areas ranging from classroom behaviour to attending drama rehearsals or sports practices. She also encourages her students to appreciate the need for self-control and self-discipline in order to achieve these levels of excellence. It is often noted that Jan and her staff went to great efforts to encourage student pride in their achievements through awards, newsletters, special assemblies and published articles in the region's newspaper.

Her professional work ethic is a fundamental influence on her work as a principal and on the way she expects her staff and students to perform. For example, Jan would be embarrassed to be seen leaving school earlier than any teacher. She learnt early on, in her foundational experiences, that hard work was rewarded with success and recognition, and that same value permeates her principalship. Her work demands made of staff are also high. Jan holds staff self-reliance, punctuality and job completion in high regard.

Another professional value that becomes apparent is her ethic of care, a strong feeling of support for staff (every teacher receives a principal's classroom visit each term) and students. One senior teacher commented:

> She is very concerned for kids who have, for one reason or another, had some misfortune or who have been disadvantaged. She will work very hard to assist those kids, both in a low key way but also in a higher profile way.

Jan admits that her caring approach is an integral part of establishing good human relationships. She finds it relatively easy to be empathetic and supportive on the important issues yet can get frustrated, when some of the staff demand her care and attention over what she sees as issues of self-interest.

Sense of self

A further aspect in the consideration of the person behind the principal is Jan's sense of self-worth and self-belief. All those with significant knowledge of Jan's principalship confirm her strong sense of self that is allied to her set of deeply-held convictions:

> She does have, I think, a strong sense of self. She knows where she is coming from. She has a very good understanding of her own values and commitments and as they apply to what happens in the school. So there is a strong consistency, there is a real consistency here in the decisions that she makes.
>
> (Deputy principal)

Her strength of inner conviction leads to expression of her core values in the way in which she leads the school.

Jan invests so much in her work for several reasons. First, as a former student of Otago Girls, Jan has a strong feeling for the school. Since her departure as a student, she had maintained links with the school for over 30 years and was determined, on appointment to the principalship, that it would become a high achieving academic school.

Second, Jan has a strong personal commitment to the people of her school community. She feels keenly the interpersonal nature of the job and her capacity to influence other individual lives for better or for worse. She enjoys the intrinsic reward of seeing teachers and parents happy, and students achieving their individual potential, both inside and outside school. Of all the aspects of the role she most likes, it is the connection with students.

Finally, Jan takes a great deal of personal satisfaction in, and professional pride from her job. She is passionate about her leadership role, which is built around her professional integrity and pride:

> I want to do it [the job] well. I couldn't live with myself if I was half doing it and if I was the butt of huge amounts of criticism from all around. I would be absolutely miserable. If you take it on, you've got to give it your very best shot ... Inside, you would be giving yourself hell if you didn't.

Challenges and dilemmas

Despite her leadership success, Jan still faces challenges and dilemmas. School-wide challenges include achieving a uniform teaching and learning performance across different subjects with different staff, working within financial constraints while still responding to the pace of educational change, and dealing with staff issues.

Addressing the barriers to student achievement presents an interlinked series of challenges. These include the negative impacts of out-of-school and social activities, and ensuring student cyber-safety. Jan also reflected on the challenges of meeting the human needs of her staff, providing motivation for problem-solving and the acceptance of change, and exerting her professional leadership skills to maximum advantage.

For the principal, two intrapersonal dilemmas present themselves. First, Jan is very aware of the need for her own continuous improvement, especially in view of her age and length of time at the school. Hence, the professional development focus on thinking skills and her proactive role in its implementation. Second, she is also aware of maintaining a balanced leadership style in order to avoid complacency in the job: 'I'm on a knife edge between having more experience, more confidence ... and then the other side of things – too confident, too casual...'

A legacy for the future

As Jan brings a formal end to her educational career, she reflects back on her 15 years of principalship with a quiet satisfaction. Her legacy, she believes, will rest with the girls' continued desire to love learning, believe in themselves and to achieve very high academic standards. This is an on-going aim of academic excellence that is built upon a platform of quality teaching, enhanced by a high-trust model of distributed leadership among the staff. Jan concludes that her spiral of success has been based on instilling confidence in teachers and students to 'jump across the curve' in search of new and exciting teaching and learning initiatives. The Scottish ancestors who founded Otago Girls' High School would say 'Aye' to all of that.

Reflections on the concept of values-based leadership

Jan Anderson's case study is a tangible example of an emerging theme in the literature that personal dimensions of educational leadership are influential factors in a successful principalship. Day *et al.*, (2000) had earlier proposed a values-based contingency model of leadership where effective leaders' behaviour is contingent on context and situation, and where their choices and decision-making practices are related directly to their personal beliefs, values and leadership style. Like Jan in this New Zealand study, the headteachers in Day *et al.*'s (2000) study had communicated their personal vision and belief systems by direction, word and deeds. They came across as authentic leaders; that is, leaders who were acknowledged as such by their staff, who derived their credibility from personal integrity and from 'walking their values'.

Similar findings have been reported in more recent research studies. For example, West-Burnham's (2009) large-scale study of British headteachers, together with findings from the International Successful School Principalship Project in New Zealand (Notman, 2010, 2011) and in Australia (Drysdale *et al.*, 2009; Duignan & Gurr, 2007), identified principals' critical self-reflection and intrapersonal understanding of their personal values systems as key features in a successful principalship. Day *et al.* (2009) conducted a research study that investigated the impact of school leadership on student outcomes in English schools identified to have significantly raised student attainment levels over a relatively short three-year period. In affirmation of the influence of values-based leadership and contingency leadership, the research demonstrated that

> heads in more effective schools are successful in improving pupil outcomes through who they are – their values, virtues dispositions, attributes and competences – the strategies they use, and the specific combination and timely implementation and management of these strategies in response to the unique contexts in which they work.
>
> (Day *et al.*, 2009, p. xv)

Jan's narrative also exemplifies the relational connectedness between herself, the school, and its parent community. Trust was built up and maintained among her constituents through shared beliefs in what she and the school stood for, and through positive, caring relationships. The impact of building relational trust is acknowledged in the educational leadership literature whereby relationships, connections and trust building were found to be key features in the success of principals (Duignan & Gurr, 2007; Kutsyuruba *et al.*, 2009; Tschannen-Moran, 2004).

Reflections

For current educational leadership practitioners and aspiring leaders, four key reflective questions are suggested as a 'stock-take' of one's values systems and of how such values systems might influence subsequent leadership behaviours and help build relational trust:

1 *What are your core personal and professional values?* These values represent guidelines for how one thinks and acts, and for judging oneself and other people. They are deeply-held convictions about how to live and how to best enhance teaching and learning respectively.

2 *Which of your core values align with your school/community values?* Educational leaders might use the extent of their values alignment to gauge and/or predict potential outcomes arising from their decision-making processes, and how they might go about personifying their shared values (Kouzes & Posner, 2012).

3 *How do you deal with values conflict situations when your personal or professional values are confronted?* Leaders will find it useful to review past critical incidents that present a values conflict, often in the form of moral or ethical dilemmas for resolution. The objective in this context is to 'combine the intellectual and the moral into frameworks that help transcend knowledge generation and skills development to one of reflective critique of contemporary dilemmas, and personal and professional growth' (Duignan & Collins, 2003, p. 292).

4 *How do these values shape the overall way in which you run the school or centre?* An examination of how one's values systems link to leadership behaviours can help establish a personal leadership platform that encapsulates the concept of philosophy-in-action and promotes critical self-reflection. It can also assist the leader to determine which key values are not open to negotiation in the particular educational context in which they work.

This New Zealand principal case study, together with developments in the conceptual and research literature, underlines the notion that leadership is inevitably values-driven. As Burns (2003) noted, the advent of more open, pluralistic societies has both broadened and complicated the role of values-based leadership: dilemmas and leadership-followership debates abound. However, the potential for strengthening educational leaders is profound: 'Leaders embrace values; values grip leaders. The stronger the values systems, the more strongly leaders can be empowered...' (Burns, 2003, p. 211).

References

Burns, J. M. (2003). *Transforming leadership: A new pursuit of happiness* (New York: Atlantic Monthly Press).

Day, C., Harris, A., Hadfield, M., Tolley, H. & Beresford, J. (2000). *Leading schools in times of change* (Buckingham: Open University Press).

Day, C., Sammons, P., Hopkins, D., Harris, H., Leithwood, K., Gu, Q., Brown, E., Ahtaridou, E. & Kington, A. (2009). The impact of school leadership on pupil outcomes. Research report DCSF-RR108 (London: Department for Children, Schools and Families).

Drysdale, L., Goode, H. & Gurr, D. (2009). An Australian model of successful school leadership: Moving from success to sustainability, *Journal of Educational Administration*, 47(6), pp. 697–708.

Duignan, P. A. & Collins, V. (2003). Leadership challenges and ethical dilemmas in front-line organisations. In N. Bennett, M. Crawford & M. Cartwright (Eds.), *Effective educational leadership* (London: Open University Press & Paul Chapman), pp. 281–294.

Duignan, P. & Gurr, D. (Eds.) (2007). *Leading Australia's schools* (New South Wales: Australian Council for Educational Leaders).

Kouzes, J. M. & Posner, B. Z. (2012). *The leadership challenge* (5th edition) (San Francisco, CA: Jossey-Bass).

Kutsyuruba, B., Walker, K. & Noonan, B. (2009). Importance and fragility of trust in the world of school principals. Paper presented at the American Educational Research Association Conference, San Diego, 13–17 April.

Notman, R. (2009). In pursuit of excellence: A leadership story. *Journal of Educational Leadership, Policy and Practice*, 24(1), pp. 26–31.

Notman, R. (2010). Who lies within? The personal development of educational leaders. *Journal of Educational Leadership, Policy and Practice*, 25(2), pp. 16–28.

Notman, R. (Ed.). (2011). *Successful educational leadership in New Zealand: Case studies of schools and an early childhood centre* (Wellington, NZ: New Zealand Council for Educational Research Press).

Tschannen-Moran, M. (2004). *Trust matters: Leadership for successful schools* (San Francisco: Jossey-Bass).

West-Burnham, J. (2009). *Developing outstanding leaders. Professional life histories of outstanding headteachers: Summary report* (Nottingham: National College for School Leadership).

Chapter 11

Cyprus

Trust in leadership: keeping promises

Petros Pashiardis and Vassos Savvides

Who is Myra Johnson?

All the people we spoke to about the principalship of Myra Johnson (not her real name) indicated that she is a successful principal. Indeed, one needs only spend ten minutes with her in order to conclude that she is the right person in the right position.

Myra has been the principal of the Anassa Primary School since 2006. She is a woman in her mid-fifties and has been a teacher for 30 years and a principal for six years. She graduated from the Pedagogical Academy of Cyprus and earned a BA and an MA in Education in the USA. She has also worked for the Pedagogical Institute of Cyprus and the Curriculum Development Unit for five years. Her rich academic and professional background seems to have paved the way for her to become a successful and committed educator.

In Cyprus, promotion is based primarily on seniority. Principalship was not something which was deliberately pursued by Myra, but over time, opportunities for promotion arose, and when she was able to be principal, she readily assumed this role because she reasoned that from a position of greater influence she would be able to support student learning and serve the needs of the school community in a more effective way.

Setting the stage

The school is set in a rural area 16km from Nicosia, the capital of Cyprus. As is the case with all primary schools in Cyprus, the age of the 108 pupils varies from 6 to 12 years old.

The socio-economic status of the school could be described as moderate since most of the inhabitants of the area are high school graduates who work on their farms or in the private sector. They do not seem to be facing any serious economic problems. In addition, whilst there are single parent families, and some families have parents originating from a foreign country, the proportion is low. Whilst some children have one of their parents coming from a foreign country, the school does not consider them to be foreigners since only one of their parents is not Cypriot.

Moreover, there is little relative disadvantage as they were born in Cyprus and their Greek language skills are comparable to that of the other children in the school.

The physical environment of the school is pleasant and appealing. For example, the building and sitting areas of the football stadium are painted with various pictures. One can also find a number of toys in the yard that children make use of during breaks. The school building is a three-storey building with a long staircase. This staircase is covered on the top so that children are protected from adverse weather.

There is no local board in charge of formulating policy for the school or monitoring its implementation. The school is centrally governed by the Ministry of Education and Culture through the Inspectorate. Personnel and administrative management, curriculum issues and money allocation are mostly exercised by the Ministry without any significant deviation. The principal of the school is obliged to obey, without really questioning the system.

Major challenges of the school

When Myra began her tenure as the school principal, she was confronted with discipline problems characterised by frequent expressions of aggression and disobedience. This was a common concern of both pupils and teachers at the school. Pupils themselves reported fights taking place among their peers whereas teachers attributed this kind of behaviour to serious family problems that these children face on a daily basis.

Upon her arrival at the school, Myra also identified low levels of student achievement, especially with regard to performance in Greek language, both verbal and written. The teachers attributed this weakness to the bidialectism, which is a characteristic element of the Cypriot linguistic context. At this point, it would be useful for the reader to explain what bidialectism is. In Cyprus, Greek is the spoken language of the majority of the population, however, the Greek-Cypriot dialect is different from the Greek language as spoken in mainland Greece, and is very similar to the Greek-Cretan dialect. Therefore, when children in Cyprus speak, they use the Greek-Cypriot dialect. However, the books are written using mainland Greek, and this creates some confusion for students when reading and writing mainland Greek.

> We also have the problem of bidialectism, which takes us one step backwards, and when they have to express themselves in writing it seems that most children use the Cypriot dialect.
>
> (Teacher)

According to teachers, bidialectism combined with low motivation for learning explained the low levels of student outcomes in the domain of language learning.

The inconsistent behaviour of parents was also reported as a challenge by the principal. In particular, the parents seem to have no fixed schedules for their children, and their parenting role is exercised in a 'laissez faire' mode. For example, according to the principal 'it might be 19:00 and the children would be grubby, tired, watching T.V. and having done no homework.'

Addressing school challenges – the importance of trust

Myra used a variety of strategies in order to address the challenges that were previously described. However, a basic strategy seemed to permeate her whole behaviour and practice, and that is building trust (Pashiardis, 2009). Trust may be defined as 'one's vulnerability to another in terms of the belief that the other will act in one's best interests' (Hoy *et al.*, 2006, p. 429). Hoy and Tschannen-Moran (2003) conducted a review of the literature on trust and concluded that there are multiple facets of trust – benevolence, reliability, competence, honesty and openness. Taking a closer examination of Myra's relationships with other individuals and groups, it is evident that she managed to create an authentic profile comprising the aforementioned dimensions of trust. Next, we will consider how each aspect of trust was portrayed in Myra's personality within the specific context of the Anassa school community.

Benevolence

Benevolence refers to confidence that the trusted party will not harm one's well-being (Hoy & Tarter, 2004). This facet of trust was mainly secured through Myra's persistence in building harmonious relationships with teachers, parents and students. Myra describes herself as being passionate about school life. She is motivated by love for children and a desire to help others. She feels like a mother embracing all people who come to her with a problem.

Myra exhibits the same kind of benevolence towards her teachers. She described an incident where a teacher called her in the afternoon at home to make a complaint about the school inspector's visit during the same day in her class. Myra listened to the teacher patiently. According to Myra, she was there to support her, find out what had happened and what had gone wrong. This kind of approach was guided by a strong belief of giving to others. It is very important for her to be able to use her authority for the benefit of the people in the school. This is mirrored in the principal's own words: 'I believe that we are here to offer, and by offering you receive things. Nothing goes in vain. This is my philosophy. Whatever you do it comes back to you.' For example, when a school inspector has some negative comments about a teacher's lesson, Myra is very discrete in conveying this information to the teacher. The purpose is to encourage the teacher to improve and not downgrade him or her. As a result, the teachers felt empowered to perform their work in the best possible way.

The parents themselves verified this approach of the principal and indeed showed much satisfaction with her behaviour.

we see her approach with us. That she will call us on the phone and the way she will speak to us. There is no distance between us, anything she needs she will ask for it. We have a very harmonious relationship.

(Parent)

Being divorced in Cyprus carries enormous social stigma, especially for women in the rural areas. Myra described how she was able to support a divorced parent. She talked to her, made her feel accepted by the school community, and persuaded her to see the priest of the local church to receive further support. Building close relationships with parents has meant that parents work to support Myra in promoting the school's mission.

In the case of students, the principal showed tolerance, understanding and support. According to Myra, students react negatively when being persistently opposed, whereas by showing patience and benevolence towards them and trying to understand their behaviour, problems are more easily resolved.

If you try to show understanding and ease things out and tolerate some things at that time so that (pupils) calm down and then explain things to them, the problems are more quietly solved out, there is no aggravation.

(Principal)

The principal seemed to have a very delicate way of approaching children so that she ended up in winning them over to do what she wanted and moreover, what was right for them. In this way, problems of disobedience and disorder were minimised and children focused more effectively on their learning.

Reliability

Reliability refers to confidence that the other party will act in a consistent way to ensure the benefit of the trustee. This facet of trust was first manifested by the principal through ensuring that the necessary teaching and learning resources were available for all students and teachers. The teachers of the Anassa School knew that they could always rely on Myra to provide them with the necessary teaching material or other resources in support of their work. The pupils themselves seemed to acknowledge that it was the principal who took immediate action to supply them copies of the English books that had not yet arrived, or ensure the presence of a specialised music teacher at the school. It was common belief of school stakeholders that their principal would never leave them on their own to deal with a lack of resources.

Myra's consistent behaviour is further illustrated through her approach in addressing disorder at the school. Her clear and consistent approach to student welfare had improved student behaviour. Myra was very specific and firm in her stance on appropriate behaviour, something that the school community had not experienced for many years. According to a teacher,

The principal tries to explain to them (pupils) their mistakes and make them understand that whatever we do has its consequences and that the negative consequences that follow some wrong behaviour are due to that behaviour and not due to a revengeful teacher.

Teachers stressed the fact that problems during assemblies or excursions had decreased to a significant degree since the principal arrived at the school. Pupils also referred to the setting of rules by the principal in an effort to improve their behaviour: 'We used to have problems of children fighting between themselves while now they do not fight as they used to do before.'

Beyond school discipline issues, Myra was consistent in her personal approach with teachers. Teachers knew that the principal would not disclose any personal or professional information to the rest of the school members. For example, if a teacher had some form of illness this would certainly not be circulated around the school. It was a personal piece of information that had to be kept only among the interested parties. Moreover, Myra might have observed a lesson in a teacher's class, yet she would not reveal what happened in class to the other teachers. She was very clear with teachers that she would not release any information that was important and personal to them. According to Myra, 'you have to be aware of what you want to say to someone, who is this person, and in what way you express yourself. In any case, you have to protect what the others have entrusted you with.'

Competence

Another critical ingredient of trust is competence; that is, the ability to perform in accordance to set expectations and standards appropriate to a task. Competence is mainly portrayed through the principal's strong instructional leadership. First, Myra developed a vision for improving student learning. This vision related especially to the language skills of the children, a domain that had proven to be in need of extra consideration. To this effect, Myra communicated her vision that 'whatever happens in class should emphasise the functional development of language.'

The achievement of this purpose was enhanced by Myra performing model lessons, providing feedback to teachers on instructional methods, and praising outstanding practice. Parents were invited to school where they were informed about the vision as well as the instructional strategies employed for its implementation. Not many principals in Cyprus will invite parents in order to speak with them about instruction and other pedagogical matters. When principals do that, it is a sign of exhibiting great competence and confidence on behalf of the school leader.

Even more, according to the teachers, Myra herself had arranged to teach some lessons in all of the classes in an effort to have a personal contact with all pupils. In relation to this last practice one of the teachers noted:

by entering the classroom to have a lesson it is very easy to look at the notice boards, see if the work is renewed, observe whether the students' behaviour has improved, check their exercise books, ask them some questions or evaluate the teacher who takes on the lesson during the following period.

It is also important to mention that the principal observed some lessons in the sixth grade and concluded that the students had developed their language ability at a satisfactory level. The instructional strategies were also judged to have been successful: 'And I noticed phrases written on pieces of paper glued on the wall, which were used in order to improve their speech' (Principal). It is through these processes of teaching and observing that Myra is able to gauge the progress of the school on a daily basis.

As for the parents, they claim that the principal and teachers are responsible for a significant proportion of the improvement in students' learning. The following quote is characteristic of the parents' standpoint:

> I believe that 50 percent (of the school success) is due to the principal and the teachers and the other half due to the students and parents.
>
> (Parent)

On the whole, the parents seemed to appreciate the beneficial effect of the principal in their children's learning.

Honesty

Honesty alludes to the truthfulness, integrity and authenticity of a person or group. Myra has been shown to possess strong qualities that demonstrate an honest and authentic person in leadership. She has a passion for school life driven mostly by her love for human contact, especially with children. She perceives herself as a motherly figure that makes use of her authority in order to offer to others. That is why she exhibited individual consideration to all those who were in need of her support. She was caring and understanding as well as committed to the well being of all school members. She showed respect for all people and never intentionally offended them. Instead, she had a delicate way of approaching and resolving difficult situations. At the same time, she insisted on telling the truth to parents about their children's own performance without trying to 'beautify' the situation as many teachers try to do in Cyprus in order to be liked by parents (Pashiardis, 1998). The following quote of the principal is characteristic of her leading behaviour inspiring this aspect of trust:

> You have to take some things seriously, especially with regard to student learning. If you just say that these children cannot learn despite any efforts, then the other people won't take you seriously as well. At the same time, you cannot say that all students are excellent. You have to say the truth to parents with regards to their children's academic achievements.

This genuine interest in the school community was appreciated by all school stakeholders. Everybody knew that Myra was not seeking to promote her own image to the community but that everything she was doing was intended to benefit student learning. She really cared about the school and her whole behaviour was not an act but came directly out of her heart.

Openness

Openness concerns the extent to which relevant information is shared. This facet of trust was mainly manifested through a participative and inclusive style of leadership. Indeed, Myra is very approachable and always kept an open door for everyone who wished to discuss any issue with her. This holds both for internal stakeholders such as teachers and students as well as for external agents such as the parents and the community.

Myra adopted a consultative form of leadership where decisions were collectively made by the school staff. More specifically, the principal states:

> I want to have my colleagues' opinions. I would never do something they don't want to do because in this case it won't be done in the right way. If you force them to do something they will react negatively upon it.
>
> For example, when I write a communication letter to the parents I give it to everyone to have a look at … I don't want someone to read it and tell me that it is good to give away. I want them to read it and tell me that there is a mistake here or maybe it is better to put it this way. By advising me they protect me.

In this way, Myra received the support and cooperation of the teachers in promoting the development of the school. This plea for participative decision-making was also extended to stakeholders other than the teachers. For example, the cleaning lady, who had been working for many years at the school, was invited to express her opinion in relation to school issues.

> I might call her (the cleaning lady) to my office and read to her the invitation for a school celebration. And she says to me: You know, it is quite cold at this time up here and you should set the time of it at 14:30 instead of at 15:00, until everybody gathers … while if you make it at 15:00 you will begin at 15:15 … I sometimes share more things with her rather than my assistant head.
>
> (Principal)

This participative and open culture was also stressed by the teachers. They agreed that the majority of the school staff made decisions collectively, while all stakeholders made the more serious decisions in a cooperative manner.

> She does not tell us this is the theme, that's what is going to happen, it's over. She says to us that there is an issue and we have to make a decision. Everybody

says his/her opinion and in the course of time she does not impose her own opinion. We take into account the positive and negative points and decide ... and later on there will be no muttering or anybody accusing the others.

(Teacher)

Myra has managed to create an inclusive and open culture where everybody's opinion was valued and where the majority decided on the issues concerning the school and its people.

The principal was also open to the parents and the community. Myra kept close contact with the parents and made them feel comfortable to talk to her. She tried to pass on the message that she wants the parents' collaboration in accomplishing the school's mission. Moreover, she involved them by performing sample lessons in their presence, or she invited them to educational lectures taking place at the school.

Last year, we had brought a young psychologist from the Pedagogical Institute and he talked to them in a very nice and friendly manner. He wrote some things on the board and the parents were satisfied with those five things that they learned.

(Principal)

In addition, Myra informed parents about educational programs and invited them to take an active part in them. It is evident that the principal had established an effective form of partnership with parents, thus creating an atmosphere of openness and belongingness and indicating that the school is inviting and open to everyone.

Myra had also expressed her strong desire to become a member of the Anassa community. In this effort of hers, she attended the community church on Sundays or took part in the community parades. Moreover, she even became a blood donor thus enhancing the community's humanitarian aims: 'By donating blood I was giving the message that I belong to their community and that I am not just a morning visitor who leaves on the Fridays' (Principal). This approach of hers is also reflected in an incident where she invited some high school children wandering outside the school to a lecture on road safety given by the police.

In turn, the community council and the parents' association, appreciating Myra's commitment and efforts, reciprocated by contributing to the enrichment of the school's infrastructure. The community members actively demonstrated their appreciation of the principal's work by publicly honouring her for her services only a year after she obtained her tenure.

The way forward and some reflections

Myra is an exceptional principal inspired by her strong beliefs in people and trust. In her talk, it is evident that she is motivated by her love for children and her authentic will to support their learning and well-being in general. She is driven by an 'ethic of care' towards the individuality of all children and she is committed to creating an inclusive, child-centred learning environment. Furthermore, she works on establishing close relations with teachers and parents. As we articulated in the case of the Anassa School, Myra is consistent in her effort to establish, build and sustain a trusting relationship between herself, teachers, and other school stakeholders through the five aspects of trust, specifically benevolence, reliability, competence, honesty and openness. This allowed her to set high expectations that everyone agreed with; it also helped teachers to develop their teaching skills because of a strong sense that their school leader trusts them to be the best they can be; finally, it helped her improve her school through gaining community support.

What do all of the above mean? Are they mainly about trust when leading a school (or any organization for that matter)? Is trust the alternative to external accountability? What we can suggest is that high levels of trust allow school members to embrace the school vision for improvement and participate more actively in its implementation. In order for a principal to be successful, he or she needs to build not just on the attainment of the school's goals, but also on their attainment within a certain realm of good relations, colleagueship, and friendship with the members of the organisation. Friendship is built on the foundation of trust; therefore, for leaders to be successful they also need to create a minimum level of trust (Hersey & Blanchard, 1988).

Seashore-Louis (2007) found that in high trust schools, teachers were willing to work with administrators in order to implement quality management practices in their school and classrooms. On the contrary, in low trust schools the change vision was seen as a distraction or something irrelevant that was brought 'through the back door'. Thus, this distrustful setting in fact impeded any efforts to bring about change. In another case of an English secondary school principal, trust constituted an important component of capacity building and the sustained development of the school (Day, 2009). Specifically, the principal earned the trust of the school community by combining a personal and academic interest in staff and students. A key feature of the principal's approach was the initiation of opportunities that enabled the development of individual and collective leadership capacities, something that was strongly manifested in the case of Myra as well. What is clear from all cases is that placing trust at the core of an organisational set of values empowers all stakeholders to work on achieving the school goals for improvement.

Questions to ask

Myra's focus on creating an open and trusting environment enabled her to build arenas for collaboration and negotiation with all school stakeholders. Democratic processes of decision-making were set in place in order to bring about real and long-lasting change at the school. For her, school improvement is a collective responsibility that all school stakeholders should be concerned with. Power and authority is not held in the hands of the principal alone but rests within all those who are committed to bringing about deep rooted change in the lives of all children at the school. Myra, first and foremost, feels accountable to all of these people who are engaged in the process of school improvement. For her, accountability is not about complying with an external impersonal mechanism but about serving the needs of all those who have placed their trust on her. The main questions to reflect upon here are which accountability is more important, useful, and effective? Is it a process of accountability from outside or the one that emanates from the inside, when trying to be the best you can be?

It is important to note that trust building takes time and continuous effort on behalf of the principal. For example, Day (2009) found that in the case of a secondary school principal in England, trust was broadened and deepened over a long period of time. Moreover, the principal intentionally focused his attention and repeatedly fostered trust to achieve success and improvement for the school. Similarly, Seashore-Louis' (2007) research shows that violations of trust may occur at any point and therefore, principals should not assume that they will continue to share a trustworthy reputation. According to Tschannen-Moran and Hoy (1998), trust is like studying a moving target because it can easily be altered over the course of a relationship as the level of interdependence increases or decreases. With reference to our case, although Myra managed to build a culture of trust among school members, she will need to persist in her efforts to maintain and sustain this trusting nature of relationships, especially in view of unanticipated challenges that might emerge in the future. That is, trust should not be taken for granted but should be continually cultivated, nurtured, and strengthened. Therefore, what actions and behaviours should be distinctive of school leaders who try hard to sustain (and even raise) the level of trust that has been created in their schools? What kind of mechanisms are necessary so that this kind of trust is an enduring quality of the school ethos?

Finally, school leaders need to understand the dynamics of trust in order to develop and sustain a climate that is conducive to excellent teaching and learning. To this effect, school leaders should first scrutinise how their own practice is interpreted by others (Seashore-Louis, 2007) and then act upon those perceptions to improve the quality of trust in their relationships. Central to this process is the question of 'How can a school leader build and sustain trust?', especially within the context of their own school unit. Then, school leaders need to consider how they can gradually build trust both at the *individual* as well as at the *collective* level; this is how the relationship moves to a more mature level (Pashiardis, 2009). Therefore, school leaders need to respond to the following question as well: 'To what extent can trust at the individual level lead to trust at the collective level?' No single answers or recipes can be provided in regard to these questions. Certainly, Myra's and other cases can provide us with important reflections on the significance of trust at the school place, yet we strongly believe that principals should shape their own perceptions of how trust can be fostered through a continuous learning cycle and personal development.

References

Day, C. (2009). Building and sustaining successful principalship in England: the importance of trust. *Journal of Educational Administration, 47*(6), pp. 719–730.

Hersey, P. & Blanchard, K. (1988). *Management of Organizational Behaviour: Utilising Human Resources* (5th ed.). Englewood Cliffs, NJ: Prentice Hall.

Hoy, W.K. & Tschannen-Moran, M. (2003). The conceptualization and measurement of faculty trust in schools. In W.K. Hoy & C. Miskel (Eds.) *Studies in Leading and Organizing Schools* (pp. 181–207). Greenwich, CT: Information Age Publishers.

Hoy, W.K. & Tarter, C.J. (2004). Organizational justice in schools: no justice without trust. *International Journal of Educational Management, 18*(4), pp. 250–259.

Hoy, W.K., Tarter, C.J. & Woolfolk Hoy, A. (2006). Academic optimism of schools: a force for student achievement. *American Educational Research Journal, 43*(3), pp. 425–446.

Pashiardis, P. (1998). Researching the characteristics of effective primary school principals in Cyprus: a qualitative approach, *Educational Management and Administration, 26*(2), pp. 117–130.

Pashiardis, P. (2009). Educational leadership and management: blending Greek philosophy, myth and current thinking. *International Journal of Leadership in Education, 12*(1), pp. 1–12.

Pashiardis, P. & Ribbins, P. (2003). On Cyprus: the making of secondary school principals, *International Studies in Educational Administration, 31*(2), pp. 13–34.

Seashore-Louis, K. (2007). Trust and improvement in schools. *Journal of Educational Change, 8*, pp. 1–24.

Tschannen-Moran, M. & Hoy, A. W. (1998). A conceptual and empirical analysis of trust in schools, *Journal of Educational Administration, 36*, pp. 334–352

Chapter 12

Sweden

Teachers make the difference: a former principal's retrospective

Helene Ärlestig and Monika Törnsén

Introduction

River School is a school for students between 13–16 years of age and is situated in a small municipality in Sweden. At the beginning of the 1990s the school was underperforming with low student learning outcomes and a poor reputation in the community. Over a period of only five years learning outcomes improved and the school was regarded as successful. The person who instigated the dramatic change was the new principal, Olof. He stayed as principal at River School for five years and then moved to a position as superintendent, in charge of many schools. This chapter is based on his retrospective reflections on his leadership at River School. It describes his main views about students and teachers, views that formed his work in improving River School, and how his leadership led to a positive and successful school culture through focusing on enhancing the learning capacities of students and staff.

Setting the stage

Sweden has a national curriculum and syllabus (www.skolverket.se/sb/d/493). At the beginning of the 1990s Swedish municipalities became responsible for schooling, and the employment of principals and teachers. In 1994, a new curriculum was introduced that provided concise guidelines on academic knowledge and social values. So, although principals and teachers are recruited and paid by their municipality, they are also expected to implement a national curriculum. The curriculum indicates that the principal should act as the pedagogical leader and manager in relation to the school staff. The role as pedagogical leader is described in the national curriculum and in the School Act in various ways. The principal is, for example, expected to set directions towards national goals, to actively work with following up and evaluating the results, and to continuously work with school improvement (Törnsén, 2009). To fulfil their task as pedagogical leaders, principals must be democratic, learning, and communicative leaders (Johansson, 2004). To be a democratic leader means to be knowledgeable about contemporary educational practice and to work actively to fulfil the schools mission regulated in the School Act and other policies i.e. to prepare students to be active and knowledgeable citizens in a democratic society. A principal should act as a role-model and involve staff, students and parents in decisions and responsibilities concerning the school's work. Important values like equity, respect for others, participation and free speech are a part of the expectations for education and enacted in practice by staff and students. These include building collaborative processes inside schools and with external interested parties, without abandoning the responsibilities of the principal, which are to see to that students gain academic knowledge in and through a democratic school setting. The concept of learning not only focuses the principal as a learner, but as someone with a responsibility to enhance the learning and development of teachers. This is carried out, for example, by means of annual individual development talks and regulated professional in-service training. Finally, leadership is mainly conducted through communication. What and how principals communicate will affect how they are perceived and what results they will contribute to. Organizational communication can be viewed from several perspectives such as individual style, organization within a school, and content (Ärlestig, 2008).

From industrial work to principal leadership

River School had at the time around 300 students, 25 teachers, and support staff such as a school nurse, a social welfare officer, a careers counsellor, administrative and maintenance staff. The geographically widespread municipality where the school is situated has a low density of population. Whilst the educational level of the population is low, education is seen as important and parents are on the whole engaged. Some students strive to continue in local businesses often established by their parents, while others leave the municipality for further studies.

Olof had worked for five years outside education before entering a teacher education college to become a teacher of children aged between 10 and 12 years old. After one year as a deputy principal, at 30 years of age, he became the youngest appointed principal in the municipality. This appointment was at the same school where he had been a teacher. Olof did not apply for his first position as a principal. He was asked by the outgoing principal to step in. He remembers being curious and wanting to explore what a principal does.

After five years as principal, Olof was asked by the superintendent to become the principal at River School. At first he hesitated. River School was known as a non-functional school, where everyone – staff members, students, parents, local politicians – was dissatisfied. The national media reported negatively on the situation in River School on several occasions. The principal in charge had left due to problems, such as arson in the school and student fights. Olof hesitated also because of his own background. As the principal of River School, his teaching staff would have more higher education qualifications and experience than he had, and he had no experience working in a school with students in their final years of compulsory schooling. To take on leadership when the school had a bad reputation, and not being able to rely on the legitimacy provided by having the same level of education and experience as the teachers, could create difficulties for his credibility and this might result in him not getting a mandate to lead. In his time as principal however, he had met some of the teachers at River School, and they indicated that they wanted the new principal to assist them and help them to realize the positive values base which many, although not all, staff members held. The positive values had, according to those teachers, been hampered instead of being promoted under the leadership of the previous principal.

After some thinking Olof decided to take on the challenge. The first years he described in retrospect were exciting and very strenuous. His first impressions were of a school with frightened, risk averse grown-ups who did not dare to show who they were. They did not care about others, did not take responsibility for students when they left the classroom, avoided students in the corridors, and avoided any unnecessary contact with students. Instead they walked quickly into the staff room and locked the door. The internal environment, together with a focus on teaching academic knowledge, had contributed to a culture in which teachers were most concerned about their own problems and their own class. River School, Olof remembers also, consisted of groups of adults and students gathered in the same place trying to limit contact with each other outside the classroom. The students too had the feeling that many of the teachers did not like them.

Leadership for change: the importance of seeing and respecting students

Olof decided to make both structural and cultural changes at River School. His leadership for change was based on his fundamental values and beliefs. By respecting every individual regardless of age, recognizing their capacities, and acknowledging their feelings, Olof wanted to create an environment of open communication and trust among the teachers and students. He saw this change as necessary for creating a good learning environment. Olof made it clear that everyone working in the school needed to understand that every student was a person with expectations for the main part of their life ahead of them and were full of possibility and potential. The school and what happened there would affect not only the current situation but also the future of students. Students were entitled to expect teachers to contribute positively to their lives and futures. Olof introduced a mentorship system where every teacher was responsible for 10–12 students. The teachers were expected to contact students and parents if the student didn't show up, and also to meet with the students to have short individual conversations several times during a semester.

Because of the history of River School, Olof was fully aware that some students had severe problems and a poor attitude to school. If teachers worked with a person's strengths and provided adequate support he was convinced that every student had the capacity to improve their situation. Showing respect for the individual student would, he believed, make them understand that the school could be an interesting and important place, not a prison. One example of how Olof worked to get a more respectful learning environment to enhance student capacity to learn was to open up a study room in the middle of the school. If the ordinary work in the classroom became too difficult, or students ended up in fights, they could choose to come to this room where teachers for special needs education were always available. The class teacher could never force the individual student to go to this room; it was not the teacher's decision; instead it was the student's responsibility to make the best of their situation. In the room they worked on something they needed to improve, although not always equivalent to what their classmates did. Still, students were provided with sufficient knowledge and experience to qualify them for high school. Students and teachers soon noticed that Olof believed in a school that was warm and friendly but with purpose, and not a place where it is acceptable just to 'kill time'. Instead students needed to perform in a range of different subjects. If they failed, teachers needed to react and act.

Olof believes that a school is not successful until students exceed their own expectations and the expectations of others. He is not totally in favour of today's focus on results and accountability. When he was working as a principal much of the emphasis of external accountability was missing, and they relied on teachers' tests and student evaluations to get a sense of how the school was progressing. He was not adverse to using data though, and one thing he did was to contact the high school and look into their former students results. These were later discussed in staff meetings. Even though results and quantitative data are important, the assessment of quality is much more subtle, according to Olof. Quality also needs to be expressed as a feeling sensed when looking at something and finding it better, funnier or more interesting. It can be about major school outcomes, and also minor accomplishments such as a student who performs a long-jump for the first time in front of their classmates. To gain an understanding of the meaning of quantitative data, there is a need to make a deeper analysis using qualitative information. In today's climate of increased accountability there are more quantitative data tools for principals to use, but the basic issue remains the same – to provide outstanding teaching and learning that meets the needs of students.

Another group that is crucial for supporting students at school are parents. Olof expressed a high respect for parents, and he spent a lot of time informing and meeting them, especially parents of students that needed support. If there were problems at school with a student he would visit the parents in their homes, sitting at their kitchen table talking to them and the student about what to do next. In the small municipality the fact that the principal as a person in authority would spend time and talk to everybody was appreciated. His communicative skills and ability to build relationships helped in this regard.

Teachers can make a difference

As soon as he arrived at River School, Olof began to focus his improvement efforts on supporting teachers. He believed strongly that his teachers had the capacity to create an excellent school if they got the right support. He found that many of the teachers had a will to do well and to create something good. However, the pervading culture of distrust and poor communication structures did not always allow these individuals and their beliefs to be expressed. The negative culture was supported by some teachers who treated students in ways that counteracted the values that Olof believed should characterize an improving and successful school. This was something which Olof as a new principal had to handle, and he was successful in setting free the inner strengths of people, their energy and internal motivation. Olof modelled openness through his own behaviour, gave people the possibility of being represented by colleagues or participate themselves in various groups, initiated dialogues, provided everyone with minutes from meetings, all of which created trust among staff. His way of leading called for participation by all. Everyone had to contribute. Through communication and feedback people actually started talking to each other instead of talking about each other. The strong driving force and ambition to 'do well' soon overshadowed the existing destructive forces.

One keystone in Olof's work was to make teaching a collective work. To manage and fulfil the school's mission, teachers needed to work in teams. Olof provided the teams with time and in-service training to improve their collaboration and their team process. Of course there remained some conflicts and frictions, but the longer they worked together the more obvious it became that the teams appreciated their colleagues even if they had different opinions and views. Besides working, teachers needed to have fun together, and so social evenings became important. Some of the activities created back then are still alive and of importance at River School today.

Olof's support of individual teachers and the collaborative work between teachers made the teacher teams strong and independent. All professionals, according to Olof, need to become aware of the theories and fundamental values that underpin their actions and activities. He recognizes a need for a solid connection between the school mission, teachers' actions, and an awareness of who they are there for. To be professional means to take responsibility for who you are and what you are hired for from a national, municipal and local school perspective, and to integrate all three perspectives. To stay professional calls for ongoing support for activities where teachers keep updated, collaborate with others, identify a common direction and decide together what actions to take in order to progress.

In the beginning, Olof's and the teachers' work at River School was challenging. Students did not show up, or they often acted in ways that were not acceptable. Olof made it very clear that in those situations it was the teachers' responsibility to act. If the problems were too big, the teachers had to seek assistance. Earlier when somebody ran into a problem that was too hard to handle they tried to pass it on to others, like the healthcare team or the principal. This is understandable, Olof says, especially concerning students with severe problems:

> If a student, as well as the student's parents, have lots of problems you cannot just tell them to try harder, they need something else. Teachers need to give them help and try other strategies. To be able to do so, teachers also need help to find strategies and tools. It is never enough to just encourage teachers to go on without giving them ideas of how to do it. Teachers who are managing children with special needs need to feel that they are not alone with all the problems. Teachers with competence and education to handle students with special needs are important in the organisation. At the same time, it is essential that class teachers realise that they can never give up on a single student. Again teachers need to understand that it is a collaborative work effort to ensure the support of every single student.

Even if teachers in their daily work do not feel that they are important, Olof points out that they can make a big difference in the lives of students. For teachers not to be able to see results at once can be discouraging. A phenomenon that teachers need to be aware of, talk about and remind each other of, is that it is long-term results that count. To see a student who has experienced difficulties succeed is one of the most rewarding feelings a teacher or principal can perceive. A teacher needs to understand that students may talk about him or her several years later either as a teacher who gave support and saw the person in the student, or as a teacher who never cared and who was disliked.

To support his ideas, Olof attempted to create structures that fostered a supportive culture. Working in teams, showing respect and encouraging different opinions was supported by an open building design. When River School was rebuilt, the entrance to the school with a cafeteria nearby served as a natural place for staff and students to meet. This open meeting place encouraged interaction and communication. The aim was to make everyone visible and feel welcomed. Simple solutions like having the photocopying machine in one corridor and the coffee machine in the other made the teachers move around among the students. When people move around it leads to numerous meetings and a calmer atmosphere. A positive culture developed and the teacher teams started to believe in their capacity to affect others. Their mission became a joint adventure where everyone could find support working together and respecting diversity.

Reflection: the steep learning curve of early years principalship

When Olof was appointed to his first position as a principal his lack of knowledge about leadership was vast. He believed that just as long as people are decent, kind, and have the same goals, all would work out well. After a while however, he discovered that this was not sufficient, and so the first five years in office as principal were years of apprenticeship when he learnt many things the hard way.

The platform that he established became a solid ground for actions. His leadership platform was based on his view that school is for human beings, for students with faces and feelings. Through a 'close to people' leadership style, a leadership based on values and with respect for diversity, he worked to establish a positive view on students and their capacity. This phase of establishing trust with a 'close to people' leadership style, sometimes met resistance that created conflicts. Once, when Olof decided on a matter concerning a teacher that was not supported by the staff, they turned against him. All teachers intended to make an official written complaint on 'the leadership of River School' to the municipal board. When Olof asked them to address him by his name instead of hiding behind the formal position of principal, they objected by saying that it was not him personally they were complaining about, but his leadership. They needed to depersonalize him to voice their complaint, much as they did when complaining about students. When they became aware that Olof as an individual was ready to take responsibility for the situation, the complaint was not sent. Step by step he gained trust and the ear of the superintendent and the school board, parents and finally the whole staff.

Olof made a decision not to work as an instructional leader, even though he tried to have more general discussions about students and learning. Most of the teachers had more higher education than Olof had, and so whilst he deferred to their expertise by not visiting classrooms, he still had high expectations and used his knowledge of the working of the school to talk to teachers about these. Although Olof did not spend much time visiting classrooms, he spent a lot of time walking around the school corridors talking to students and teachers. This gave him a good picture of how the school was working and where there were problems. Teachers regarded classroom visits as a means of surveillance and control, but with the information from the walkthroughs in the corridors, Olof was able to talk to the teachers about the effects of their behaviour and work over a cup of coffee. However this was not enough.

When Olof looked back, he saw that there was a need to take the school to the next level, and to achieve this there should be a stronger focus on the teachers' work with students inside the classroom. Olof would, if he returned to River School, focus more on the teachers' work with students inside the classroom, working, for example, on teachers' competence in their subject and consequently focus on the content and how teaching is conducted. The quality of the content and the working forms in each subject are crucial and teachers need continual in-service training and time to discuss their teaching. They need to find and try new working methods related to research and new findings. By improving teachers' didactics they can offer even more. It is also essential to convince and provide opportunities for teachers in the same subject to visit each other and discuss teaching in order to give teachers a broader perspective on their own teaching and learning performance.

When Olof is talking about his own strengths as a principal he says that he is good at supporting individuals and makes them grow to be better as students and teachers. This was tough, a fight and a struggle at times but also carried out with joy; and it involved a lot of fun! He sees himself as a role model. Olof's strengths can, however, also become a problem or an impediment in his leadership. His belief in people, understanding them and accepting their shortcomings sometimes led to him giving individuals too many opportunities. He reflected on how he tried to influence and give directions to people with too little guidance when they probably would have benefited from more boundary-setting. There is a need to figure out when boundaries and no more chances are the best help for the individual.

Olof believes that the principal's role is very important, especially in relation to the prevalent school culture and in relation to school improvement. He recognizes that informal leaders can disturb and delay change processes but believes that in the long run the principal's impact on culture contributes to how the school as an organization deals with students, and this directly or indirectly will affect school results.

There is no doubt that Olof and his leadership contributed strongly to turn around River School so it became successful. He managed to be a democratic, learning and communicative leader. His first step was to be brave enough to take the challenge of the principalship of a dysfunctional school, even if he wasn't sure he was going to succeed. This story shows that with the right person in place, positive change is possible.

Reflections

Based on Olof's narrative several areas for reflection can be identified, and a few are suggested here.

1   *The importance of trust:* Olof was met with distrust but managed to build trust as a principal with all stakeholders and interested parties, inside and outside school. How do you start to build trust when the trust is low?
2   *Dialogue and boundary-setting:* as a principal, Olof had formal power that needed to be used in a professional way. he was also clear that as a principal you should not underestimate the power others believe you have, and use it to help people around you to develop. It often helps to give people a second chance. This requires a balance between dialogue and boundary-setting and it is useful to reflect on examples where it is more important to use dialogue rather than boundary-setting and vice versa.
3   *Instructional leadership:* Olof set directions, developed teachers, redesigned the organization, built coalitions and he also managed the instructional program. But, his instructional leadership did not include classroom visits, and therefore he did not have first-hand information about teachers' work with students. How important are classroom visits and instructional leadership in the work of a successful principal?

4 *Academic knowledge and social justice:* today there is a big emphasis on effectiveness and good academic results. For many students good academic knowledge and results make a difference later in life. Olof put all his emphasis on trust and making students visible and regretted afterwards that he didn´t work more with the teachers in relation to students learning. What obstacles do you see in relation to work that emphasizes social justice, good academic knowledge and school effectiveness?

The Swedish case gives an example of how values affect our actions from the day a principal enters his or her position. It also shows how meta-reflection and a retrospective view can provide new insights and visualizes changes over time e.g. in what you emphasize as well as your values. To reflect on how you are, what you do and why you do it is to make good use of one's time.

References

Ärlestig, H. (2008) Communication between principals and teachers in successful schools. Doctoral thesis, Umea University. This can be retrieved from http://umu.diva-portal.org/smash/record.jsf?pid=diva2:142460

Johansson, O. (2004) A democratic, learning and communicative leadership? *Journal of Educational Administration,* 42(6), pp. 697–707

Törnsén, M. (2009) Successful principal leadership: prerequisites, processes and outcomes, Doctoral thesis, Umea University. This can be retrieved from http://umu.diva-portal.org/smash/record.jsf?searchId=1&pid=diva2:211453

Chapter 13

Singapore

Building on the past: connecting with others

Loke Heng Wang, David Gurr and Lawrie Drysdale

Introduction

This chapter is about Mdm Linda, the principal of a successful primary school in Singapore. Mdm Linda is not her real name as her story comes from research we conducted as part of an exploration of successful school leadership in Singapore (Wang, 2010).

Dimmock and O'Donghue (1997) used a life history approach as they felt that understanding how a leader is formed helps to understand current successful leadership practice. Taking this more extended approach to thinking about leadership formation, Mdm Linda's current work practice was heavily influenced by her supportive family who ensured that she had the financial means and moral support to advance in her educational career. With this support Mdm Linda is able to give herself to something that she enjoys doing – education.

How she came to be a primary principal is somewhat unusual as her teaching career began with a six-year appointment at a primary school but she did not stay in this sector. She went on to teach literature to college students for about eight years. During this time she was perplexed by the problems that college students had in learning about literature. To help understand this further she decided to seek an appointment in a secondary school, and here she headed the literature department. Finally, after several years in this role, she returned to the primary sector, first as a vice-principal and later as a principal. She is currently in her second principalship. Such diverse educational experience gave her a rich view of the educational landscape in Singapore and served her well in her primary principal role. Her formation as a principal involved her having experience teaching across three of the four sectors of education, and leadership experience in two of them, and multiple principal roles.

A leadership model to explore Mdm Linda's work

This chapter is based on the first author's attempts (Wang 2010) to make sense of four case studies by using the 6Es Singaporean model of successful school

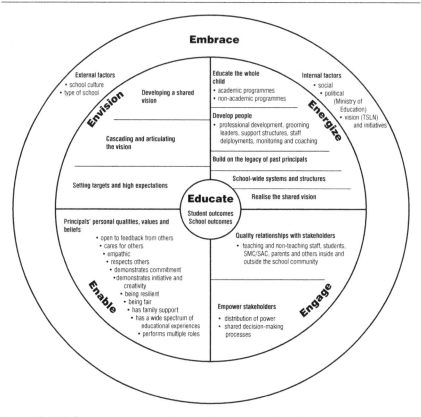

Figure 13.1 6E Singaporean model of successful school leadership

leadership (Figure 13.1). The 6Es ('Educate', 'Envision', 'Energize', 'Engage', 'Enable' and 'Embrace') lie in three concentric ovals. We will explain each of these and show how Mdm Linda's leadership has contributed to the success of her school.

The model begins at the centre of the three ovals with 'Educate', which is the core purpose of schooling in any education system. In Singapore, student outcomes are indicated by academic achievement and by student development in the social, affective and psychomotor domains. School outcomes are measured by effectiveness and efficiency in school strategic planning, staff management, resource management, and teaching and learning as stipulated in the School Excellence Model (www.moe.gov.sg). Since 2005, Mdm Linda has been the principal of Robin Primary School, which is a government school situated in a neighbourhood area in the southern part of Singapore. The school is a co-educational English medium school with a roll of about 2000 students. Taking over from the previous principals who had set high standards for the school, Mdm Linda continues the transformation of Robin Primary School into a highly regarded and successful school. The school has attained prestigious national awards presented by the Ministry of Education (MOE), Singapore, including the Sustained Achievement Award (SAA) for Aesthetics (2007) and Physical Fitness (2008), and the Best Practice Award (BPA) for excellence in Teaching and Learning (2008). In recognizing the school for its excellence in providing a holistic education, in 2008 the MOE presented the school with a special award, the School Distinction Award (SDA).

Fostering a collaborative culture

The next outer oval constitutes the foundations of the principals' leadership characteristics and practices which impact on the realization of the student and school outcomes. Within this oval are the components 'Envision', 'Energize', 'Engage' and 'Enable'. The first component, 'envision', represents collaborative visioning. In the original four case study schools, the principals developed the school vision with the stakeholders such as the staff and parents.

Mdm Linda demonstrates an ability to develop a shared vision within the school community. She understands the importance of envisioning to provide coherence and direction for the school. When she first became the principal of Robin Primary School, an early initiative was to look at the existing vision and see if that vision had served its purpose and whether there was a need to re-envision to take the school into the future. Mdm Linda did not work alone in this process. She said:

> I believe in top-down, bottom-up. So, the vision was crafted from bottom-up which supports the school values. And again, the values were from bottom-up. I believe in ownership ... Because I believe in ownership, my philosophy is to work with people.

Mdm Linda believes in wide participation in crafting the school vision. She asserts that everyone has an intellectual capacity to think and that everybody has ideas to contribute. The school vision is formulated and endorsed collectively by all within the school.

The school community, including the staff members, students and parents, jointly praise the principal for working together with them. Her approach is to work in harmony with them to establish positive relationships in making decisions and implementing programs for the school. One teacher explained that proposals submitted by middle managers are discussed at length at middle management and senior management level, debated and finally endorsed by the whole management team. For this teacher, it was clear that the principal works in collaboration with the staff to decide on school matters.

Mdm Linda also finds that staff members work better in teams and she creates opportunities for them to work in this manner such as forming teacher study groups, and making time for teachers to discuss professional issues such as how to teach a particular topic, and how to engage students in learning. She believes that teachers derive support from working in a team. She said:

> It is the power of synergy that allows the people to tap on one another's ideas to generate a high level of plans, programmes and strategies. The school culture is such that the staff members are comfortable working in teams as they like doing things together like in a family.

As principal, Mdm Linda, fosters positive relationships with the students. She establishes close contact with them by visiting classes to find how students are doing, walking through the school and interacting with the students during breaks. To further build relationships, Mdm Linda published a book about the school so that students could connect more strongly with the school. The book illustrates such things as the history of the school, how the school name came about, and the school's achievements. The principal aims to create a bond and a sense of attachment for the students with the school. It is part of her efforts to build a positive relationship with the student body.

The principal also works in partnership with the parents by communicating with them to establish rapport. The school has a parents' support group which acts as a link between the school and the parents. Parents' whose children study at the school are welcome to join this group. Parents indicated that this helps to make them more aware of the school's activities and it builds a bond between the parents and their children. Mdm Linda also has frequent breakfasts with parents to listen to their concerns. At these sessions, she gathers feedback from parents about the school programmes and activities.

To further establish relationships with parents, the school conducts programmes for parents, such as English and science workshops. The objective of the workshops is largely for parents to understand the school syllabus and expectations so that they can help their children at home. Activities like this help to foster a partnership between parents and the school in providing an education for the children.

Mdm Linda also collaborates with the community at large. In particular the school builds bonds with the community to work on major events. For example, the school and the neighbourhood collaborated in celebrating community festivals.

Building the capacity of others

The second component, 'Energize', indicates the principal's ability to improve the school by implementing vision-oriented and comprehensive strategies and interventions for school improvement. These strategies and interventions include educating the whole child, developing people, building on the legacy of past principals, creating school-wide systems and structures and realizing the shared vision.

In this account of Mdm Linda's success, she valued working together with others. With the school community, she fostered positive relationships with staff members, students and parents. Mdm Linda builds the capacity of others. One such way was building on the success of her predecessors. Mdm Linda, like other successful principals in Singapore, carried on with some of the school programs of here predecessor and added new elements to suit the school's current context. She also affirmed the school direction set by her predecessor and continued to strengthen the school image and identity. Staff members who showed potential were given opportunities to take on higher positions. Mdm Linda also developed the professional capacity of the staff.

Mdm Linda's story of success is built on the past success of several of her predecessor principals who have paved the way for her to take on the leadership of the school. As Wang's (2010) research noted, this is a feature that is rarely acknowledged in other studies of school leadership. She is grateful for the leadership and contributions of these principals. Her sincerity is shown in her strong commitment to building the capacity of others to take on leadership roles. Mdm Linda sees herself as being a mentor in this process. She guides people to uncover their strengths, to build their confidence-levels, promote aspirations, find meaning in their life, and ultimately to feel good about themselves. Her role is to help others realize their dreams. For example, she recounts the experiences of three teachers she has help to develop into successful principals. In working with her senior leadership group, she partners them, sharing her experiences and giving these vice principals opportunities to develop their own successful educational beliefs, knowledge and practice so that they may feel confident to apply for principalships. Mdm Linda also sees the potential of her middle managers in becoming future school leaders. Through her nurturing efforts, middle managers are promoted to vice-principal positions.

Mdm Linda cherishes all staff members. They are exposed to extensive and well-planned professional development. The school has been accredited as a People Developer institution for demonstrating organizational excellence in valuing, managing and engaging people in the school, and challenging them to scale new professional heights for the organization and themselves.

Mdm Linda's focus on building the capacity of others is targeted at providing a good education for students. She rightly believes that a highly skilled staff will lead to better student learning outcomes. This supports leadership models developed in the ISSPP research, in which principal leadership action is focused on capacity building across four dimensions: personal, professional, organizational and community capacity (see Gurr et al., 2006).

Building a collaborative culture

The third component, 'engage', is concerned with building a collaborative culture. The principal established quality relationship with stakeholders within (e.g. staff, parents and students) and outside (e.g. companies and community centres) the school community through formal and informal settings. She also empowered the stakeholders within the school community through distributing power and sharing decision-making processes which signified elements of distributed leadership in these schools.

Mdm Linda relies on others for school success, much as she has built her success on the success of past principals. She readily admits her lack of knowledge and skill in some areas. She adds that the strengths of the vice principals complements hers, as her strength is in the areas of systems, structures and innovations, while the vice principals' strengths are in human relations. Mdm Linda also depends on the middle managers for school success. She explains that each middle manager manages a department and a team of staff. For her each department is like one of seven arms in the school. Believing in the importance of having cohesive and powerful departmental middle managers, as one weak department may weaken the whole system, she sees the value of developing the leadership of the middle managers. She believes that a lot of focus, money and time must be spent on them. She said:

> If you want to take leaps for the organisation, they [middle managers] are the ones you have to look out for. They are the ones you have to motivate, support, pour resources into, and do a lot of training because they are the ones managing all the critical arms. When they come together, they will become very powerful.

The principal adds that besides the vice principals and middle managers, she also relies on the leadership of other staff members. She explains that principals should be able to identify staff members who are leaders in their own right. She acknowledges that these leaders are able to form their own groups and taskforces, and as a result they are powerful energy sources complementing the middle managers. She feels that everyone in the school must feel that he or she has a role to contribute to the school. For example, a teacher who is people-oriented can be appointed as Head of the Staff Welfare Committee. Mdm Linda appointed leaders according to their abilities.

Connecting with people

The fourth component, 'Enable', denotes the principal's personal qualities, values and beliefs which impact on the execution of the other three components, 'Envision', 'Energize' and 'Engage' and characterize their leadership practices. Among her many attributes, Mdm Linda believes strongly in communicating with her staff to make clear policy and practice expectations, and she likes to connect deeply with people.

The principal likes to be with the staff and students to understand their needs and concerns. She enjoys talking to the staff and going to the grounds to be with the staff and students. To accommodate the large enrolment of students, the school operates two sessions, one session starts at 7.30 am and finishes at 1 pm while the other starts at 1 pm and finishes at 6.30 pm. As such, Mdm Linda tries to be present at both sessions in the school. She wants the school to know that whenever they need her, she will be there for them. Mdm Linda also sits among the teachers at informal sessions. She does things together with them so that she understands them better and to foster positive relationships with them. This work also supports the research evidence that principals can have a major effect on student learning outcomes by participating with teachers in professional learning (see Robinson, 2007).

Mdm Linda finds opportunities to connect with people in meaningful and respectful ways. For example, with the School Advisory Committee (SAC), she speaks the many languages of the members. The members are from diverse educational and social backgrounds, and so she communicates using different languages and dialects during meetings. She has to be sharp in understanding their needs and has to adopt different approaches for different groups of people as their needs vary:

> I have to switch gear and be a chameleon. I have to approach different groups of stakeholders differently. I need to look at the context of the stakeholders and look at their needs ... The way I carry myself, the tone that I use and the words I use, changes. As school leaders, we must be able to adjust our behaviour and actions when we are needed to.

Mdm Linda also works with principals locally and overseas to collaborate, exchange views, to learn together, and to ultimately benefit the school.

Connecting with the external environment

The oval furthest away from the centre, 'Embrace', exemplifies that regardless of conditions, successful school leadership practices are limited by uncontrollable internal and external factors.

In this Singapore example, internal factors include school culture (e.g. school direction, school image and school identity) and type of school (government or government-aided). At Robin Primary School, there is a culture that has promoted the use of technology to support teaching and learning and this orientation leads to connections with the wider environment to support this, but within the constraints of being a government primary school (refer to the next paragraph).

External factors include the uncontrollable economic and political contexts in which the school operates. In Singapore, accountability to bureaucracy is viewed as not only legitimate but important, as it is a small country with only people as the resource for creating economic prosperity. All schools then have to operate within an environment of economic and political demands which shape leadership practices such as endorsing the national vision, Thinking Schools Learning Nation, and realizing it by implementing the initiatives introduced by the MOE such as the Teach Less, Learn More, and school self-appraisal using the School Excellence Model.

Reflections

Mdm Linda's leadership is characterized by: her acknowledgement of the successes of previous principals and building on them; her skill in enabling others to take develop professionally; her ability to establish leadership throughout the school; and her ability to develop a collaborative culture. All this can be summed up by her capability of connecting with people.

Mdm Linda acknowledges the successes of past principals and builds on their successes. A feature of the ISSPP Singapore study, and shown in Mdm Linda's work, is the acknowledgment of the good work of previous principals, such as the school programs and the positive relationships with students and parents that had been developed. Mdm Linda saw her work as adding new elements to suit the current school context, and to further improve the school.

Having built upon the legacy of previous principals, Mdm Linda develops the capacity of her staff and worked with her stakeholders collaboratively. Mdm Linda values every member of staff in the school, as evident by a structured professional development plan. She develops leaders by building on the leadership and intellectual capacities of the teachers and middle managers. People development is vital in Singapore as the government makes it clear in its policies and schemes. At the national level, investing in education is on the national agenda to enhance human capacity which underpins Singapore's economic transformation and growth (Goh, 2005).

Mdm Linda's leadership is also characterized by working in collaboration within and outside the school community. Within the school community, Mdm Linda reaches out to the students. She listens to their voices through interacting with them on a daily basis. She believes in empowering the staff through shared decision making. Mdm Linda values parents as partners in education in supporting the learning and development of their children. She involves parents in school activities. Outside the school community, Mdm Linda builds bonds with the community such as during festive celebrations. As supported by research in Singapore (Khong & Ng, 2005; Ng, 2003) and from other studies, including research from several countries in the ISSPP (Notman & Henry, 2009; Raihani, 2007), successful principals typically develop and sustain positive relationships with stakeholders inside and outside the school community. In Singapore, the MOE advocates a tripartite partnership which involves the school, home and the community through the Community and Parents in Support of Schools program (Ministry of Education, 2000). Such partnership

> enables parents to get a better understanding of school goals, and develops a closer relationship with the teachers and principal; provides teachers with invaluable support in the process of educating our young; enriches the school environment and reinforces its mission; and allows the community to contribute to the life of the school and to establish lasting and meaningful links.
>
> (Ministry of Education, 2000, p. 4)

Schools in Singapore view stakeholders in education as vital partners and allies in the common journey of enhancing the quality of learning for all students through a deep sense of shared responsibility to create a learning environment for the children (Khong & Ng, 2005).

As a people-oriented leader, Mdm Linda believes that principals need to be selected and developed to emphasize service and moral purpose:

> school leaders must be somewhat well chosen and carefully chosen, if not it can corrupt the system. When we [principals] identify potential leaders to take over our seats, we also have to be very careful what we are looking for, if not we can tilt the scale and it will affect the landscape of education in Singapore. To me, I don't care about how well educated you are and what your IQ is, my main concern is they must have the heart for people and they must be willing to sacrifice and serve. If you cannot do that, you cannot be a school leader. Other organisation leaders look for other things but a school leader must be giving, must be able to sacrifice and must really care about the people, and that is the first step and other things can be learned.

This case demonstrates how appropriate values are an essential component of successful school leadership. Mdm Linda's values were formed from an early age, closely tied to family values, and continually shaped by a diverse range of experiences. The key value that stands out is respect for the students, families, staff and the wider community. This is demonstrated through honouring the past, encouraging all to be involved in the development of school values, building social capital to support students, building staff capacity, a commitment to developing the whole child, and transparent and open communication. Trust and commitment were established through 'walking the talk', and as such, Mdm Linda's espoused values were closely aligned to her actions and behaviour.

Four areas for reflection are suggested:

1 *Have you aligned your actions with your espoused values and beliefs?* Argyris and Schon (1998) outlined the importance of alignment between one's espoused theory and theory in use. It is important to reflect on your own value statements and examine how consistent they are with your actions. Understanding and closing the gap will promote trust and credibility between you as a leader and the followers in your school.

2 *How respectful are you to your colleagues, students, families and community?* Principals relate to a wide range of stakeholders who will inevitably have different perspectives, values and beliefs. Yet the principal needs to recognize and understand these differences, and demonstrate an understanding of each person as an individual (Bass & Avolio, 1997).

3 *As a principal do you engage in systems thinking?* Leaders are required to know how people, structures and processes connect. Senge (2006) noted the importance of systems thinking – understanding the interrelatedness within

organizations, and between organizations and the wider environment. Effective leaders see organizations as holistic, not fragmented, and are sensitive to change across a range of situations and environments. Leaders need to ask themselves how existing processes and systems get reviewed and improved over time.

4 *Do you act with integrity?* In other words are you true to yourself? Integrity is regarded by many as a corner stone of leadership (Badaracco & Ellsworth, 1993; Covey, 1993; Morrison, 2001). Integrity is the quality of being honest and having strong moral principles. Acting with integrity is not simply about how others see you, as it is also a way for leaders to stay true to themselves. The majority of leaders want to be able to look in the mirror and know that they see someone who is ethical, fair, and honest: someone with integrity.

While this case shows a number of qualities and behaviours that successful leaders demonstrate; the heart of good leadership comes from within. Based on her values, beliefs and personal qualities Mdm Linda remained true to herself while at the same time developing others and insisting on high expectations.

References

Argyris, Chris & Schon, Donald A. (1998) *Organisational Learning II: Theory, Method and Practice.* New York, Addison-Wesley.

Badaracco, J. L. and Ellsworth, R. (1993) *Leadership and the Quest for Integrity.* Boston, MA: Harvard Business School Press.

Bass, B. & Avolio, B. (1997) *Manual for the Multifactor Leadership Questionnaire.* California: Mind Gardens.

Covey, S. (1993) *Principled Centred Leadership,* New York and London: Simon & Schuster.

Dimmock, C. & O'Donoghue, T. (1997) *Innovative School Principals and Restructuring.* London: Routledge Falmer.

Drysdale, L., Goode, H. & Gurr, D. (2009) An Australian model of successful school leadership: Moving from success to sustainability, *Journal of Educational Administration,* 47(6), 697–708.

Goh, C.T. (2005) *People – A precious renewable resource.* Keynote Address by Senior Minister Goh Chok Tong, at the Jeddah Economic Forum on February 21, 2005,   S a u d i Arabia. Retrieved June 20, 2010, from http://app.mfa.gov.sg/pr/read_script.asp?View,4170,

Gronn, P. (1999) *The Making of Educational Leaders.* London: Cassell.

Gurr, D., Drysdale, L. & Mulford, B. (2006) Models of successful principal leadership, *School Leadership and Management,* 26(4), 371–395.

Khong, Y.L.L., & Ng, P.T. (2005) School–parent partnerships in Singapore. *Educational Research for Policy and Practice,* 4(1), 1–11.

Ministry of Education (2000) *Home, School and Community Partnerships.* Singapore: Ministry of Education.

Ministry of Education (2010) *Nurturing Our Young for the Future: Competencies for the 21st Century* (Singapore: Ministry for Education). Available at: www.moe.gov.sg/committee-of-supply-debate/files/nurturing-our-young.pdf

Mok, K.H. (2003) Decentralization and marketization of education in Singapore: A case study of the school excellence model. *Journal of Educational Administration*, 41(4), 348–366.

Morrison, A. (2001) Integrity and global leadership, *Journal of Business Ethics* 31(1), 65–76.

Ng, P.T. (2003) The Singapore school and the school excellence model. *Educational Research for Policy and Practice*, 2(1), 27–39.

Ng, P.T. & Chan, D. (2008) A comparative study of Singapore's school excellence model with Hong Kong's school-based management. *International Journal of Educational Management*, 22(6), 488–505.

Notman, R. & Henry, A. (2009) The human face of principalship: A synthesis of case study findings. *Journal of Educational Leadership, Policy and Practice*, 24(1), 37–52.

Raihani. (2007) Successful chool leadership in Indonesia: A study of the principals' leadership in three successful senior secondary schools in Yogyakarta. Unpublished Doctoral thesis, TUniversity of Melbourne, Australia.

Robinson, V. (2007) *School Seadership and Student Outcomes: Identifying What Works and Why*, *Monograph*, 41. Melbourne: Australian Council for Educational Leaders.

Senge, P M. (2006) *The Fifth Discipline: The Art and Practice of the Learning Organization* (Revised ed.). New York: Doubleday/Currency.

Wang, P. (2010) Successful school leadership in Singapore government schools. PhD thesis, University of Melbourne.

Part IV

Social justice

Chapter 14

Norway

Leadership for social justice: educating students as active citizens in a democratic society

Jorunn Møller and Gunn Vedøy

Introduction

The Nordic countries have exemplified a strong commitment to comprehensive education and social justice, inspired by social democratic politics for ensuring equality. The main justifications for democratic leadership in schools are grounded in the ideological purposes of education with a focus on promoting democracy as a fundamental social value and an ethical guide to citizenship. There might be disagreement about how to define democratic education, but most definitions will include the following set of qualities: recognition of the basic values and rights of each individual; considering other people's perspective; deliberation in making decisions; embracing plurality and difference; and promoting equity and social justice. In addition, a focus on developing a democratic community entails acknowledging that schools are sites of cultural and political struggles, and it is important to support interactions and negotiations that are characterized and distinguished by mutual trust and respect (Beane & Apple, 1999; Møller, 2006).

The following narrative of a Norwegian principal is based on data from one of the Norwegian schools that participated in the International Successful School Principalship Project. The school was also revisited five years later and the continuity of success was reflected in the principal's capacity to promote good relationships among staff members. The moral imperative of developing the whole child was still at the forefront. In the interview material as a whole there were many accounts that spoke of a strong dedication to cultivate an environment for learning that was humanly fulfilling and socially responsible, and teachers were expected to take significant responsibilities and decisions in their everyday work (Møller et al., 2009). It is a story of a principal who is very committed to working for social justice.

Brief description of the school and the principal

Brage is a combined primary and lower secondary school (grades 1–10) with 575 students, located outside Oslo in a town with roughly 30,000 inhabitants. The school has about 20 per cent students with minority language background and there are altogether 16 or 17 different first languages in the school. The enrolment area includes students from both high and low socio-economic status groups. One area consists of detached and terraced houses and has a high socio-economic standard. The other area consists of blocks of flats, inhabitants living under poor socio-economic conditions, many single parents, recipients of social welfare, and a high number of ethnic minorities. The principal, Birger, male and in his fifties, has a dual educational background; in special needs education on the one hand, and in economy and administration on the other. He has been principal of this school since it was opened in the late 1990s. Previous to his appointment at Brage he was a teacher and later the principal of a special needs education school for ten years. In addition he has been active in the teacher union and involved in project work for the local education authorities. Birger highlights his work with special needs education students and challenging students as experiences that have shaped his commitment to social justice and given him an eye for the challenged student that does not always fit in. He lives in the same municipality as the school, but in a more affluent area.

A story of leadership for social justice

At Brage we are met by an experienced and charismatic principal who is optimistic and committed in his pursuit of high expectations of achievement for all. He is also particularly well known in the local community for his successful work with students who require special needs education. In telling his story to the researchers about leadership, the principal is also negotiating who he is for others as well as for himself (Giddens, 1991). His story of leadership centres on the students with behavioural and learning difficulties. He demonstrates consideration for the weak, and portrays himself as a sort of spokesperson for people without a voice. This is shown in the way he talks about leadership in a language of values, where social justice, respect and equity can be described as core values. It is also shown through his emphasis on diversity and difference as values, in creating a school where there is space for everyone and where everybody feels that their voice is being heard and that they are taken seriously. His mission is reflected in the way the teachers are given supported responsibility in their jobs, and how participation and representation are treated in relation to matters of the parent council at the school.

Staging himself as a school principal through values

Birger's approach to leading a multicultural school may be characterized by an ethic of care for individuals as well as a concern for social justice. He portrays himself as very close to students. He emphasizes that he cares and has respect for both children and adults (Møller et al., 2009).

'Respect' is the key term for descriptions of relationships between majority and minority, or more specifically between people in general. Birger argues very strongly that one should not establish a dichotomy between discourses of social justice and working for high academic achievements among the students. Through an explicit discourse of critical multiculturalism based on respect, the principal is open to democratic processes (Vedøy & Møller, 2007). Birger's solution to success is structure, respecting the students, and focusing on learning processes, learning outcomes, and hard work. He has a clear sense of purpose about how to create a learning environment in which all children may not only feel they belong, but also in which they may be successful. He is proud of what he has accomplished. He comes across as energetic, humorous, engaged, and has a strong presence in the school. To the question about what qualifies and motivates him for the job, his answer is courage and commitment.

> It is all about courage and commitment. I am completely clear and consistent in that matter. I have told people around me that the day you see that I lose my commitment you have to tell me because then I have nothing more to give. Actually, I could in fact let go and sit in my office with budgets. There is more than enough to do, everybody would have understood. It is a big school with 70 employees and millions of budgets. ... But the day I do that, that is really the day I have to quit. Because then I have lost the spark. When I arrive in the morning and there is garbage on the stairs, I pick it up and throw it in the bin. The day I don't do that anymore, that is when I have to start to consider finding something else to do.
>
> (Birger)

Birger's motivation above all is probably to make a difference in children's and adolescents' lives, and to stand up for the values he is convinced are right and important. This is evident in the way the organization of teaching and education as a whole has been carried out at the school.

Equity and social justice as personal commitment

Birger is a hard-working principal, who works long hours every day. The students have the impression that he is everywhere in the school, and when we ask the teachers what would happen if the principal resigned, they answer:

Teacher 2:   I think it would be a disaster.
Teacher 1:   I think the school would have fallen apart.
Interviewer: Why?
Teacher 1:   Well, yes. It is Birger, he is a part of everything that is going on in this school ... from the individual young student to the largest team. He has a part in everything, he ...
Teacher 3:   He's here from you come till you leave, and he is here after you leave as well; you find much of his spirit in the walls here.

His presence and participation in the everyday life of both staff and students are emphasized. His expressed aim is that the students will do well later in life, and get to live meaningful lives, with as many prospects as possible. Everyone's responsibility for the community is strongly emphasized. Another aspect is that there should be room for everyone, and that everyone can participate with their bit and receive respect and recognition for that. This has resulted in a very low number of students who receive special needs education outside the school's mandatory work with adapted education. In addition the school has a group (ROT) constructed to work solely for adapted education where students who have behavioural or learning difficulties from time to time work with their individualized curricula. Birger stresses that the students connected to ROT have a high status in the school community. He explains this with the low tolerance for bullying. There are few instances of bullying at Brage, and the instances that occur are taken very seriously.

Ten per cent of the student population has transferred from other schools, after parental application. Birger states that they very often have one thing in common: They do not fit in anywhere. They are bullied and excluded in other schools. He makes clear that the tolerance for diversity is very high at Brage and that all students are entitled to respect and to be part of the school community.

This ideology of belonging and meaningful work is also applicable to the staff. As a principal he is persistently emphasizing that learning is hard work, and he has clear expectations of staff members and students concerning responsibility, challenge and support.

> If you take a look at our organization, the aim is to get a structure and climate that gives the staff support, help, advice, and guidance all the way. The senior-leadership team is extremely available; we never close our doors, you can turn up whenever you like. There is no case too big and no case too small. We support and help all the way.
>
> (Birger)

Through parent, student and teacher interviews, this impression is reinforced. They all give the impression that the level of trust in the principal and between groups in the school is very high.

Embracing plurality and difference

Birger's discourse has many similarities with critical multiculturalism (Kalantzis & Cope, 1999). He stresses the school's qualifying mandate; high expectations for minority students' language needs are in focus; the pedagogy is clearly formulated and made accessible; and the teachers' professionalism is emphasized (Vedøy & Møller, 2007). Although the argument in this section is about minority language students, it does not differ much from the argument concerning all students or students and teachers in general.

Birger: We have clear focus on the fact that we need to have high expectations of the minority language students, of their parents and of the teachers who give this type of tuition. We are on our way to reaching that goal, but we have very clear ambitions in getting better every day in that area. I think that this distinguishes us from the majority of schools that treat this area as an appendix to what they do ordinarily. And they have, in my opinion, a wrongly formulated goal. Their goal focuses on the differences; to nurture the differences instead of having clearly defined educational goals; goals related to nationality and being a student in Norway. They want to focus on the fact that a student is Pakistani, and want to nurture that part of the student. To us that is not satisfying. To us it is interesting what kind of educational needs that student has. And for the Pakistani student the aim is always to improve in the Norwegian language. In other schools, however, there is a sort of idea about grasping the cultural side and nourishing that, so that, and in many ways I think that deprives these students of the opportunity to learn Norwegian, by focusing on that …

Interviewer: By focusing on culture?

Birger: Yes, and paradoxically, it becomes an obstacle for improvement instead of the opposite. But we don't say that we don't want to focus on culture. We want to focus on culture when it is pedagogically right and necessary … But we have respect for the individual and each individual student. I think this pervades Brage School, too. And I think that this to a great extent has been essential when the school's pedagogical platform has been shaped in that we have enormous respect for our students, independently of ethnic background, cultural background and socio-economic background … it is something which has strong roots here, and I think that I, as the principal of this school, to a very large extent have influenced this mission.

The principal at Brage considers the school's task as providing their students with the best possible platform for living in Norway where language is the key to success both in higher education and occupationally. Hence, the school's priority number one is to promote the students' fluency in Norwegian. The focus is on possibilities and opportunities for students' future lives in Norway. The principal states that the students' home cultures are subordinated to this primary goal. This does not imply any form of neglect of students' home cultures. The individual minority home cultures are often referred to and spoken about in order for teachers to develop the understanding and respect necessary to help all students reach the primary goal. The principal also emphasizes that all students are different, and that this is an asset for the school. In that respect all students are included in the school community despite their differences.

Birger also regards difference and plurality as assets amongst the teachers. The staff consists of a heterogeneous group of teachers, but with focus on young teachers aged around thirty. In addition, teachers with minority backgrounds are recruited and there are almost as many men as women. Birger has had the opportunity to influence the employment of teachers at Brage. The plurality of teachers is a deliberate choice. The school is rather new, and the principal reports that they since the beginning have had lots of qualified applicants for each advertised position. Teacher teams are based on the concept of complementarity. It is expected that different teachers have responsibility in their subject of specialization. In that respect, all team members are mutually dependent on each other in order to give the students the best education possible.

Opportunities for open dialogue among staff

Leadership of the daily pedagogical work is delegated to teachers who have different functions in the school. The teachers are organized into six teams, led by a team leader. The team leaders are recruited amongst the teachers, and interested teachers can apply for the position at a yearly basis. Each team has in addition one teacher responsible for special needs education, and one teacher responsible for minority language education. The teams are the arenas for discussion. Matters of importance, also at school level, are to be discussed at team level. All team leaders have a seat in the school's extended leadership team, which meets every week. The senior leadership team at Brage, wants the team leaders to be active, to question practice, to provide time for reflection, and to lead the team in a professional manner. At the same time it is stressed that conflicts of loyalty might occur. Is the team leader's loyalty to the senior leadership team or to their fellow teachers? This has been a matter for discussion, and there is a consensus that the team leader needs to balance his or her loyalties as best he or she can.

Birger highlights the importance of effective systems and structures, and underlines that one has to focus on the resources one has, and make the best of it, instead of complaining about missing resources and regard that as an impediment. Teachers have the mandate to make their own decisions in most matters.

> We need to focus continuously on what we have, the opportunities we have. Then we will manage to exploit the energy in this system more positively. Decisions of actions are to be made at the lowest level possible. I am not preoccupied with details. If people have a problem, they have to solve it where they are in the organization. They don't have to ask me at all. I like to be informed of what is happening, but I have no desire to decide. We work in a systematic model, which says who does what, how, why and when.
>
> (Birger)

He makes the following reflections when it comes to the decisions he himself has to make:

Birger: … All matters which are important for running the school are to be discussed at team level. At the same time, I, as the principal, can say that this is a matter we do not discuss. I decide, and there is no need for a discussion. If I involve you in a democratic process now when I already have made up my mind, that is deceitful, that is "pretend – democracy". I have decided in the matter, I am the principal at this school and have authority to do so, in matters that are completely meaningless to discuss.

Interviewer: Do you often use your authority like that?

Birger: I think most of the teachers here are happy that I have a very clear view of direction. I think so. But I never interfere with details. Never details!

With this statement, the principal is very explicit. He presents himself as a leader who wants and takes responsibility, at the same time as the importance of democratic processes is highlighted. Birger acknowledges that not all teachers agree about every decision, but in the teacher interviews it appears that they find this overall to be a convenient arrangement.

Teacher 1:   I discuss with friends that work at other schools, and I believe we have much more freedom with responsibility. We have a very unique trust between top and bottom, so to speak. The trust between each other is very strong at this school. We trust each other and believe in each other and when you do something you're not supposed to, it is spoken about in an OK manner.

Teacher 2:   I remember Birger asking me what I thought about school discussion events. You know, when you have a meeting between teachers and the principal, and in many places everybody has to say something, whatever, even if it is the same thing as the last speaker. I remember answering no; I didn't think that was very effective. I am happy for that. … He decides on the big issues; he is the boss and I find that very reassuring as an employee.

Both teachers and the principal stress the high level of trust in the school

Active relationship with the local community

Democratic education entails an active relationship with the community (Starratt, 2002). When it comes to the school building, it is an important arena for the locals. After school hours, local clubs and organizations use the premises. Norwegian schools are legally obliged to cooperate with parents and the local community at group level through parent councils, as well as at the individual level. At Brage the principal stresses the importance of the individual relationship to parents:

Birger: And I tell them in everything I do, and in everything I write, if there is any kind of problem, please, contact us. Parents are invited to come out with even the smallest matter, really.
Interviewer: Do they?
Birger: Sure, but as I said, first, you ought to bring things up with the primary teacher. Always at the lowest level possible. There have never been conflicts at this school between parents and teachers like you find in other places. Never! We invite a high degree of openness, and a high degree of trust, and parents have a lot of confidence in us

Contact with parents is high and frequent at the individual level. At group level Birger reports an attempt to establish extensive student and parent participation in a management council when the school was new. Students, parents and teachers were represented together with the formal leaders in the council, and were supposed to have a say in all matters of importance at the school. According to Birger, this did not work well, and the school has reverted to the regular student and parent councils.

One of the matters they found problematic was that parents who got elected for council work were from the higher socio-economic group. The school had also experienced that elected parents were primarily engaged with their own children, and did not necessarily think in terms of the best for the school as a whole. Even though the enrolment area includes students from both high and low socio-economic status groups, only one socio-economic group was represented. The question whether it was most appropriate to relate to the parents as one single group, or as parents as consisting of different interest groups was raised. This became a dilemma for the leadership team. Their way of handling the dilemma was to create a committee with parents from different interest groups in the community. The function of this committee is advisory in matters where there are conflicts between parents and the school. According to Birger this is something that almost never happens.

Reflections

Birger is an experienced and charismatic principal. When he talks it is possible to distinguish quite defining narratives. First, he emphasizes persistently that learning is hard work, and that everyone has to accept that fact. A second narrative is about the importance of systems and structures at the school. As a principal he has clear expectations of staff members and students related to responsibility, challenge and support. But first and foremost, this is a narrative of a principal who is driven by his commitment to social justice and who works hard within the system to balance all the demands placed on his shoulder in order to ensure more equitable learning environments for all students. He has a quite distinct approach to leading a multicultural school with focus on the existing resources and making the best out of them, instead of complaining about missing resources. He is optimistic and persistent in his pursuit of high expectations of achievement for all.

Democratic education implies recognition of the basic values and rights of each individual; considering other people's perspectives; deliberation in making decisions; embracing plurality and difference; and promoting equity and social justice (Beane & Apple, 1999). The principal at Brage School has participated through trial and error in developing a school with a high degree of respect for the individual student. The goal has been to educate students as active citizens in a democratic society, where everybody has a responsibility to the community, but also vice versa. The daily work at Brage is built on the idea that a democratic education has to be lived. To enable students to reach this goal, students' basic skills are emphasized, and the teachers emphasize an open, accessible pedagogy. When Birger talks about student learning, he refers to educational theories about learning. It is possible for all stakeholders to agree or disagree, and it opens up opportunities for professional conversations and discussions at school level. The school's procedure is for open and democratic processes to explain and give reasons for educational practice. Ideas and values in the pedagogical practice are thus made explicit and accessible for the parties involved. When decisions are made from those open and democratic processes, the main rule is that all stakeholders pull in the same direction. By showing a will to engage in problematic issues, the concept of democracy is given substance. To a certain extent, an exception is the parent council decreed by law. The argument for choosing a different strategy in this area is an idea that the parent council works undemocratically.

In this chapter we have presented a narrative of an individual school principal; it is about his mission and how he is taking responsibility for leading the school. To him leadership is about values, processes, relationships, substance, and hard work. One problem with such a narrative is that the focus on individual actions fails to capture the significance of interactions and that the leadership practice may be enabled or constrained by structures, routines and tools (Spillane, 2006). But the fact that leadership practice extends beyond school principals, does not undermine the vital role of the principal in school leadership, and school principals actively engage in creating the persona they want to become, and the persona they think their staff and superiors expect them to become.

The narrative of Birger is not meant to be a universal possibility, but an *inspiration* to think about school leadership. Individual agency is important. As a school leader one has to work within the dominant structures of power and authority. A challenge is to demonstrate responsiveness to this context rather than compliance. The way school principals respond to the external accountability probably depends on their capacity of being professionals and involving themselves in internal evaluation of practice (Elmore, 2006).

Based on Birger's narrative about leadership for social justice, six areas for reflection are suggested:

1   *What is the driving force for you as a principal? What motivates you to pursue new educational opportunities, and how can you make a difference in students' lives?* It is important to reflect on how and what shapes one's leadership identities.

Identity integrates the meanings behind the skills and knowledge of leaders and reflects the rationale for enacting the role as well as influencing the ways the role is enacted by individual leaders (Sugrue, 2005).

2   *What is considered as successful principalship in your context?* How the principal frames a successful school will probably influence his or her approach to getting involved with teaching and learning. Therefore, it is important to reflect on what is a good school for you?

3   *How can you include stakeholders at the local level in the struggle for a more democratic and just society? Whose voices are allowed to be heard? Which stakeholders are listened to, and how is it possible to facilitate arenas for the many voices?* Leadership for social justice calls for a collective endeavour in the local community and the wider society, but how do you cope with such a challenge?

4   *How does your leadership in your school generate and support social justice, and how much can be expected of you as a principal?* Working for social justice is in many ways a thankless task, considering the goal is more or less impossible to reach. The job as such can therefore never be completed, and the workload can become heavy. As a school leader one also has to work within the dominant structures of power and authority. Is it possible to initiate and exercise oppositional power to become voices for change and transformation in your context?

5   *How would you describe the present model of accountability in your context and to whom and in which ways are you accountable?* The meaning of 'good work' is contested across contexts, and often economic interests or demands of efficiency overshadow collective and public interests. The focus can be on raising test scores instead of serious concern about how to promote good education for all children. The challenge is to find ways of combining working for high academic achievement on the part of the students with working for social justice in your context.

6   *What steps can you take to foster trusting relationships with teachers, students, parents, and the local community, and what are the signs that trust is present in your schools?* Trust is critical to the achievement of goals that require sustained collective effort. Trust is the glue that holds things together and it creates the conditions and mobilizes people to action and collaboration. The principal is probably crucial in building these conditions for encouraging democratic participation since trust and power within an organization are so closely interrelated.

Successful leadership should not be separated from deeper philosophical and political questions because education is essentially a moral enterprise. Success always requires that we ask: Success in or for what? Success for whom? Who benefits? And finally, success under what conditions? At a time when performance measurement and managerial accountability are at the forefront of educational policy across countries, the principal's conscious construction of his or her leadership identity is crucial. The Norwegian principal case study emphasizes that it is important not to lose those aspects of leadership that make it ethical and capable of sustainable and deep-rooted change.

References

Beane, J. A., & Apple, M. W. (1999). The case for democratic schools, in M. W. Apple & J. A. Beane (Eds.), *Democratic Schools: Lessons from the Chalk Face* (Buckingham: Open University Press), pp. 1–26.

Elmore, R. (2006). Leadership as the practice of improvement, in B. Pont, D. Nusche & D. Hopkins (Eds.), *Improving School Leadership. Volume 2: Case Studies on System Leadership.* (Paris: OECD Publishing), pp. 37–69.

Giddens, A. (1991). *Modernity and Self-Identity* (Cambridge: Polity Press).

Kalantzis, M. & Cope, B. (1999). Multicultural education: Transforming the mainstream, in S. May (Ed.), *Critical multiculturalism* (London: Falmer Press), pp. 245–276.

Møller, J. (2006). Democratic schooling in Norway: Implications for leadership in practice, *Leadership and Policy in Schools*, 5(1), pp. 53–69.

Møller, J., Vedøy G., Presthus, A. M., & Skedsmo, G. (2009). Fostering learning and sustained improvement – the influence of principalship, *European Educational Research Journal*, 7(3), pp. 359–371.

Spillane, J. P. (2006). *Distributed Leadership* (San Francisco, CA: Jossey-Bass).

Starratt, R. J. (2002). Community as curriculum, in K. Leithwood (Ed.), *Second International Handbook of Educational Leadership and Administration* (Dordrecht: Kluwer Academic Publishers), pp. 321–348.

Sugrue, C. (Ed.) (2005). *Passionate Principalship: Learning from Life Histories of School Leaders* (London: RoutledgeFalmer).

Vedøy, G. & Møller, J. (2007). Successful school leadership for diversity. Examining two contrasting examples of working for democracy in Norway, *International Studies in Educational Administration*, 35(3), pp. 58–67.

USA

Culturally-responsive leadership

*Betty Merchant, Encarnacion Garza
and Elizabeth Murakami Ramalho*

The principal and the school

Laura Martinez is in her third year as a principal at Grande Academy. We have been observing her leadership for the past six years when she transferred from Stephens Elementary School located in the center of a large urban area in South Texas, to a newly constructed school in the southern portion of the same district. In both schools, her culturally-responsive leadership is evidenced in her advocacy for the children and families she serves, the majority of whom are Hispanic. As a Hispanic native of the city, Ms. Martinez's background is similar to that of her students, and the community knows that Ms. Martinez and the students understand each other well.

Although the purpose of this chapter is to examine Ms. Martinez's leadership experiences at Grande Academy, a brief overview of her experiences at Stephens Elementary is helpful in understanding the continuity that was evidenced in her leadership style, as she moved from one school context to another. During the eight years she was principal at Stephens, the school received incrementally higher ratings each year for the students' performance on state-mandated achievement exams by the Texas State Accountability System (TEA, 2010).

The high performance of students at Stephens did not go unnoticed; one year, there were allegations of cheating on the state standardized tests. Stephen's third grade students scored in the top 5 percent of the state, which was much higher than the consistently high-scoring schools in the surrounding districts and state. Accusations of cheating were made by members of affluent communities who could not believe that the students in a poor, predominantly Hispanic school could outperform the students in more affluent, predominantly White schools. The district, in response, instituted an Integrity Review to examine records, performance indicators, and testing procedures. The committee reported that the accusations were unfounded. "We were just doing a good job with our kids," attested Ms. Martinez, "but the allegations hurt our reputation and our trust in the system."

When we visited Ms. Martinez at Stephens Elementary, her promotion of community relationships was very apparent. As Gurr *et al.* (2005) indicated, it is important that principals create an ethos of schools as "community-centered organizations" when building social capital within a school (p. 545). To achieve such an ethos, Ms. Martinez organized important community-building events. For example, there was a poster announcing a Dad and Daughter Dance, for which godfathers, grandfathers, uncles and dads signed up to dance with students at the annual Fall Festival. Such activities provided important and greatly needed family connections to the school, as well as invaluable opportunities to build relationships with students and their families. All of these important community-building activities were contextually and culturally relevant, and sensitive to the fact that families in the community were often struggling economically (For a detailed description of Ms. Martinez's leadership experiences at Stephens Elementary School, see Murakami *et al.*, 2010.)

In addition, Ms. Martinez carried high expectations, monitored student progress, supported teachers and parents, and assisted students academically and socially. Teachers at Stephens confirmed that Ms. Martinez had high expectations from them, but they also acknowledged that she "meant business." In her last year at Stephens, the teachers awarded Ms. Martinez with a little trophy representing a lightning bolt, engraved with the letters TCB (Taking Care of Business). We believe that Ms. Martinez was instrumental in the continued success of the school, through her mentorship of the principal who succeeded her.

Ms. Martinez left Stephens in 2008 to assume the principalship of the newly constructed Grande Academy, the only campus built in this district since 1966. The school is located near one of the 13 historic frontier Missions built along the city's river in 1718 by the Franciscans, the Spanish colonizers, and Native Americans. The student-decorated campus reflects its rich local history. This campus is designated as an academy, that serves grades Pre-K-8; while the other elementary schools in the district serve grades Pre-K-5. During the first year of operation (2008–9) the school served only grades PK-6. Grades 7 and 8 were phased in one year at a time. According to the state Academic Excellence Indicator System (TEA, 2009, 2010), the total student enrollment in the first year was 425. The total enrollment in the second year (2009–10) was 570, and in the third year (2010–11) 620 students.

Experience in becoming a principal

Laura Martinez is a product of the Mira Vista Independent School District (MVISD) in which she has served as an educator all her professional life. She was born deep in the inner city in a community commonly referred to as the "Westside." Ms. Martinez is the only child of parents who emigrated from Mexico in the early 1950s. Upon their arrival from Mexico, her parents rented a home and a few years later bought a home in the Stephens Elementary School neighborhood.

Her family lived in the district all their lives and Ms. Martinez attended and graduated from MVISD schools. Her parents were very involved with her education during her elementary years and they encouraged and supported her the best way they knew. However, they could not protect her from the low expectations imposed on students like Ms. Martinez in high school, where her counselor told her that she should not even attempt to apply for college:

> I didn't know that college was a priority in my life when I graduated because I remember hearing over and over again that I just wasn't college material as many of us were told in high school ... I didn't think I was going to go to college because I was told I was probably not going to make it.

She was encouraged, like so many of her classmates, to consider secretarial work, and she was enrolled in shorthand and typing classes. In spite of the lack of guidance and support from school, Ms. Martinez went to junior college after graduating from high school:

> I went to college and found out that everything they told me was kind of true. I had to take remedial courses and everybody I knew was in the class taking remedial courses. And nobody really prepared us for college. I don't know if it was because we're Hispanic ... I don't know because I wasn't a failing student, but still I did show up and I went. Yeah I did go. I went to college for about a year only.

Ms. Martinez quit college and went to work for the MVISD as a library aide at one of the inner-city middle schools. After about a year on the job, she took pregnancy leave for what she thought would be a few months, but she did not return to the district until 18 years later:

> I stayed home for 18 years ... when my baby was in fourth grade I told my husband I needed to go back and do what I've always wanted to be, and that was a teacher. I wanted to go back to school and get my degree ... I guess I was in my late thirties.

Once Ms. Martinez decided she was going back to college, she was totally committed to her studies. She enrolled in a private university and earned her bachelor's degree in less than three years. Without taking a break, she enrolled in graduate school and received a master's degree with a major in curriculum and instruction. Ms. Martinez continued with her studies and earned a second master's degree in administration and bilingual education.

Ms. Martinez was determined to come back to start her teaching career in the MVISD. Even though the private university she attended did not place any of their student teachers in this district, she found a way to get them to approve her student teacher placement in the MVISD.

> I got my Bachelor's degree and I said, "I want to work with the MVISD district" and they said "No, the school we're wanting you to go to is in the

Suburb School District." Knowing that my heart was over here I wanted to come back to MVISD, I drove myself up to an MVISD elementary … spoke to the principal and I told him "I'm getting ready to do student teaching and I'd really like to do it in your school"… He introduced me to a teacher there and I started student teaching there.

Laura Martinez' path to the principalship was not traditional. She took time to raise her children as a stay-at-home mother and did not earn her bachelor's degree until she was in her thirties. Ms. Martinez was hired as an elementary teacher at Stephens and taught only three years in the classroom before she was encouraged to apply for an assistant principal position. She served as an assistant principal for three years, and then her principal decided to retire. When she expressed interest in applying for the position of principal, her principal said that she was not ready, and that he would not recommend her. Instead, he explained, he was going to support and recommend the curriculum instruction coordinator.

Despite her principal's lack of support, Ms. Martinez submitted her application anyway. While the decision was being considered, she was reassigned to another campus to serve as assistant principal. She did not have much hope that her application would be seriously considered, so she accepted the challenge of her new assignment and decided that she would make the best of this new opportunity. While attending a working breakfast with Mr. Alvarez, her new principal, at a local restaurant, she unexpectedly met the superintendent. She knew who he was but had never met him personally. Her principal introduced her to Dr. Gonzalez, the superintendent, and they shook hands, exchanged a few words, and he left. A few minutes later, the cashier came to their table asking for Ms. Martinez. "Not more than 15 to 20 minutes later the cashier comes to me, the girl at the register comes to the table and she says, 'Are you Ms. Martinez? Yes, you have a phone call.'" She had no idea who it could possibly be because nobody knew she was at this restaurant. To her surprise, it was the superintendent asking her to come to his office. Her principal told her she was going to be a principal if the superintendent was calling her personally. She was nervous; she did not know why he wanted to meet with her:

> Mr. Alvarez says, "You're going to be principal", and I said "Mr. Alvarez if you only knew the problems I was having with the other principal … I don't know, I don't think so … maybe there's something else going on." I was real nervous about the visit. Dr. Gonzalez opens the door and I walk in to meet with him … he says "So you're Laura Martinez? You've kept us real busy, we've had so many calls from the community and the teachers, they want you back as principal at Stephens. Do you want to be principal at Stephens?" "Yes I do sir. Yes I do!"

The superintendent told her that he was going to recommend her at the school board meeting that same evening and warned her not to tell anyone. The school board accepted the superintendent's recommendation and Laura Martinez became principal at Stephens Elementary.

Ms. Martinez's key accomplishments at Grande Academy

At Grande Academy, as at Stephens Elementary School, it is possible to observe Ms. Martinez's commitment to parents and families. Her experiences growing up in the district, and her bilingual skills provide her with emotional and cultural connections to the families with whom she works, the majority of whom are Hispanic. This, in turn, contributes to her success in creating a school where families felt invited, and welcomed. It is evident to us that Ms. Martinez's leadership is a major reason for the success of Grande Academy. Her commitment to children is non-negotiable; she demands and earns the same commitment from her teachers, students and parents.

Ms. Martinez was born in this school district, it is where she went to school, and it is where she will work until she decides to retire. She expressed what she hoped she would be remembered for and the legacy she hopes to establish:

> Well what I would truly like to leave is pride in the students. I want the students to feel proud to say they were here at Grande ... that they had good experiences. I want them to be proud of where they are and who they are.

Facing challenges in the principalship

The first group of children who were required to enroll in Grande Academy adapted quickly, but the parents and especially the teachers, initially resisted the changes associated with re-locating to a new school. This presented a significant challenge for Ms. Martinez. Initially, she thought that it was going to be exciting to open a new school, but she underestimated the resistance she would encounter from the adults.

Many inner-city school districts in the United States face the out migration of families to the suburbs, and this is also the case in MVISD. As a consequence, such districts face declining enrollment, and the families who do remain, often do so because they lack the financial resources to move elsewhere. In the first year at Grande Academy, most of the students came from schools that were closed due to low enrollment, while others came because of redrawn attendance boundaries. Although most students were excited about coming to a new campus, many parents were not happy about the closure of their neighborhood schools. The district's methods for re-locating students to the new school were often unsatisfactory to parents who had other children enrolled in middle and high schools that were located in their neighborhoods but were far from Grande Academy.

Staffing the school was another challenge that Ms. Martinez faced. She was really hoping to bring teachers from Stephens Elementary, her former school. The district required that before she could hire any new teachers, she would first be required to recruit teachers from the six elementary schools that were being shut down because of significantly declining enrollment, as well as the other schools whose enrollment was reduced because of redrawn attendance boundaries. Principals who had to cut teachers because of lower enrollment viewed this as an opportunity to "get rid" of their less effective teachers. And Ms. Martinez had no choice but to accept all of these teachers who were reassigned to her campus.

> I never had an opportunity to at least interview some of the teachers. [The principals were] having problems with the majority of the teachers that were sent over. So they were like hand-picked [by principals who essentially told them] "If you're causing me problems, you're going …"

In the first year, all the teachers came from another campus; which made it impossible for Ms. Martinez to select her own staff: "They didn't allow me to bring anybody from Stephens. They said it would be a conflict." Most teachers were resistant, they did not want to be there and they manifested their discontent openly:

> it truly was a battle every step of the way. Anything I wanted to do just wasn't right. It looked like everything that I was doing, that I wanted to do, just wasn't good enough, that I was not going to replace that principal they had.

A third challenge pertained to the lack of support that Ms. Martinez's district-level supervisor provided to her during the staffing process. This lack of support was manifested throughout the first year, as evidenced in the supervisor's disregard of requests for materials and basic supplies as well as her unresponsiveness to telephone calls and emails from the school. Ms. Martinez expected her supervisor to help her get the school off to a good start, but she got the sense that she did not want her to be successful in her new position. "You know I felt again … unsupported by my … the person that I'm supposed to rely on to say you know we want to make sure this is going to be a successful school."

Ms. Martinez's resilience and persistence helped her navigate and overcome the challenges she encountered as the new principal at Grande Academy. The greatest challenge, however, came from the state and federal accountability systems. In MVISD, principals have been informed that they will be removed and reassigned if they do not achieve at least a recognized rating according to the state accountability system. This pressure was evident in Ms. Martinez; she expressed that she was experiencing high levels of stress related to meeting the standards associated with the federal No Child Left Behind Act (NCLB) of 2001 and the Texas state level accountability systems.

The stress of the state and federal accountability systems was a recognizable source of high anxiety. However, we learned that even under the most severely stressful conditions resulting from high stakes testing and the accountability system,

Ms. Martinez was not willing to let students fail. As we observed and interacted with Ms. Martinez and her staff, it was not difficult to detect the pressure they felt from their supervisors to maintain *recognized* and *exemplary* ratings. We also observed her self-imposed commitment to stay at the top of these ratings. Martinez's loyalty to the district and passion to serve in this community is evident: "I want to tell you in spite of everything, in spite of all the lack of support that I've experienced, my heart is in this district. I love this district with a passion."

We are struck by the strong sense of personal efficacy that Ms. Martinez displayed early on, when she enrolled in junior college despite her high school counselor's exhortation that she was not "college material." The fact that her parents were very supportive and involved in her schooling undoubtedly strengthened Ms. Martinez's resolve to achieve higher educational goals than those suggested by her teachers or counselors. Despite the fact that she left college after a year, she remained committed to becoming a teacher, and after 18 years of marriage and several children, she entered a four year college in her late thirties, completed her bachelor's degree in less than three years, and, without a break in her studies, went on to earn the first of two master's degrees. Not only was she able to enjoy the unwavering support of her parents, she also had the encouragement and support of her husband.

In considering the nature and extent of support she received from her district, the direct intervention of the superintendent was certainly instrumental in obtaining her first principalship, but he played no obvious role in her being selected for the second principalship. There was, however, one individual from the district's central office that played a significant, albeit highly negative, role in Ms. Martinez's efforts to lead her new school. The direct supervisor assigned to her was extremely unsupportive during her transition to Grande Academy, but Ms. Martinez never informed the superintendent about her conflicts with this supervisor. Instead, she waged a seemingly unending battle with her the first year, in order to obtain vital supplies and the additional teachers needed to respond to the school's growing student population. Ms. Martinez found ways to secure the resources she needed, but the stress associated with the lack of support from her supervisor exacted a significant toll on her that was evident in her conversations with us. Fortunately, a different supervisor was assigned to her in the third year of the school, and the relationship between them is proceeding smoothly.

With respect to the teachers who were involuntarily assigned to her, rather than becoming confrontational with them, Ms. Martinez made a conscious effort to understand their concerns and actively sought ways of easing their transition to the school. Asking the teachers to share the things that worked well in their previous schools, for example, gave them an opportunity to integrate some of their favorite activities and procedures into their new environment.

Although she was frustrated and challenged by the attitudes of the teachers, she knew that she needed to acknowledge their concerns and feelings. She decided that in order to move ahead, she had to nurture her teachers and gain their trust and support:

They're here, and I have to give them time to grieve because they were comparing me [to their previous principal]. "That's not the way we did things" [they'd say]… When we met, I said, "I want you all to submit anything that you did at your other school that you feel we should do here because I want to make this ours."

Ms. Martinez created an environment of collaboration, but she was also clear about her expectations:

I had to create an environment. I had to create a culture; I had to somehow together come up with the rules, the expectations. I had to share with them the things I've done at my school and I said I'm not willing nor will I stop at any measures not to be exemplary. We will be exemplary. Although they came from low performing, from acceptable, recognized campuses none of them had ever experienced exemplary.

This respectful and sensitive approach to her teachers was critical to her ability to co-create an environment in which everyone felt welcome and valued.

Ms. Martinez continues to be deeply involved in her community, and knows the families of all of her students. She organizes social events at the school that attract large, enthusiastic crowds of people, and she participates in the activities that the community sponsors. She is well known by parents and is immediately recognized as she moves about the community.

Reflections

Ms. Martinez's case provides an example of culturally-responsive leadership. We used Johnson's (2007) lens of culturally-responsive leadership, which considers social justice practices that recognize the students' diverse cultures, considers community and family involvement, and aims to advocate for societal change. We believe that her uniform perception of the children is strong evidence of her predisposition to view all students in a respectful and positive manner. This belief in the students permeates the culture of Ms. Martinez's schools and significantly shapes the interactions of faculty, staff and students within these schools.

This culturally-responsive case provides a better understanding of the factors that have contributed to Ms. Martinez's success as a principal of two schools in very different circumstances. Although there were significant differences in how she described her initial experiences with the parents and teachers in each of the schools, she described the children in both schools as "excited" about being there. As we reflected on our work with Ms. Martinez, we came to realize and understand that "successful" school leadership is more than high test scores; it is about commitment to students from a social justice perspective. We learned that, even under the most severely stressful conditions that resulted from high stakes testing and the accountability system, Ms. Martinez and her teachers were not willing to let their students fail.

As we observed and interacted with Ms. Martinez and her staff, it was easy to detect, not only the pressure she felt from her district supervisor to maintain the recognized and exemplary ratings, but also her self-imposed commitment to staying at the top of the achievement scale. Although the pressure of the state and federal accountability systems was a source of high anxiety, what actually motivated this principal and her teachers was their intrinsic motivation to serve children and their passion for providing students with all the opportunities they needed to experience success.

The district viewed Ms. Martinez as a successful principal because her students performed exceptionally well on the state exam. What made her an extraordinary leader, however, was her genuine sense of care that helped to form meaningful relationships among all the stakeholders in the school community. Parents felt invited, students felt good about themselves, and the teachers felt supported and appreciated.

Ms. Martinez felt that it was her moral obligation to make sure that all her students performed well on these assessments in order to get political permission to teach them more than the "basics." She was convinced that her students needed to know more than what was measured in the state assessments if they were going to be prepared to respond to the challenges and opportunities they would encounter in life. For Ms. Martinez and her teachers, learning the "basics" was not enough to be successful in today's global society.

Additionally, we learned that Ms. Martinez was a hands-on leader who was involved personally with her students, teachers, parents, and all of her staff. She was Hispanic and communicated with her parents in Spanish if they did not speak English. Ms. Martinez trusted her teachers and gave them autonomy; she did not worry about the "how" but she was extremely clear about the "what."

1   *Principals' personal experiences can play a critical role in the development of their personal and professional ethics. How do these experiences enrich and inform the leadership practices of principals?* Engaging principals in reflecting on the ways in which their personal experiences shape their interactions with students and their families, teachers and staff members can provide principals with important insights into how these experiences: a) both limit and enhance their effectiveness in working with others, and b) illustrate the need for specific areas of improvement in their leadership practice.

2   *It is frequently argued that effective school leadership in an increasingly diverse society requires principals who are culturally-responsive to their various constituents. What are some of the attributes that principals should possess to be successful in schools with diverse populations of students? How is culturally-responsive leadership different from other leadership styles?* In high poverty schools with large proportions of students from groups historically marginalized in mainstream educational settings,

it is crucial that principals insist on a positive, responsive school culture that holds high expectations for all students

3   *Today's educational environment requires principals who can integrate social justice practices with demands for accountability. What social justice practices can motivate students and teachers to improve the academic performance of students?* Ms. Martinez was aware of the low expectations that were associated with predictions of her students' performance on the state's high stakes assessments but she did not accept this view of her students' ability. Although other principals in the district did not commonly participate in the kind of outreach activities in which Ms Martinez engaged, her work with parents and community members was critical in gaining their support for improving the achievement levels of the students in her school.

We believe that Ms. Martinez's success as a principal is rooted in a strong sense of self-efficacy that is nurtured by a supportive family, a passionate and unwavering commitment to her students, and a strong belief in the importance of reaching out to community members to enlist their assistance in promoting high standards for their children. Less so, but still important, is the fact that Ms. Martinez's superintendent was attentive to the parents in her first school, responsive to their positive opinions of her, and willing to use his authority to appoint her to her first position as principal.

After reviewing the findings from this case study, we conclude that, more than any single factor, it is the combination of the factors described above that that has contributed to Ms. Martinez's ability to effect consistently high levels of student performance and to earn continued recognition from the state for the academic achievement of the students in the schools she leads.

References

Gurr, D., Drysdale, L. & Mulford, B. (2005). Successful principal leadership: Australian case studies. *Journal of Education Administration*, 43(6), pp. 539–551.

Johnson, L. (2007). Rethinking successful school leadership in challenging U.S. schools: Culturally responsive practices in school-community relationships, *International Studies in Educational Administration*, 35(3), 49–57.

Murakami. E., Garza, E., Merchant, B. (2010). Successful school leadership in socio-economically challenging contexts: School principals creating and sustaining successful school improvement. *International Studies in Educational Administration*, 32(2), 1–24.

TEA (2010). Academic Excellence Indicator System. Accessed January 2011, at http://ritter.tea.state.tx.us/perfreport/aeis/index.html.

Chapter 16

Indonesia

Leading an Islamic school in a multicultural setting in Indonesia

Raihani, David Gurr and Lawrie Drysdale

Introduction – a culturally diverse setting

In the International Successful School Principalship Project school leadership has been explored in contexts as diverse as Cyprus, Norway and the United States of America (Johnson *et al.* , 2011). One of the tensions indentified by principals in these countries has been finding the balance between honouring student home cultures whilst emphasizing student learning outcomes. Johnson *et al.* (2011) show that it is a complex leadership responsibility to lead culturally diverse schools. There is a need to be culturally responsive, but also a social justice imperative to improve student learning outcomes. The problem in many contexts is that the student learning outcomes that are most valued are those that privilege the dominant cultural group.

In this chapter we explore the work of Mr Mulyono, the principal of *Madrasah Aliyah Negeri* (MAN: public Islamic senior secondary day school) school in Palangkaraya, Central Kalimantan. This study extends our knowledge of successful school leadership in Indonesia (see Raihani, 2007; Raihani & Gurr, 2006) and was part of a research project Raihani has been involved in about education for multicultural and tolerant Indonesia funded by Australia Research Council (ARC). In this study, six different secondary schools were selected in two provinces, Yogyakarta and Central Kalimantan. In these schools, we interviewed the principals, teachers, students, parents and community figures to explore amongst other aspects how the principals exercise leadership in the context of multicultural society like the two provinces. For the purpose of this chapter, however, we present only MAN in Palangkaraya for its constant outstanding improvement relative to other similar schools in the province.

Indonesia, the largest Muslim country in the world in terms of population, also has great cultural diversity. The Palangkaraya area is rich in diverse cultural groups and a little of the history of this area is needed to understand why Mr Mulyono's work is worth attention. Whilst MAN is a school for Muslim children staffed by Muslim teachers, both students and staff come from diverse cultural backgrounds that reflect this complex part of the world.

Background

The province of Central Kalimantan was established in 1957 after negotiation by its people to have their own province independent from the whole Kalimantan, which at that time was centred on Banjarmasin, now the capital of South Kalimantan. The population in this province represents less than 1 per cent of the total population of Indonesia, and it was, until recent times, relatively under-developed. The major cultural group is the indigenous Dayak, which has several tribes and many sub-tribes who have been known to fight amongst each other at least up to the end of the nineteenth century. More recently, unresolved long-standing social and economic conflicts between Dayak and the migrant Madura people (an ethnic group from East Java) resulted in a civil war in 2001. The capital city of Central Kalimantan in Palangkaraya is inhabited by people of more diverse backgrounds compared to other districts in the province, and includes ethnic groups such as Java (the dominant Indonesian ethnic group), Banjar (a dominant ethnic group in South Kalimantan), and Batak (from North Sumatra). People of these groups adhere to different religions and faiths (such as Islam, Protestant Christian, Catholic Christian, Hindu, Buddhist, Kaharingan, and Confucian), but the majority of population in Palangkaraya are Muslims, with Protestants the second largest group. Despite the number of Muslims, the Protestant Dayaks have major political control in the area, and this is often a source of tension between groups. So, the area in which My Mulyono is a principal is a melting pot of different cultural groups, and there are tensions within and between these groups.

As well as this, people from outside the area are sometimes regarded with suspicion. This is a problem as the need to develop this area has meant that the central Indonesian government has sent many people from more populated and developed areas to run government agencies, and in particular, to be teachers and school administrators. This was particularly true at the time of the New Order (1966–1998) where a transmigration policy was intensively implemented, and Central Kalimantan, lacking in capable human resources, was the subject of an influx of qualified outsiders taking over responsible positions such as school principal. Mr Mulyono is one of these people, and the local people would already know this by his name, which indicates he is of Javanese background. Mr Mulyono is therefore not only charged with leading a school in a culturally diverse community, but doing as an 'outsider'.

There is more complexity to Mr Mulyano's role and this concerns the type of school he leads, which we now describe.

Islamic day schools

Indonesia has dualism in education with general or secular schools administered by the Ministry of Education and Culture (MOEC) and Islamic schools administered by the Ministry of Religion (MR). Islamic schools in Indonesia comprise less than 20 per cent of all school enrolments, but in a country as populated as Indonesia nevertheless serve a large number of students. There are two major types of Islamic school in Indonesia, namely *madrasah* or Islamic day schools and *pesantren* or Islamic boarding schools. In 2007, the total number of *madrasah* across Indonesia constituted nearly 40,000 schools (17.4 per cent of all schools excluding kindergarten and tertiary levels; see, Pusat Statistik Pendidikan, 2008). While all *pesantren* are owned by private groups or individuals, a few *madrasah* are public. Since the majority of *madrasahs* are privately owned, *madrasahs* have suffered from a lack of proper attention from the government. After the issue of the regional autonomy law in 1999, both *madrasahs* and general schools continued to receive funding from the central government. But, unlike the general schools, madrasahs cannot receive funds from local district government because it is considered a vertical institution which remains under the central government's control. This situation has made *madrasahs* like a second-class school system. Some local governments, however, are willing to support *madrasahs* in their jurisdiction through non-education funding schemes or other schemes that are not characterized as education programs.

The school that Mr Mulyono leads is a public *madrasah* operating at a senior secondary level. The students enrolled in this madrasah are aged from 15 to 18. When he came to this school as a teacher in 1988, eight years after its establishment, it only had 82 students across the three years of senior secondary schooling. The building and facilities were very poor, which made Mr Mulyono ponder how the school was left behind compared to similar schools in Java. Transportation from and to the school was difficult and unreliable so that there were frequent delays in students getting to school. He further admitted:

> I still remember, I was crying at one mid-semester exam in my early years here to see teachers write all the exam questions on the blackboard. This was a real backward sign as in Java they already used exam papers at that time. I then initiated to change this by persuading the principal and parents to provide funds for the exam administration.

Since 1998, the school has become a model school cited by the MR for its outstanding performance among the 14 public Islamic day secondary schools in Central Kalimantan. In 2010, it enrolled more than 640 students through tough selection processes including administrative checks, and written, oral, and psychological exams. Since 2009, the school has developed some of the natural science classes to be 'international classes'. These classes are designed to comply with the MR determined criteria for schools with international standards in terms of curriculum and instruction, facilities, teachers, evaluation and so forth. Mr Mulyono has been working on this project with his curriculum improvement and student affairs teams to eventually have the school become a *Rintisan Madrasah Bertaraf Internasional* (RMBI: Islamic day school with international standards). If he succeeds, it will be the first Islamic day school in the province with these international standards. Regardless, it is a sign of his concern to ensure that there are high expectations in regard to student learning and the school as a whole. For Mr Mulyono it is important the school improves student learning outcomes and opportunities.

Being humble, showing empathy and respecting others

Mr Mulyono obtained the principalship in February 2005, two years after his completion of a Masters of Education degree from Universitas Negeri Padang (Padang Public University) in West Sumatra. This qualification, together with his outstanding performance as a teacher, drove the provincial MR to appoint him as the school principal (principals are appointed by the controlling authorities and not locally selected).

Since he became principal, as acknowledged by many teachers, the school has achieved several distinguished results including the improvement of student learning outcomes, increased teacher professional development, and improved physical facilities. The school has recorded a 100 per cent success rate for the last three years in the national exam, which is better than the best general public school in the province. In his time as principal, eight teachers have complete Master's degrees, happening at a time when other general secondary schools were just starting programs to enhance the qualifications of their teachers.

In terms of facilities, the use of information and communication technology in learning has been remarkable. Every teacher has a laptop and most of them are used during teaching. Data projectors are available for use by teachers. In some classrooms, multimedia facilities are installed and used for student learning. There are two computing laboratories, with one for students to improve computing skills or to search online references for their learning, and the other is for them to learn computer assembling as a vocational subject of the school curriculum. All of the computers are connected to the Internet, and the school provides two WIFI points respectively for teachers and students so that they can always access learning resources through the Internet. The principal relentlessly encourages and provides his teachers with ICT training so that they can use this facility effectively. Compared to other schools we visited in the city of Palangkaraya, the quality of provision and use of ICT was high.

The school employs Muslim staff from many different cultural backgrounds, reflecting the cultural diversity in the area. Mr Mulyono discussed how difficult it was to lead teachers and staff with different cultural backgrounds, and to establish networks with people from very different cultures and religions. As he explained, the key to the success is developing good relationships, and the key to good relationships is, as he stated, 'how to put yourself in the context of difference'. He has upheld a common assimilationist principle of 'di mana bumi dipijak, di situ langit dijunjung', which literally means 'wherever one stands, s/he holds up the sky'. From when he first came to the school, he has gradually learnt local cultures and traditions particularly in terms of building harmonious and effective relationships with others. He wanted himself to be accepted by all, so that he is able to contribute and make a difference to the school.

> I think being different from others is no problem as long as we communicate effectively. To me, I have no problem with it because I can accept [the differences] and I am a keen person to learn other cultures. There are many things good in here, like the concept "rumah betang", which literally means a long and big house. This is a philosophy of Dayak people who accept other people to live in the big house (a metaphor for area or province).

To be accepted, Mr Mulyono emphasizes that people may not show off as if they are better than any other person. A person needs to be humble and should not look down on others because they come from a more advantaged place or have more qualifications than others. He believes that if someone has quality skills and dispositions, and they work hard, people will respect them. Personally he has experienced this as his work for the school has been highly regarded by the provincial higher authorities including the Mayor of Palangkaraya and the Ministry of National Education (MNE)'s heads in both the province and municipality. He has become one of the few local educationists with whom these high profile figures consult on matters of education.

Putting quality teaching over ethnicity

The principal has experienced difficulty in involving his teachers from the indigenous Dayak and Banjar groups. There seems to be a stereotype in this city that the indigenous teachers are not as diligent as migrants to the area. Mr Mulyono did not accept this stereotype. Indigenous teachers constitute about 50 per cent of the total teacher population and are therefore an important feature of schools in this area. What Mr Mulyono has done is to work with these teachers to improve their performance, and to construct reward systems for those who are performing well. Teachers commented that this performance and development program has driven many teachers to improve their performance. We observed several schools in Palangkaraya. In Mr Mulyono's school we rarely saw classrooms without teachers during lesson hours. In other schools, however, we found many students at the school canteen during lesson hours because their teachers had not come to class. Anecdotally then, the teachers in Mr Mulyono's school seem to be more committed and diligent than in many other schools. Mr Mulyono has himself become a role model for teachers in that he arrives at 6 am and returns home at 4 pm, whereas the usual school hours are 6.30 am to 2 pm.

A teacher of Banjar background explained:

> Indeed, some teachers said that the principal prioritises teachers from his ethnic background. But I think it is not true. He just wants to show that whoever is willing to work hard will get rewards, like to be given some other

assignments. Like me, I am trusted by the principal to manage student organisations with other teachers. So, if you want to advance, you should go with him, but if you stay [where you are now] you will be left behind no matter what you are.

According to one of his vice principals, Mr Mulyono believes in gradual improvement of his teachers. This means that those who seem to be stagnating are personally persuaded to improve, and helped to do so through encouragement to be actively involved in the school, and to try new tasks and responsibilities. He continuously evaluates his teachers' performance mostly through informal means (such as the impressions he gains in the normal course of his work) and provides appropriate and supportive feedback and professional development solutions.

Working with religious differences

As indicated previously, *madrasah* in Indonesia have suffered a lack of attention and support by local government due to, among other aspects, the impact of the 1999 regional autonomy law (Parker and Raihani 2009). Local governments take advantage of this law so as not to provide financial assistance to *madrasahs* even though the role of the *madrasah* in educating children in the area is never doubted. Here the role of Mr Mulyono in lobbying provincial and district decision makers for support for his school is significant and applauded by the school and wider community. As mentioned above, he does not mind being as humble as possible to get to the hearts of the decision makers, and he has done this lobbying for the sake of his school and other Islamic schools in the province. He wanted these schools to be inspected and treated equally. His commitment is very strong, even though the political context in Central Kalimantan is not fully supportive as Muslims seem to be inferior politically despite their majority. Within this context, however, Mr Mulyono demonstrated exceptional competences and skills to establish good relationships with people of different religious backgrounds. He said that it was a tradition for him to visit them during Christmas season, and he also received them during Eid celebrations (the most important Islamic holiday). This has proved to be an effective way to foster close relations among people of different faiths. More importantly, as he and teachers admitted, these efforts have resulted in the local provincial and municipal governments providing support to *madrasahs*. The teachers enjoy the same incentives from the local governments, as their counterparts in general schools receive.

Developing students' multicultural awareness

An Islamic school in Indonesia cannot legally enrol non-Muslim students (although again it is worth noting that whilst the students are all of one faith, they come from diverse cultural backgrounds reflecting the cultural richness of the area). It is therefore important to ensure students are exposed to religious differences and so the school has developed many programs that provide opportunities for students to interact with students from other schools with various religious backgrounds. For example, every two years the school hosts a scout convention which brings scouts from 11 different general and religious schools together to further develop their scouting skills. Ethnically and religiously diverse teams are arranged so that students can learn to work together. The teams are involved in various competitions and activities through which they learn fairness, justice, and sportsmanship. For example, there is a traditional dancing competition that promotes understanding whilst doing an activity that the students enjoy. There is sensitivity to religious needs with the school providing Christian students with a room to use for worship on Sunday morning, and the school committee members (who are Muslims) serving them and providing necessary assistance. This demonstrates the concern of the school to develop religious understanding and tolerance among students.

Mr Mulyono emphasizes the importance of ensuring that his school community understands the importance of living in a place with cultural diversity, and that they develop the beliefs, understandings, attitudes, and behaviours that reflect acknowledgement and engagement in such a society. He often said that he wants to make (peaceful) 'jihad' here, with 'jihad' taken in its broader meaning to contribute to the advancement of Palangkaraya and its people as a whole. He enjoys his work at the school and in the city and is not interested in returning to his place of origin, Yogyakarta in Java.

Reflections

The story of Mr Mulyono is about a principal who is responsive to the needs of those he serves, and in particular the students and staff of the *Madrasah Aliyah Negeri* school. Unlike many of the case studies in the ISSPP, there is cultural diversity in both the students and the staff; much of the early research on culturally responsive leadership was focused on the mismatch between diverse student populations and teachers who were from the dominant cultural group (Johnson *et al.*, 2011). Mr Mulyono is from the dominant cultural group in Indonesia, and an outsider in Palangkaraya despite having worked there for 24 years. Yet this is what makes his story worthy of attention – How can a privileged outsider work with a diverse staff group to develop a successful school for a diverse student population?

It is evident that he exercises a democratic style of leadership through: recognizing the basic value and rights of each individual; taking the standpoint of others into consideration; fostering deliberation in making decisions; embracing plurality and difference; and, promoting equity and social justice (Møller 2006). An example is how Mr Mulyono diligently seeks consultation with his staff, holds regular meetings with them, and has several development teams, each consisting of teachers with their own cultural uniqueness, to which he delegates jobs and leadership. He takes criticism, which sometimes comes from teachers, as forces that drive him to serve the school better.

There is evidence that Mr Mulyono understands critical multiculturalism (Kalantzis & Cope, 1999) in that he is concerned to develop a school that:

- has high student learning outcomes and acknowledges the dominant culture so as to enhance the chances for social mobility;
- develops the full potential of students regardless of culture and ethnic backgrounds;
- has a school culture that respects diversity of staff and students and which seeks to foster cultural and linguistic diversity;
- exposes staff and students to religious and cultural pluralism through school intra- and extra-curricular programs;
- develops teachers as professional educators.

There were two important conclusions about leading in culturally diverse settings from the Johnson *et al.* (2011) study: school leaders are, and should be, catalysts for change; and, honouring home cultures and promoting student outcomes can both be achieved. On the first point, Mr Mulyono believes that it is his responsibility to help improve the school, with this most evident in improved learning and social outcomes for students. Most of his effort as a teacher and principal has been directed at this. However, and this relates to the second point, he does so in a culturally sensitive way, helping to explore and honour the cultural diversity whilst encouraging staff and students to adopt behaviours that will see them succeed in the majority culture and pedagogy. It is a balancing act but one that Mr Mulyono seems comfortable with, even when he has to adopt actions that are controversial. An example of this is that the school has developed classes based on wealth and ability in which families pay extra for the privilege of having their children in these classes. The rationale for this is that it secures extra financial resources for the benefit of the whole school, and creates model classes in which students will succeed in gaining entry to reputable universities, and so these students become a role model for other students (and teachers). Whilst he is aware of the problems this creates (such as adverse reactions from students who are excluded from these groups), he believes that overall student socialization has not been disturbed by this program, and that the benefits outweigh any disadvantages. It is a brave choice to create this program, which in many other contexts would be very controversial, but which is an example of the concern Mr Mulyono has to improve his school and the circumstance of the school's students.

Our observation of Mr Mulyono's leadership reflects an important pattern of successful school leaders in that they are culturally and contextually sensitive. This echoes our previous findings on successful school leadership in Yogyakarta, Indonesia (see Raihani, 2007, 2008). The principals in both the current and previous study demonstrate considerable skills and competences in analysing the immediate context of society where the schools exist, acting appropriately upon the contextual requirements, and being flexible in connecting with people. The difference is that in the previous study, the principals exercised their leadership in a relatively homogenous Javanese society, while in the current study Mr Muyono is bounded within a strong multicultural/religious society.

Three areas for reflection are suggested:

1   *Can you enhance your personal qualities to make you a more successful school leader?* Leadership is a complex phenomenon based on the interaction of many situational, contextual, organizational and personal factors. Whilst often not given due regard, personal qualities are important in thinking about school leadership, and the research of the ISSPP has consistently shown a strong link between leaders' personal qualities and leadership success. Mr Mulyono showed exemplary character. He showed people-centred core values, emotional intelligence, resilience and conviction. He also showed a great deal of integrity, humility, and impartiality. While some of these factors may be a natural part of his personality, many were developed, such as his tolerance and respect for cultural diversity.

2   *To what extent do you understand your moral purpose?* For Barber and Fullan (2005) moral purpose is a fundamental element in bringing about school improvement, and they describe the central moral purpose of school leadership as constantly improving student achievement and removing achievement gaps so that all students were achieving at high levels. In the case of Mr Mulyono, the focus of his moral purpose was on promoting equality and respect, and improving student achievement for all. School leaders need to be clear about their moral purpose and consistently articulate this on a regular basis. This enhances integrity and trustworthiness and helps to promote improvement plans.

3   *To what extent do you as a school leader embrace difference?* Diversity in the workplace comes in various forms and can include consideration of difference based on such features of the workforce as gender, age, language, ethnicity, cultural background, educational level, religious beliefs, family responsibilities, marital status, socio economic status, geographical location and personality characteristics. Valuing diversity is recognising and respecting individual and group differences. Being able to lead in such circumstances is the new reality of successful school leadership. The success of Mr Mulyono in leading a culturally diverse school community is one example of the importance of embracing diversity and working with it to develop and sustain successful educational outcomes.

The story of Mr Mulyono's leadership is an exemplary case study of culturally-responsive leadership. Coming as an outsider from a different cultural background and leading a culturally diverse school community (staff and students), he embraced the context of difference, learnt the local cultures and traditions, raised expectations and standards of the school, and won the respect of all those around him. He achieved this through his personal qualities and hard work. He earned the respect of the school community by his integrity, humility, and impartiality.

Finally he was a role model for teachers and sought to understand and satisfy the needs of the students and the broader school community.

References

Aspinall, E. & Greg F. (2003). *Local Power and Politics in Indonesia: Decentralisation and Democratisation* (Singapore: Institute of Southeast Asian Studies).

Barber, M. & Fullan, M. (2005, March). Tri-level development: It's the system. *Education Week*, 24(25), pp. 32, 34–35.

Johnson, L., Møller, J., Pashiardis, P., Savvides, V. & Vedøy, G. (2011). Culturally responsive practice, in R. Ylimaki & S. Jacobson (Eds.), *US and Cross-national Policies, Practices and Preparation: Implications for Successful Instructional Leadership, Organizational Learning, and Culturally Responsive Practices* (Dordrecht: Springer-Kluwer), pp. 75 – 101

Kalantzis, M. & Cope, B. (1999). Multicultural education: Transforming the mainstream, in S. May (Ed.), *Critical Multiculturalism: Rethinking Multicultural and Antiracist Education* (London: Falmer Press), pp. 245–276.

Møller, J. (2006). Democratic schooling in Norway: implications for leadership in practice. *Leadership and Policy in Schools*, 5(1) pp. 53-69.

Parker, L. & Raihani (2009). *Policy Briefs: Governing Madrasah* (Canberra: Australia Indonesia Governance Research Partnership (AIGRP) – The Australian National University).

Pusat Statistik Pendidikan. (2008). *Ikhtisar Data Pendidikan Nasional Tahun 2007–2008* (Jakarta: Departemen Pendidikan Nasional).

Raihani & Gurr, D. (2006). Value-driven school leadership: An Indonesian perspective, *Leading and Managing*, 12(1), pp. 121–134.

Raihani (2007). *Successful School Leadership in Indonesia: A Study of Principals' Leadership in Successful Senior Secondary Schools in Yogyakarta* (Pekanbaru: Suska Press).

Raihani (2008). An Indonesian model of successful school leadership. *Journal of Educational Administration*, 46(4), pp. 481–496.

Chapter 17

Thinking about leading schools

David Gurr and Christopher Day

The principals in this book can all be considered as leading successful schools. Some of the schools are amongst the highest performing in their countries (e.g. Trinity Grammar in Melbourne, Australia; Public Secondary School No. 50 'José Vasconcelos' in Monterrey, Mexico), others are performing at a level beyond expectations (e.g. David's school in England and Westminster Community Charter School in Buffalo, USA). There are many stories of dramatically improved performance, be that in terms of typical student learning outcome data (e.g. Juarez Elementary School in Southwestern Arizona, USA) or more fundamentally having the basic technical, human and educational features in place to allow for success (e.g. Kiptai Primary School, Kenya). In all cases, it is the exemplary work of the principals that have been central to the success of these schools.

A key attribute of principal leadership is sense making and so we see one of our roles as editors to help the reader to make sense of the many wonderful stories of success presented in this book. Here we present the key themes that arise as we consider the chapters in their entirety. We do not claim that a theme is evident in the work of every principal, but nevertheless, these themes are those that have sufficient representation to be worthy of attention. Our synthesis has been helped by the reflections of two graduate classes who read an early draft of the book.

High expectations

Having high expectations has been one of the key features identified in the effective schools research for many years. All the principals have high expectations of staff and students. However, they also have high expectations of parents and of themselves. It is high expectations mixed with a belief that the expectations can be achieved by the school community that helps define the work of these leaders as this commentary by Merchant *et al.* on the work of Ms Martinez suggests:

> We believe that Ms. Martinez's success as a principal is rooted in a strong sense of self-efficacy that is nurtured by a supportive family, a passionate and unwavering commitment to her students, and a strong belief in the

importance of reaching out to community members to enlist their assistance in promoting high standards for their children.

In Chamuada's leadership of Kiptai Primary School, there are high expectations for the community, but tinged with a sense of reality that reflects the particularly challenging context of the community the school serves:

> We have yet to take a student to a national school. However, my greatest hope is that the success in this school will outlive me. ... That many of the children I have here today will live better lives than their parents, and that this community will look back and be proud of what we have achieved together.

The expectations translate into a restlessness in the principals to always do better – for the school, for the people within the school, and for themselves as this comment from Villafuerte-Elizondo suggests:

> I am not the kind of person that sits down and waits for things to happen. I go out looking for solutions, not problems. I don't sit on the side of the road crying. If the road doesn't lead to a solution I take another road.

The following quote from Villafuerte-Elizondo indicates that confidence she has to surmount obstacles, the high expectations she has for all in the school, and the supreme confidence she has in the teachers to achieve these expectations:

> When obstacles don't stop you from where you want to be, when you are continually discovering and taking advantage of new roads and ways of doing things, that is the true meaning of success. Life will always be full of what seem to be obstacles. What is great is that you, me, anyone, everyone can find a new path, and new paths must always be explored, regardless of where one ends up at. I really believe that we can do anything we set our mind to if we have a positive outlook on what we do, on who is around us, on why we are doing what we do. Education is a noble profession and if all of us, all of us educators, were committed to make our children successful, our country would be a very different place. There is no doubt in my mind that teachers are the key to all, so half my job is done. The other half is simple: remind all my teachers, every day, that they are the key to all.

For David, in his second spell of principalship, his initial work in raising the historically low aspirations of staff, pupils and community was:

> as much about changing perceptions as about changing actions. Much as my experiences had pushed me to develop distributed leadership styles, it was clear to me that I would need to place myself at the centre of change and

tie my own character and credibility into the process, allowing the staff to personify the Academy.

Post-heroic leadership

In the ISSPP we have in recent years been considering the extent to which our successful principals might be considered as displaying heroic leadership. Many of our principals are certainly heroic in the way they challenge the status quo, fight for the best opportunities for their students, and have a positive and empowering view of what is possible for a school community, whatever the circumstances. The use of the term heroic leadership itself has become a problematic concept. This is in part because it is often associated with earlier concepts of charismatic leadership (e.g. Conger & Kanungo, 1988) in which a single person – the principal – drives change and improvement. The creation of such a dependency model does not build the capacity of others, does not promote succession planning and, so history tells us, the effects do not last much beyond the tenure of the particular 'charismatic' principal. Apart from these flaws, it does not fit well in countries which are committed to democratic ideals. Moreover, this kind of leadership is simply not practical in the complex worlds of today's schools as they strive to respond to the changing demands of policy and the needs of young people. Yet it would be true to say, as evidenced by accounts in this book, that much of what these principals do is heroic, or as David, the English principal states, brave:

> Leadership means not only having answers (to problems of the changing curriculum, staffing structures, building management, pastoral systems) but also having the courage to stand by them when they are questioned. It also means being prepared to hear these questions and change your mind if you need to, without losing the strength of those original convictions or confidence in yourself. It's a fine line, like everything else in leadership. The brave leader must show a positive face, an unstinting outward belief that not only is the battle eminently winnable but that it is practically won.

These successful principals also emphasize that others can do what they do, given opportunity and support, and they repeatedly mention how much they rely on the good work of the many people in their schools. For these reasons we suggest that a better label may be post-heroic leadership. Thus, whilst there is an obligation on principals to exercise leadership , leading a school requires collaborative and aligned effort by all. Ragan, Villafuerte-Elizondo, Chamuada, David, Yaakov, Birger and Martinez are all principals that exhibit this type of post-heroic leadership; firm in their leadership but also engaging of the school community. The reader will recall that Wasonga in writing about the work of Chamuada, provided a framework for reflecting on this directive yet inclusive style of leadership. The framework consists of five elements: first, establishing a common purpose; second, developing conditions of work that provide a context for co-creating with members of the community, students, and teachers; third, constructing the school's social architecture (the social networks, scheduling and communication systems created to enhance and sustain school improvement); fourth, constructing school processes that encourage collaborative decision-making and actions; and, fifth, developing personal dispositions that engage constituents, such as humility, patience, collaboration, resilience, active listening, cultural anthropology, trust, and subtlety.

Collaboration/collective effort/shared vision/ alignment

School improvement is a collective effort involving senior and middle-level leaders, teachers and other staff, students, parents and the wider community (including systemic support where relevant). In many cases the principal stories demonstrate how these leaders were the key story-tellers and sense makers for their school, and how they painted a compelling vision of what their schools should be like. However, they were careful to ensure that the vision was one that could be embraced by the whole school community, with this typically taking time and effort to develop and sustain. The reader will recall the story of Lute Ingalls who, with the help of parents and teachers, developed 'bottom lines' that emphasized academic success, good behaviour and staff collaboration. This was the vision that drove the improvement of Juarez Elementary, and Ingalls was the one that kept this vision at the forefront of all decisions, including the decision to adopt the literacy improvement program, *Success for All*. Martinez had a passion for improving schools that was conveyed in how she talked about her efforts at Grande Academy:

> I had to create an environment. I had to create a culture; I had to somehow together come up with the rules, the expectations. I had to share with them the things I've done at my school and I said, 'I'm not willing nor will I stop at any measures not to be exemplary. We will be exemplary.'

Wasonga in describing the work of Chamuada used the term co-creating leadership to emphasize the need for collaboration and shared leadership. The 6E framework described by Wang and used to consider the principalship of Mdm Linda is a way of conceptualizing this empowered view of principal leadership. The 6Es include educate, envision, energize, engage, enable and embrace. Even though collaboration was emphasized, typically, the principals were the glue that bound the school community to the school visions. They were the champions of change, the gatekeepers and custodians of school direction, and were adept at ensuring the whole school community was aligned and in agreement as this quote from Minor-Ragan indicates:

> Everyone must be kept abreast of the school's plans, and of its progress or lack thereof. When committees and groups are working together, I provide

the 'glue' to keep everyone on track and aligned with our vision, goals and mission. Committee work and shared decision-making can easily become compartmentalised. My role is to assure that we all understand how each group's piece of the puzzle helps to create the larger picture.

Whilst the principal tended to involve others, there was also a sense of responsibility to make decisions, and on some matters to be very directive. This was evident especially in the narratives of Ingalls, Frandsen, Anderson, and Birger.

All matters which are important for running the school are to be discussed at team level. At the same time, I, as the principal, can say that this is a matter we do not discuss. I decide, and there is no need for a discussion. If I involve you in a democratic process now when I already have made up my mind, that is deceitful, that is "pretend – democracy". I have decided in the matter, I am the principal at this school and have authority to do so, in matters that are completely meaningless to discuss.

Symbolic role

The role of story-teller and sense maker is an important part of the symbolic importance of the principals. It might be a simple message – we want to be the best school we can be – and it might influence the whole community. For example, Mr Chamuada had a simple message at Kiptai Primary School, 'We need to create this school together.' His vision of the school's future, his persistence in improving the school, his trustworthiness and integrity in an environment full of corruption, and the quiet way he engaged the whole school community led to remarkable success. He is the symbol of the efforts to create a viable and successful school in very challenging circumstances. He is a story teller of hope as this extract from the chapter describes:

He uses stories, analogies, and experiences in everyday life to help people connect the purpose of school to their lives. For example, at a meeting with parents, he explained how a new statute – all Members of Parliament would need to have a college education and all ministers must have a Bachelors Degree – would impact the community. He said, "the grumbles of a frog will not stop a cow from drinking water. If we continue this way, if our children cannot go to high school, we will never have a representative in parliament. Other communities will." A parent later told me that he could now figure out the purpose of school and its larger impact. He would encourage children to stay in school.

At River School, Olof emphasized to teachers that students were on a journey with the main part of their life ahead of them, and that it was the responsibility of the teachers and school to contribute positively to their lives and futures. In defining his role as Headmaster of Trinity Grammar, Tudor commented:

As Headmaster, I am the leader of the school community and that is the key thing, and people look to the Headmaster as being the leader of the community in all senses. In every word that you say, you are judged and you are reacted to and so on.

David used the metaphor of gardening to portray his work:

in the early stages the head gardener has to play a huge part in putting the vision onto the area, using the skills to decide what works where, what doesn't, to move things when they're needed and to really look at the whole landscaping and how it is. There's then a very frenetic bit where there's preparing the ground the moving the seeding the propagating all those kinds of things, when eventually you look at the garden and you say wow isn't this amazing, the actual gardener's hand should actually be disappearing and is not clear.

The emphasis placed on the symbolic role could mean that when these principals leave, there might be a mission/purpose gap that will be difficult to replace. Yet many of the principals sustained school success for many years and so even if this was an issue, having them lead a successful school for a decade or more must be worth it; generally they are not short-term principals. In some ISSPP cases, reported elsewhere (e.g. Drysdale *et al.*, 2011), there is evidence of sustained success once the principals have left. In the case of Mdm Linda, there was a sense of continuity of successful leadership at the school, with Mdm Linda acknowledging the work of the previous principals, and seeing herself as the custodian of the school at the moment, with a strong expectation that whoever succeeds her will continue the school's success. Whilst she was an important part of the journey of the school, the story of success was bigger than her, and there was an assumption that success would be sustained when she left.

Integrity, trust and transparency

A standout characteristic of the principals is the degree to which they were respected and trusted by their school communities. They acted with integrity, modelling good practice, being careful to ensure fairness in how they dealt with people, and enduring respect and trust through the integrity and transparency of their values and actions. In the case of the Cypriot principal, Johnson, the trust that she had was described in terms of Tschannen-Moran's (2003) trust dimensions of benevolence, reliability, competence, honesty and openness. In some contexts such as Indonesia and Kenya, without respect and trust the principals could not have done their work. In Mulyono's school, there were many different ethnic groups involved (both amongst the students and teachers), and it was important to bring these groups together in a climate of open communication, respect and trust as indicated in the following quote:

> I think being different from others is no problem as long as we communicate effectively. To me, I have no problem with it because I can accept [the differences] and I am a keen person to learn other cultures. There are many things good in here, like the concept "rumah betang", which literally means a long and big house. This is a philosophy of Dayak people who accept other people to live in the big house (a metaphor for area or province).

As much as possible, principals were concerned to make decision making transparent and involving all others; the school becomes a place that is trusted because there is a culture of inclusion. When decision making is transparent and involving of many people it may enhance trust. Frandsen spoke of the need to promote democracy in schools, such as ensuring that teachers had involvement in most decisions, even those that required quick solutions:

> You have to balance the fact that sometimes you as leader have decided upon something and you therefore can be action minded, and at the same time make sure that teachers feel they own things. This balance is very important in the everyday life of school and it is important for democracy in schools. It is important for each individual to be participating the whole way through.

Sometimes though, teachers cannot be involved, and the following quote from Minor-Ragan, illustrates how even when decisions cannot be made collaboratively, in a climate of transparency and trust there is little concern by staff:

> In my role as leader, some situations must be solved with quick decision-making and do not allow for collaboration. My staff knows, understands and accepts that I reserve this right. There is no resistance to following top-down decisions when they occur, because we have been careful to build a foundation of trust and respect.

People centred

The principals were focused on helping students to learn and develop. As Chamuada said:

> I was so angry with what I saw in this community. I decided to channel my anger to work for these children who, I think, are paying for the sins of society. How could I turn my back on children?

They gain great satisfaction from the changes they see in students. They were also excellent in helping staff to learn and develop, and gained equally great satisfaction with this. Notman described Anderson's work with staff and students:

> Jan has a strong personal commitment to the people of her school community. She feels keenly the interpersonal nature of the job and her capacity to

influence other individual lives for better or for worse. She enjoys the intrinsic reward of seeing teachers and parents happy, and students achieving their individual potential, both inside and outside of school. Of all the aspects of the role she most likes, it is the connection with students.

The reader will recall that an important element in the work of Mulyano was his focus on developing staff, and to do so in a manner that was, whilst still aware of the need to improve the school, respectful of the person, both in terms of who they were as a professional and a person, as explained in this comment from a teacher:

> some teachers said that the principal prioritises teachers from his ethnic background. But I think it is not true. He just wants to show that whoever is willing to work hard will get rewards, like to be given some other assignments. Like me, I am trusted by the principal to manage student organisations with other teachers. So, if you want to advance, you should go with him, but if you stay [where you are now] you will be left behind no matter what you are.

Without exception, the principals were people centred and genuinely enjoyed the engagement with the many people, students and adults that they meet daily. This is evident in a student's description of Tudor:

> He's open, he's welcoming and he's nice. He's really friendly and always interesting to talk to. He's also a really honourable guy. He doesn't promote himself. He tries to cater for everybody not just purely academic or purely sport. He tries to get a range of things and interests. He's genuinely interested in like everything that goes on, and he's always looking for ways to make things better, and he gets the respect of everyone.

In some cases it seemed that this engagement with people is what gave them the energy to work the long and intense hours typical of a principal..

The power of 'AND': transformational AND instructional leadership

There has in recent times been a revival of the transformational/instructional leadership debate (e.g. Robinson *et al.*, 2008). Our principals were invariably both. They were concerned to motivate and support staff, but also concerned to ensure that teaching and learning was happening in an appropriate way. Whilst they typically weren't the hands-on instructional leader wished for in the 1980s (Murphy, 1990; Murphy & Hallinger, 1992) and perhaps evident in the work of Lute, they were educational leaders, ensuring improvement in curriculum, pedagogy and assessment by most often working with other school leaders to influence teacher practice (e.g. Yaakov). One principal, Olof, deliberately distanced himself from the instructional leadership role, although he was a very visible leader nevertheless and emphasized the relationships he had with students and teachers. On reflection, Olof wished he had been more concerned with the quality of teacher's work in the classroom, a reflection that recognizes the need for instructional and transformational leadership (Moos *et al.*, 2011a). A counsellor at Kiptai Primary School spoke of the teaching and learning culture that Chamuada had established:

> Our teachers are empowered through constant conversations about teaching, learning, and the community around us. We all feel that we have enough information and knowledge about our school, students and parents. And even though sometimes we lack resources, we are happy that we do our best.

All our principals seem to exhibit transformational leadership qualities (Bass & Avolio, 1997; Avolio, 2011), such as motivating and supporting staff (e.g. Villafuerte-Elizondo), understanding them on a personal level (e.g. Tudor), and encouraging them to have a voice in decision making processes (e.g. Frandsen). There were also elements of the transactional element of transformational leadership. This is the aspect that uses learning theory to reward appropriate behaviour and to act upon concerns. The following quote from Villafuerte-Elizondo illustrates some of the transactional element based on a clear sense of what is expected, and ways of understanding when the expectations are met:

> Each one of us has a particular role. Each can contribute in his or her own way to meet the school's goals. So what we need is a plan with clear goals known to all, so each one of us can know how we can contribute to achieve those goals. And a clear set of measures so that each one of us knows if we are contributing. Then each one simply does what s/he is willing to do and knows if s/he is contributing or not.

Improving schools in challenging circumstances

Many of the chapters in this book tell stories of school turnaround. Some of our research groups, particularly those from the USA, England and Mexico, have focused on successful school leadership in challenging contexts, and so there are many examples of a principal being appointed to a school with low performance and dramatically improving performance, sometimes over a relatively short time, but often taking several years for substantial and sustained success. For some principals it seems to be a calling to serve in schools in challenging circumstances, and examples include the stories of Ragan, David, Ingalls, Villafuerte-Elizondo, Chamuada, Birger, Olof, Martinez and Mulyono. Some of the stories describe how the principals have a history of being able to transform schools (Ragan, Villafuerte-Elizondo, Martinez) or have gone on to superintendent roles to use their knowledge to improve other schools (Ingalls, Olof). Consistent in the stories of those that have improved schools in challenging circumstances is an initial focus on ensuring that there is at least the basic requirements of an adequate school – it is emotionally and physically safe for all; there are adequate physical resources; the teachers and other staff are appropriately qualified and committed, and there is a structure to the curriculum. Once these are in place, then they attend to establishing an empowering direction, improving curriculum, pedagogy and assessment, supporting staff development, acquiring and using resources well, engaging the school community in a collaborative effort to improve the school, and so forth.

Developing as a leader

The development of successful leadership characteristics, dispositions and qualities takes time. When we came to study the principals in this book, they were mostly experienced educators who had taken many years to become successful principals. Some had early leadership opportunities, but their success as a principal was generally crafted through a blend of on-the-job learning, formal and informal professional learning, mentoring or sponsorship by significant others, and serendipity in the pathways to leadership (consider the story of Laura Martinez). Whilst formal graduate programs were not emphasized (although cases such as that of Martinez and Mulyono emphasize the importance of formal learning), nevertheless the principals demonstrated a capacity for life-long learning, were inquisitive and restless, and were always looking for new opportunities for their schools. Most importantly, all the principals seem to be concerned to develop themselves. For example, this could be by accepting a challenging position (e.g. Ingalls, Tudor, Olof, Martinez), engaging in formal or informal professional learning (e.g. Frandsen, Anderson), or by participating in research; some of the principals (Minor-Ragan and Tudor) have been involved in the bi-annual ISSPP Research and Practice Conferences (the first was held in Nottingham in 2009, the second in Boston in 2011 and the third in Umea in 2013). The mix of formal and informal learning evident in the ISSPP principals is further explored in the second and third volumes of the ISSPP books (Moos *et al.*, 2011b; Ylimaki & Jacobson, 2011).

Personal qualities, beliefs and values

In addition to these themes there are some overriding features to the work of the principals. In this section we explore some of the personal qualities, and beliefs and values that seem to contribute to successful school leadership.

Personal acumen

Acumen is concerned with sharpness of mind, a quality that our principals seem to possess. This is shown powerfully when considering their problem solving abilities. Our principals seem to be expert problem solvers, both in terms of typical problems, and the swampy problems that sometimes emerge and challenge the best educational leaders (Leithwood & Steinbach, 1995). Our principals do not typically see problems as unresolvable, but rather they see them as challenges that can be worked with and overcome.

> I am not the kind of person that sits down and waits for things to happen. I go out looking for solutions, not problems. I don't sit on the side of the road crying. If the road doesn't lead to a solution I take another road.
>
> (Villafuerte-Elizondo, p. 44)

They are good at listening to people, helping them to work through issues and problems and become better problem solvers.

Qualities and dispositions

In a summary of previous ISSPP cases, Moos *et al.* (2011a) identified personal qualities of leadership that seemed to be key factors in success. These included personal commitment to making a difference, resilience, motivation to sustain their efforts over time, high self-efficacy, high expectations of themselves and others, emphasis on establishing excellent personal relationships with the school, and an emphasis on whole-child development and establishing a supportive school environment. Supporting these findings and the long history of trait theory in leadership, there are many features of the qualities and dispositions of the principals in this book that seem important for success including: optimism, persistence, trust (behaving in a way that promotes the attribution of trust in the leader by others, and also displaying trust in others), tolerance, empathy, alertness (shown through high levels of physical and mental energy), curiosity, resilience, benevolence, honesty, openness, respectful, and humbleness.

The principals worked hard. They did this for several reasons; the job demands it; it models appropriate behaviour to others; many had a belief that hard work will bring rewards. Related to this are some personal qualities such as courage, commitment and energy. Birger comments:

> It is all about courage and commitment. I am completely clear and consistent in that matter. I have told people around me that the day you see that I lose my commitment you have to tell me because then I have nothing more to give.

Similarly Tudor comments on the need for sustaining energy:

> As a principal, you need to keep renewing your energy, to be one step ahead, to be proactive never reactive, so you need mental energy and resilience, while you can do that, people are happy with you and will come with you, otherwise dissatisfaction will set in and the school will run down, relationships will run down.

As mentioned previously, they worked collaboratively. Whilst the principals displayed all the qualities of good educational leadership (such as setting direction, developing people, developing the school and managing and improving teaching and learning), they also knew they couldn't lead a school by themselves, and they genuinely valued the contribution of teachers, parent and students to the success of their schools. As Tudor states, 'through working with others, people achieve more and learn more effectively, and ... people grow by being of service to others.' Chamuada wanted to share the leadership of the school with parents and teachers and build their capacity so that, 'leadership will outlive me'.

The principals had self-belief and understanding. In regard to Anderson's leadership at Otago Girls' School, a teacher noted:

> She does have, I think, a strong sense of self. She knows where she is coming from. She has a very good understanding of her own values and commitments and as they apply to what happens in the school.

Chamuada at Kiptai Primary School, knew that what he saw happening when he first went to the school was wrong, and he knew that he could change this even though there was no compelling reason to do so as his predecessors and many of the teachers he saw did not seem to care. Nevertheless, despite his young age of 28, he believed that he could work with this community to bring about significant and sustained change. He did this through developing a strategic plan and engaging the community in a collective process to improve the school.

Beliefs and values

In the research that led to the construction of the ISSPP, Day *et al.* (2000) proposed a values-led contingency model of leadership. This emphasized the importance of context to the enactment of leadership, and how personal and school values influenced the choices and decisions made. A values framework used by Leithwood and Steinbach (1991; cited in Leithwood *et al.*, 1994: 103) describes four categories:

- *Basic human values* (principles, terminal values referring to end states of existence)
- *General moral values* (those relevant to judging the ethical dimensions of decisions)
- *Professional values* (those relevant to guiding decisions at work)
- *Social and political values* (those that recognize the social nature of human action)

The categories are not mutually exclusive but the discussion below follows broadly the sequence of categories as listed.

An ethic of care was evident in all the stories, and this extended to all in the school community. Related to this was a sense of social justice. These qualities transcended contexts and were, for example, as evident in the work of Tudor and Anderson in more privileged contexts, as they were in the challenging contexts experienced by principals such as Chamuada and Minor-Ragan. The principals displayed a genuine empathy for others. By this we mean that there was a genuine desire to understand people so as to best help them. It was not related to external demands (such as test scores) but a genuine desire to want the best for all of those in the school community, be they students, parents or teachers. The principals valued individuality and exhibited the transformational leadership quality of individual consideration. A belief in freedom and democracy pervaded many of the stories (e.g. Frandsen, Mulyono). There was a strong and persisting sense of responsibility to provide an educational environment that will set students well on their life paths (e.g. David, Olof, Birger), with many principals seeming to have a passion for working in challenging contexts to help those most in need (Minor-Ragan, Ingalls, Chamuada, Villafuerte-Elizondo, Yaakov, Martinez, Mulyono). Even in more privileged contexts, a strong sense of working for those in need was evident, with, for example, Tudor working extensively at a personal and school level with Aboriginal communities in challenging contexts. Personal qualities mentioned above such as integrity, compassion, honesty, respect for others, optimism and curiosity helped them manifest these values and beliefs.

To help them navigate the ethical dimensions of decisions the principals seem to rely on certain key values. In challenging what he saw and to help guide school improvement decisions, Chamuada would often ask himself, 'Is this what I would want for my own children?' By using this standard, he constantly sought improvement at Kiptai Primary School, and used this as a tool to challenge others; 'To do to the children in this school as they would want others to do for their children.' The reader may recall the hopeful story used by Chamuada to provide a compelling reason for children to be educated, so that the community might one day have a representative in parliament. Anderson spoke of having the courage to do what is right. This might, for example, come from a spiritual or social justice base, or more simply from an understanding of what is possible in education. Balancing individual versus collective care, and considering the unwarranted harm that might arise from decisions that are made, are further elements of how the courage to do what is right might be developed. For Anderson, one of the drivers for improving the Otago Girls' High School was for the school to 'never be like it was in past days' before she became principal, and 'to pull it back to a classy girls' school.' So, for Anderson high expectations of what the school could be gave her 'the courage to do what is right'.

Aspects that have been highlighted in the themes such as high expectations of all, the importance of developing staff capacity, use of collective capacity to achieve more, a sense of the positive impact of the work of school leaders and teachers, a sense that hard work is needed for success, and focusing on developing core areas whilst fostering a well-rounded education are examples of professional values that help to guide work-based decisions.

Leadership is of course a social activity and so social and political values are important with examples already mentioned including: sharing, participation and fostering collaborative cultures, emphasizing the centrality of people, sharing the responsibility for student learning with the whole school community, appealing to moral purpose to drive decisions, developing frameworks to guide change (e.g. the 'bottom lines' of Ingalls, or the emotional thermometer of Tudor), and engaging the wider community.

Concluding thoughts

In the opening story, Steve Jacobson asked, 'Is this your right mountain?' It is a suitable point to end this book. The stories in this book tell of people who seem to have found their right mountain. There is much that is given to be on the mountain, and much that is given back as the ascent is completed. Leading schools is about the art of leadership as much as it is about developing the knowledge dispositions and competencies of successful principal leadership that the ISSPP has documented so well. It is about adaptability and passion, knowledge and compassion, about looking after yourself as well as others, about finding your own right mountain where you can make a genuine difference to those in schools. It is our hope, in creating this selection of stories of successful principals that they will provide points of connection for your own work as educators or researchers, that they provide inspiration for continuing this work, and a celebration of what is perhaps one of the most rewarding and important jobs in our society.

References

Avolio, B. (2011). *Full Range Leadership Development* (2nd ed.) (Thousand Oaks, CA: Sage).

Bass, B. & Avolio, B. (1997). *Manual for the Multifactor Leadership Questionnaire* (California: Mind Gardens).

Conger, J.A. & Kanungo, R.N. (1988). *Charismatic Leadership* (San Francisco, CA: Jossey-Bass).

Day, C., Harris, A., Hadfield, M., Tolley, H. & Beresford, J. (2000). *Leading Schools in Times of Change* (Buckingham: Open University Press).

Drysdale, L., Goode, H. & Gurr, D. (2011). *Sustaining School and Leadership Success in Two Australian Schools*, in Moos, L., Johansson, O., & Day, C. (Eds) (2011) *How School Principals Sustain Success Over Time: International Perspectives* (Dordrecht: Springer-Kluwer), pp 25–38.

Leithwood, K. & Steinbach, R. (1995). *Expert Problem Solving: Evidence from School and District Leaders* (Albany, NY: State University of New York Press).

Leithwood, K., Begley, P.T. & Cousins, J.B. (Eds.) (1994). *Developing Expert Leadership For Future Schools* (London: Falmer Press).

Moos, L., Johansson, O. & Day, C. (Eds.) (2011a). New insights: How successful school leadership is sustained, in Moos, L., Johansson, O., & Day, C. (Eds.) *How School Principals Sustain Success Over Time: International Perspectives* (Dordrecht: Springer-Kluwer), pp. 223–230.

Moos, L., Johansson, O., & Day, C. (Eds.) (2011b). *How School Principals Sustain Success Over Time: International Perspectives* (Dordrecht: Springer-Kluwer).

Murphy, J. (1990). Principal instructional leadership, *Advances in Educational Administration: Changing Perspectives on the School, 1*(1), pp. 163–200.

Murphy, J. & Hallinger, P. (1992). The principalship in an era of transformation, *Journal of Educational Administration*, 30(3), pp. 77–88.

Robinson, V., Lloyd, C. and Rowe, K. (2008). The impact of leadership on student outcomes: An analysis of the differential effects of leadership types, *Educational Administration Quarterly*, 44, (5), pp. 635–674.

Tschannen-Moran, M., & Hoy, A.W. (1998). A conceptual and empirical analysis of trust in schools, *Journal of Educational Administration, 36*, pp. 334–352.

Ylimaki, R. & Jacobson, S. (Eds) (2011). *US and cross-national policies, practices and preparation: Implications for successful instructional leadership, organizational learning, and culturally responsive practices* (Dordrecht, Netherlands: Springer-Kluwer).

Index

Made in the USA
Las Vegas, NV
11 April 2022

47261597R00129